DISTINGUISHING JONSON

DISTINGUISHING JONSON
Imitation, Rivalry, and the Direction of a Dramatic Career

George E. Rowe

University of Nebraska Press: Lincoln & London

Copyright © 1988 by the
University of Nebraska Press
All rights reserved
Manufactured in the
United States of America
Designed by Dika Eckersley
Typeset by Michael Jensen at
the University of Nebraska Press
in Linotron Garamond
Printed by Edwards Brothers

The paper in this book meets
the minimum requirements of
American National Standard for
Information Sciences—Permanence
of Paper for Printed Library
Materials, ANSI Z39.48-1984.
Library of Congress
Cataloging-in-Publication Data
Rowe, George E., 1947–
Distinguishing Jonson.
Bibliography: p.
Includes index. 1. Jonson, Ben,
1573?–1637—
Criticism and interpretation
2. Jonson, Ben, 1573?–1637—
Authorship.
3. Imitation (in literature)
4. Literary quarrels—
Great Britain. I. Title
PR2638.R68 1988 822'.3
87-13198
ISBN 0-8032-3883-5 (alk. paper)

205508

To Kathy

Contents

Preface

This study traces Ben Jonson's attempt to create for himself a literary identity—in his own terminology, a "name." Ideally, this "name" would both designate his own particular artistry and define his stature as a writer, and Jonson believed that it could be attained only by clearly separating himself and his works from his contemporaries and whatever poems and plays they had created. For Jonson, distinction is always dependent upon the ability to make distinctions; a distinguished writer is just that—distinguished, and obviously so, from other writers. As a result, his career became an energetic, sometimes aggressive, and ultimately frustrated attempt to make distinctions, despite (or perhaps because of) what he thought to be the generally imitative nature of all human activity. We are all, a passage from *Discoveries* warns us, "in travaile with expression of another." In such a world, differences are all too often fragile and momentary; in such a world, an artistic identity—any identity—is likely to be very precarious indeed.

That Jonson spent a great deal of time and effort attempting to distinguish himself from other English poets and dramatists is not, certainly, a new discovery. Thomas Dekker knew it well enough, as did (I argue) Shakespeare; much more recently, Richard Helgerson has written instructively and at length about Jonson's "laureate" ambitions. But there is more to be said in this regard—about the way in which Jonson's attempt to create an artistic persona shaped his relations with his audience as well as with other contemporary poets and playwrights; about the complex connections between this endeavor and both Jonson's readings in classical authors and his admiration for William Camden, John Selden, and Francis Bacon; about Jonson's remarkable tendency to meld his own impulses, fears, and desires into the dramas he created; about, finally, the problems inherent in the career that he envisioned for himself.

In discussing these and related topics, I have not attempted to deal with Jonson's entire canon. His masques, written for specific occasions and particular audiences, are for the most part not directly concerned with issues of this kind. Although the royal or aristocratic approval that their very existence demonstrated was extremely important to Jonson's sense of his own worth, as was his largely unsuccessful ability to prevent the form from being taken over by the dazzling creations of an architect, the works themselves do not present the complex examination of rivalry that we encounter in his dramas. It is present to some extent in Jonson's poems, several of which I discuss in Chapters 1 and 2.

My major concern, however, is Jonson's plays. The claims he wished to make for his art were at once more necessary and more problematic in the theater. To attempt to base an artistic identity on works written for the stage was, as has often been noted, an extraordinary undertaking during the English Renaissance. When Jonson began his career, the drama was hardly a prestigious literary form, and the spectators in the theater were difficult and unpredictable. Yet the drama is also, by virtue of its generic characteristics, particularly suited to an examination of questions involving imitation and rivalry. And that ability, together with the checkered reputation of the English Renaissance theater and its audience, made virtually certain the fact that Jonson's plays would become both a primary vehicle for his attempt to separate himself from other English authors and a subtle and complex examination of that endeavor.

This book attempts to examine in depth each of these aspects of his dramas. Chapters 1 and 2 establish the overall framework of the study by discussing Jonson's attitudes toward other English writers, the reasons for those attitudes, and his relations with spectators and readers. Chapters 3–5 trace Jonson's dramatic career in order to amplify and extend the arguments of the opening chapters. As will quickly become apparent, I have given some of Jonson's plays more attention than others, and have, in fact, mentioned several only in passing. Because *A Tale of a Tub, The Case Is Altered,* and *The Sad Shepherd* lie outside the boundaries of Jonson's dramatic canon as he attempted officially to define it—that is, a canon that begins with the revised version of *Every Man in His Humour* and concludes with *The Magnetic Lady*—they have relatively little to contribute to a study of Jonson's conscious attempt to shape his career. Much of what I might have said about *Cynthia's Revels* would simply have repeated aspects of the discussion of *Poetaster* in Chapter 3; *Every Man out of His Humour* is given only a partial reading for the same reason. Similarly, the extended analysis of *Epicoene* in Chapter 4 is intended to apply as well to *Volpone* and *The Alchemist,* both of which are, as a result, dealt with more briefly than the comic masterpiece that separates them.

Throughout, I assume a close relation between Jonson's art and life, sometimes reading the former in terms of the latter and sometimes the reverse. This approach may not seem valid to all readers, but I hope that the study itself will provide some compensation for whatever problems its methodology may cause. And although this book is firmly rooted in the attitudes and works of a single author, I hope that it will also have something to say, if only indirectly, about writers other than Jonson and, more generally, about activities other than artistic ones. We are all variously involved in the business of making distinctions. Jonson knew that better than most, and his career has some important things to teach us about ourselves and our own endeavors.

No one can spend much time studying the works of Ben Jonson without very quickly becoming aware of his or her debt to the research of other scholars. Jonson seems always to have had more than his share of talented readers, but the 1980s have been remarkable for the number and quality of studies that have focused either entirely or substantially on his works—studies by Anne Barton, Jonathan Goldberg, Thomas Greene, Richard Helgerson, Alexander Leggatt, Katherine Maus, Annabel Patterson, Richard Peterson, John Sweeney, and Don Wayne, among others. I have indicated in the text and the notes specific borrowings from and, yes, differences with the ideas of these and other scholars. And while doing so, I have attempted to limit my own involvement with some of the impulses of which this study is a chronicle. Obviously, the Jonson who appears in the following pages has more in common with some of the Jonsons who live in the stacks of university libraries than he does with others, but he is, in one way or another, indebted to them all.

Other obligations are more personal. This book was first begun with the aid of a National Endowment for the Humanities Residential Fellowship at Brown University during the 1981–82 academic year; a National Endowment Summer Stipend in 1984 helped move it toward completion. During my year in Providence, Barbara Lewalski provided the kind of environment in which scholarship thrives, and two other members of the seminar, Ann Imbrie and Jim Baumlin, made important contributions to this study in its early stages. In Wichita, Don Wineke was a judicious critic of some of my ideas; Diane Singer helped sort out a particularly puzzling aspect of *Every Man out of His Humour;* and Lydia Foster supplied valuable insights into that complex series of endeavors called a literary career. In Eugene, Robert Grudin and Steven Shankman graciously read major portions of the manuscript; Thelma Greenfield took the time to criticize, and improve, the whole; and Judith Engle allowed me to examine her fine analysis of Aristophanes' *The Knights.*

Two additional debts remain. Jackson Cope has been for many years a mentor, a friend. His influence undoubtedly pervades this study in even more ways than those of which I am aware. Finally, this book owes more than I can say to the patience, support, and suggestions of the person to whom it is dedicated. As is so often the case, in this preface last is assuredly not least.

1

MAKING DISTINCTIONS

Near the beginning of *The Return from Parnassus,* Part Two, a witty satirist named Ingenioso asks his friend Iudicio to describe recent literary developments in London. Iudicio, who evidently has been forced to read a discouraging amount of hackwork while employed at a local press, is not very enthusiastic. "Slymy rimes, as thick as flies in the sunne," he complains. "I thinke there be neuer an Ale-house in England, not any so base a maypole on a country greene, but sets forth some Poetts, Peternells, or Demylances to the paper warres in Paules Church-yard" (Leishman 1949, lines 151–55). England, Iudicio tells his companion, has proved all too adept at hatching mediocre poems. They rise out of mud like flies, gather into an enormous swarm, and, to his dismay, converge on London. The result is conflict—poets metamorphose into soldiers armed with large pistols or carbines ("Peternells") or light horsemen carrying short lances ("Demylances")— and, thus equipped, take their places on the battlefield at Paul's (that is, post their poems for others to see and commend).

Although Iudicio appears to be speaking sarcastically, his choice of imagery is neither frivolous nor accidental. The decade preceding the 1601 or 1602 performance of *The Return from Parnassus* had been characterized by an extraordinary amount of artistic conflict, by quarrels that may have had their origins in personal animosity but also involved (or came to involve) literary questions as well. The Gabriel

Harvey–Thomas Nashe controversy during the first part of the 1590s was the earliest of these conflicts—one which was for Harvey primarily a matter of family honor, but for Nashe a welcome opportunity for artistic display and the pursuit of fame (Stern 1979, 85–129). In 1597 Joseph Hall precipitated a second quarrel when, in the Prologue to his collection of "Tooth-lesse Satyres," he defiantly announced his own originality—"*I first aduenture: follow me who list, / And be the second English Satyrist*" (Hall 1949, 11)—strengthened that claim in the work itself by detailing the weaknesses of other types of English poetry, and later attacked the verses of John Marston, who had the audacity to take up his challenge and so threatened the exclusivity of Hall's achievement. Before this controversy had ended, both Everard Guilpin and John Weever apparently found it necessary to join in (the former on Marston's behalf, the latter more evenhandedly managing to support each side at one time or another), and a third and more important literary quarrel had begun: the War of the Theaters, which involved Marston, Thomas Dekker, Ben Jonson, and perhaps others as well.[1] Indeed, the notoriety of these quarrels and the interest generated by them was so great that, in Arlice Davenport's words (1951, 2:viii), "literary circles . . . would not only attend theatres to see 'flyting' plays, but were so well informed that they would even buy anonymous and obscurely allusive pamphlets in sufficient numbers to make publishers interested."

The reasons for this fascination with and, in fact, the frequency of such quarrels at the end of the sixteenth century were both numerous and complex. Many of the writers involved seem to have had particularly combative personalities. Most of them wrote for an Inns of Court audience, which apparently enjoyed and encouraged such rivalry (Finkelpearl 1969, 3–80); or for the coterie theaters, where "playwrights advertised whatever innovative quality their work possessed, if not explicitly then by encouraging spectators to mock what had only yesterday been in vogue" (Shapiro 1977, 228). But neither the personal characteristics of the men involved nor the attitudes prevalent at the Inns of Court and the children's playhouses were, finally, the most important reasons for these conflicts. Iudicio alludes to a more basic cause in the answer he gives to Ingenioso: the late-sixteenth-century proliferation of poets and poems in numbers that made classification, discrimination, and evaluation both possible and desirable. It was not accidental that only at the end of this century did English writers begin attempting to define what Richard Helgerson has called a "laureate" career, distinct from amateurism on the one hand and crass professionalism on the other.[2] Nor was it by chance that *The Return from Parnassus* contained a catalogue of contemporary writers, which described their strengths and weaknesses (lines 202–326) and was reminiscent of a more famous and extensive listing that had appeared only a few years before, in 1598: Francis Meres's "A Comparatiue Discourse of Our English Poets with the Greek, Latine, and Italian Poets" in *Palladis Tamia, Wits Treasury*—a work that at once took stock of the newly created breadth of English letters and attempted to structure that richness, however ineptly and haltingly, by evaluating the relative strengths and capabilities of Meres's contemporaries.

This endeavor to evaluate was generated by the same impulses that encouraged the literary quarrels of the last thirteen years of Elizabeth's reign. The underlying function of the "paper warres" to which the author of the *Return* refers so scornfully was essentially no different from that of the same writer's censure of English poets later in the play: to create difference out of apparent similarity, to make distinctions between writers, to evaluate their skills, and by so doing to create an orderly hierarchy of authors within English letters. Admittedly, few of the participants entered the controversies with these goals consciously in mind, but the victory or approval each sought by engaging in what might be called a particularly militant form of comparison would necessarily become at least a partial basis for distinguishing one work, one attitude, from another and so an initial step toward the establishment of a series of differential relationships among authors. Moreover, as Meres recognized, these conflicts, if sustained, would become not only a basis for comparing one poet with another but also a means of preventing one kind of poetry or one poet from dominating all others: "As that ship is endaungered where all leane to one side, but is in safetie one leaning one way and another another way: so the dissensions of Poets among themselues doth make them that they lesse infect their readers."[3] Conflict is often generated by a lack of easily recognized differences; in such cases, it is an attempt to create (to enforce) distinctions. But if no final victory in the conflict is attained or allowed, the continuing rivalry serves to limit and undermine the very differences that the conflict (from the point of view of those involved) was intended to establish. I return to this paradox again in the following pages.

Not all English writers at the end of the sixteenth century were willing, however, to grant the beneficial effects of the quarrels. As early as 1596, for example, Thomas Lodge pleaded in *Wits Miserie, and the worlds Madness* for unanimity among English poets: "Knit your industries in priuate, to vnite your fames in publike: let the strong stay vp the weake," lest "besotted with foolish vain-glory, emulation, and contempt, you fall to neglect one another" (1963, 4:63). Two years later, Everard Guilpin lamented that English poets, having only recently defeated the forces of barbarism, "Puft up by conquest, with selfe-wounding spight, / Engraue themselues in ciuill warres *Abismes*" (1974, 39); and in *No Whippinge, nor trippinge: but a kind of friendly Snippinge* (1601), Nicholas Breton created a persona who—having by chance caught a glimpse of the wars at Paul's—urges that "all scholars should be friends, / And Poets not . . . brawle for pudding ends," because "our Muses sweetest musique make, / When gratious spirits doe agree in one" (Davenport 1951, vol. 2, lines 370–71, 379–80). As if in answer to the notion that conflict may lead to order and the establishment of hierarchical relationships, these poets point again and again to the envy, ambition, and malice displayed by the participants—qualities that must lead, in their opinion, to the denigration of poetry and poets. Whoever chose the problematic nature of emulation as the subject for rhetorical exercises at Oxford in 1599 and 1604 undoubtedly thought so as well (Boaseand and Clark 1885–89, 2[1]: 174–75).

Somewhat surprisingly, one of the most thoughtful and penetrating critiques of the impulses that gave birth to the literary quarrels occurs in a work not directly related to the controversies at all, Samuel Daniel's *A Defense of Rhyme* (1603). Daniel's argument is directed specifically against Thomas Campion's comments on English prosody, not against vying poets, but his essay was written only two years after the conclusion of the War of the Theaters, and much of what he has to say is as applicable to competing writers as it is to Campion.

Daniel's primary argument in favor of rhyme is a historical one, based on his understanding of custom. He states that custom, in effect, legislates what is by nature already suited to a particular society at a particular time (Smith 1904, 2:359). Conventions change according to the needs of different times and places, and thus it is foolish to attempt to force the ideas of one era or society upon those of another. Indeed, since custom is a historically determined expression of an eternal truth, no custom is superior to any other: "We haue but one bodie of Iustice, one bodie of Wisdome thorowout the whole world; which is but apparalled according to the fashion [the custom] of euery nation" (2:367, 371, 372).

What is of interest for my purposes is that Daniel's twin emphases upon the unchanging essence of truth and the necessarily but gradually changing social definitions and understanding of that truth lead him to be hostile toward innovation. In Daniel's scheme, innovation is both severely limited by custom and, at a more basic level, not possible—because truth is, after all, immutable. As a result, attempts to establish priority or distinctiveness are at once futile and potentially destructive, given the frustration that must result from the inevitable failure of those attempts. Daniel praises the Lacedaemonians for "holding the Innouator, though in the least things, dangerous to a publicke societie," and adds: "It is but a fantastike giddinesse to forsake the way of other men," because the way to perfection—which is, necessarily, defined by custom—can be attained "euer best by going on in the course we are in" (2:373).

If, for others, the desire to surpass previous accomplishments is essential to personal and social development, for Daniel it is a source of misery and maliciousness: "*Stimulos dat emula virtus,* and where there is not abilitie to match what is, malice will finde out ingines, either to disgrace or ruin it [what is] . . . and, which is the greatest misery, it [malice] must euer proceed from the powers of the best reputation, as if the greatest spirites were ordained to indanger the worlde, as the grosse are to dishonour it." In fact, Daniel continues, such a spirit "crosses all the world, rather than it will stay to be vnder her desires"—but in vain. Victory is not possible, only destruction. Even if one were somehow fortunate enough to stand apart successfully from the ways "beaten by Custome and the Time," that triumph would be only momentary, since what is today accounted admirable will tomorrow be dismissed with contempt (2:374–75). Wisdom is thus defined as a decision not to compete, as a recognition that "we must . . . be content to submit our selues to the law of time, which in few yeeres wil make al that for which we now contend *Nothing*" (2: 384).

It is against this background of literary rivalry and the various responses elicited by it that we can best begin to outline Ben Jonson's attempt to create for himself a literary identity. Just as the inflation of honors during the reign of James I led to ever greater levels of competition and unrest among the aristocracy (Stone 1965, 65–128), so the proliferation of poets and would-be poets toward the end of the sixteenth century seems to have encouraged several writers—Jonson perhaps foremost among them—to endeavor to stand apart from their contemporaries in order to define and preserve their artistic superiority.

We cannot finally determine, of course, whether key portions of Daniel's *Defense of Rhyme* were aimed specifically at Jonson; nor do we know whether Jonson believed that the tract condemned, even if only indirectly, the competitiveness that was quickly becoming a central characteristic of his artistic career. What we do know is that as late as his 1618–19 stay with William Drummond, Jonson was criticizing his fellow writer with an energy suggesting that he found Daniel a formidable rival. For despite what might be called Daniel's rather un-Jonsonian message in the *Defense,* the two men had in fact a great deal in common: both were accomplished poets and literary theorists; both tried their hands at historical writing; and both sought employment as writers of court masques (Norbrook 1984, 178–79). Daniel's fears about the destructive effects of rivalry may have led him to respond to these connections in a relatively unaggressive manner—Daniel was, Jonson assured Drummond, only "at Jealousies" with him (*Conversations,* line 152)—but Jonson apparently felt no such hesitations.[4] He belittled Daniel's historical writings, indicated that "he had written a discourse of Poesie both against Campion & Daniel especially this last," and, perhaps most damningly, described his contemporary as "a good honest Man . . . bot no poet" (*Conversations*, lines 5–7, 23–24, 211–12).

Jonson's criticisms of Daniel are certainly unattractive and perhaps even reprehensible, but their function was, in Jonson's scheme of things, extremely important. They were an attempt to make distinctions where distinctions might not readily be apparent and, as such, necessary—so Jonson believed—to the creation of social and artistic order. Whereas Daniel's response to the power of custom and the inevitability of change was, in theory at least, a glorification of "going on in the course we are in" as the only socially responsible activity, Jonson's was the opposite: a tendency to praise that which is unique and stands out from what is faceless and common. In Daniel's view, differences exist primarily in the relation of one society or era to another; within a given society, adherence to custom leads to a beneficial conformity. In Jonson's, differences must exist within a particular society as well. When at the conclusion of a long and apparently original discussion of flatterers (*Discoveries*, lines 1586–1635), Jonson adds, "Yet I know not truly which is worse; hee that malignes all, or that praises all" (lines 1632–34), the word *all* points to the source of both problems; it indicates a failure to discriminate and so a lack of judgment.

The need to discriminate ever more carefully was surely one of Jonson's central concerns—both in his dealings with society and—more important to my purposes—in his art. A cursory glance through his poems, for instance, reveals numerous examples of this tendency: his use of contrast and negative definitions in poems of praise ("Thou are not, PENSHVRST, built to eniuous show"); his decision to name only the virtuous,[5] because

> Th'Ignoble never liv'd, they were a'while
> Like Swine, or other Cattell here on earth:
> Their names are not recorded on the File
> Of Life, that fall so.
> (*Vnder-wood* 75.153–56)

In these and similar poems we sense, as Richard Helgerson (1983, 171) has argued, "the power of exclusion and the presence of the great excluder. Definition is by difference, and Jonson is always there heroically drawing the line." Such careful discrimination is necessary if virtue is, finally, to "stand forth" (*Vnder-wood* 14.29)—that is, stand apart—from a background provided by common humanity, and at times Jonson goes to extraordinary lengths to accomplish this goal.

In *Epigrammes* 94, to cite a particularly striking example, Jonson praises Lucy, Countess of Bedford, for her interest in and support of poetry. The occasion is her favorable response to Donne's satires, and that response leads Jonson to describe her virtue through a series of contrasts that delineate her special qualities with greater and greater clarity. "Rare poemes aske rare friends" (line 6), the speaker notes, and so initially distinguishes Lucy from the typical reader. She is, in her way, as remarkable as the poems before her. This judgment is emphasized in turn by the following lines: "Yet, *Satyres,* since the most of mankind bee / Their vn-auoided subiect, fewest see" (lines 7–8). Lucy is now no longer the typically rare reader of the typically rare—that is, excellent—poem; she is a reader of satire, and only the "fewest" see or understand this genre, since "most" are its subject. The contrasting superlatives once again distinguish Lucy from ordinary humanity and even more forcefully than before: the "fewest" who understand satire are presumably a subcategory of the larger group of "rare friends" that skillful poetry in general requires. In fact, Lucy's interest in this sort of poem is evidently a dangerous activity rather than simply an expression of preference or intelligence. Given that satire makes social corruption its theme,

> They, then, that liuing where the matter is bred,
>> Dare for these poemes, yet, both aske, and read,
> And like them too; must needfully, though few,
>> Be of the best.
> (lines 11–14)

The verb "dare," the conjunction "yet" (which calls our attention once more to Lucy's reasons not to read), the adverb "both" (which gives a double aspect to her daring), and the surprising addition of a third aspect of that daring ("And like them")—at once emphasized by its unexpectedness (we tend to assume that "both aske, and read" is a complete syntactical unit) and by the concluding adverb "too"—all demonstrate why this reader must necessarily be "of the best." But the speaker is not content with even this distinction; "'mongst those [the best]," he tells Lucy, "best are you" (line 14). Lucy has progressed from her status as a "rare" friend of "rare" poetry to a position among the "fewest" who understand satire, to a place among the "best" who like as well as read and comprehend this difficult genre, to a station above even the best. No poem of which I am aware moves more emphatically from the common to the uncommon, from the ordinary to the extraordinary.

Similar tendencies are present in Jonson's plays, although in more complex forms, some of which I detail in later chapters. Here I want to examine briefly the opening scene of *Every Man in His Humour,* the earliest of his plays that Jonson considered successful enough to include in the folio edition of his works. Specifically, I am interested in a change made when he was revising the drama for publication in the folio, an alteration that emphasizes one of its most important concerns: the ability to distinguish between good and bad art. Early in the quarto edition of the comedy, Lorenzo Senior laments his son's interest in poetry, an interest that he fears will interfere with Lorenzo Junior's successful completion of his studies:

> My selfe was once a *student,* and indeede
> Fed with the selfe-same humor he is now,
> Dreaming on nought but idle *Poetrie*:
> But since, Experience hath awakt my sprit's,
> And reason taught them, how to comprehend
> The soueraigne vse of study.
> (1.1.16–21)

The folio version begins similarly, but Jonson alters the conclusion of the worried father's speech (he is now called Old Knowell) in a small but significant manner: noting that he once thought poetry "the mistresse of all knowledge," Old Knowell is pleased that he has now learned otherwise:

But since, time, and the truth haue wak'd my iudgement,
And reason taught me better to distinguish
The vaine, from the'vsefull learnings.
(1.1.20–24)

The point of the revision is roughly equivalent to that of the original, but the language differs in a way I find instructive. In the quarto, experience has awakened Lorenzo Senior's "sprit's"; in the folio, it is Old Knowell's "iudgement" that has increased. In the quarto, this awakening enabled Lorenzo Senior better "to comprehend" the purpose of study; in the folio, it taught Old Knowell "better to distinguish" vain from useful learning. The folio version thus introduces much more forcefully what is perhaps the play's major theme. What Old Knowell thinks he has learned is the ability to discriminate: it is the business of judgment to distinguish rather than unite, to separate rather than join. As a result, the revision makes the father's opening statement more clearly ironic. Despite his age and experience, Old Knowell has in fact not yet learned to distinguish carefully enough; it is this inability that leads at the end of the play to the displacement of his authority by that of Justice Clement, who, for all his apparent silliness, can make distinctions that the father cannot, a skill which is represented by Clement's praise of Brainworm (for his wit) and condemnation of Matthew (for his lack of it), and which is, finally, the only source of justification true poetry needs. "Sir," Edward Knowell gratefully tells the madcap judge after Clement has contradicted Old Knowell's equation of Matthew with all poets, "you haue sau'd me the labour of a defence" (5.5.46).

As these examples suggest, one could make a good case for calling judgment the single most important human activity in the Jonsonian world. The importance of distinctions is everywhere emphasized; the ability to distinguish carefully is continually praised. Repeatedly, we encounter "the constant, sweaty effort to mark a difference" (Helgerson 1983, 183). The reason for this emphasis lies in Jonson's assessment of human nature and culture: he found judgment essential because it can at least partially counteract what he believed to be powerful tendencies toward repetition and mimicry in the human psyche and in society at large, tendencies that he (unlike Daniel) saw as pernicious rather than desirable. His most vivid and famous account of these forces occurs in *Discoveries* (lines 1093–99), with the marginal notation, *De vita humana*:

> I *have* considered, our whole life is like a *Play:* wherein every man, forgetfull of himselfe, is in travaile with expression of another. Nay, wee so insist in imitating others, as wee cannot (when it is necessary) returne to our selves: like Children, that imitate the vices of *Stammerers* so long, till at last they become such; and make the habit to another nature, as it is never forgotten.

Human endeavors are here described as the product of an incessant desire to break the bonds of the self in order to identify so completely with some other that distinctions between the self and that other are no longer possible. The result is disorder: the loss of differences and an obscuring of the dividing line between appearance and reality. The *theatrum mundi* trope that forms the basis of the passage is an especially appropriate choice, because, as Jonas Barish (1981, 87) has detailed, the theater has almost since its inception elicited "the fears of impurity, of contamination, of 'mixture,' of the blurring of strict boundaries, which haunted thousands in the Renaissance as they haunted Plato and Tertullian."[6]

In contrast, virtuous individuals, we are told in the passage immediately following this one (*Discoveries*, lines 1100–1109), are defined in large part by their ability to remain detached from this disorder. "*Good men* are the Stars, the Planets of the Ages"; they reside, like Chaucer's Troilus, in a realm somehow beyond the world of mutability, refusing to give up their self-possession, unwilling to be the "partakers, or practisers" of the madness they see below. As a result, the virtuous are not actors but audience: "But they, plac'd high on the top of all vertue, look'd down on the Stage of the world, and contemned the Play of *Fortune*. For though the most be players, some must be *Spectators*."

The opposition could not be clearer: on the one hand a world of actors desperately attempting to adopt new roles and so threatening to dissolve all difference between reality and appearance; on the other a small group of individuals who choose not to play at all but remain forever themselves, unperturbed by the chaotic activity that bustles about (or below) them.[7] The former are present everywhere in the Jonsonian canon—not only in his fools but also in the Protean figures who prey upon them. The latter are, as might be expected, less conspicuous: we glimpse aspects of the ideals they embody in *"An Ode. To himself,"* where the speaker argues, "'Tis crowne enough to vertue still, her owne applause" and vows to "sing high and aloofe, / Safe from the wolves black jaw, and the dull Asses hoofe" (*Vnder-wood* 23.18, 35–36); in characters like Horace in *Poetaster* and Crites in *Cynthia's Revels,* who attempt to ignore the attacks and enticements of the corrupt world around them; in Lovel's long disquisition on fortitude in *The New Inn* (4.4.105–221).

But the detachment Jonson associated with the highest virtue is, as he well knew, extremely difficult to sustain for very long. Jonson's own behavior is proof enough of that: no writer of his generation remained less aloof from the world of his time. A similar inability affects his most idealized characters as well (cf. Danson 1984, 183). Not even Crites in *Cynthia's Revels* consistently stands apart from the society he inhabits: he competes with the courtiers at their own games; he writes a masque for Cynthia; he assigns suitable punishments to his enemies. The same is true of Horace in *Poetaster* and, in fact, of virtually all the other characters in Jonson's works who endeavor to withdraw from the action: Surly, Quarlous and Winwife, Penniboy Cantor, Lovel and the Host. Jonson's most determined spectator—Arruntius in *Sejanus*—is impotent, if talkative. And one might argue that a major theme of *Bartholomew Fair* is the impossibility of separating oneself from the world. No one remains totally self-sufficient at the fair; no one remains uninvolved and untouched.

According to this playwright, then, even the best of us cannot escape from a world that is also a theater. To live is to adopt roles, or rather—to use the language Jonson employs in the passage quoted above—to imitate. We are all somehow "in travaile with expression of another"; in fact, the very existence of the passage demonstrates as much, for like so much of the material in *Discoveries* it is based upon the work of another writer. As Margaret Clayton (1979, 397–408) has shown, these comments on players and spectators are taken from John of Salisbury's *Policraticus*. And among the changes that Jonson made in the original, he altered John's third person to first—"they insist" to "we insist"—thus emphasizing his own involvement in the very activity the passage apparently condemns.

Jonson's imitation of John of Salisbury is, certainly, literary rather than social; he is echoing a text rather than a role. But for Jonson there was very little difference. Imitation was for him an inescapable human activity, central to all areas of human endeavor, but also a problematic one. If to live or to write is in some way to follow a model external to the self, the effect of imitation can only be a lessening of distinctions, a blurring of boundaries that may threaten the existence of virtue, since virtue in Jonson is always characterized by its difference from the normal or customary. The difficulty Jonson faced was how to create diversity out of the tendency toward repetition that is inherent in most activity—more specifically, how to make his art stand out from that of other artists. As Terence Cave has argued in another context, the concept of imitation "recognizes the extent to which the production of any discourse is conditioned by pre-existing instances of discourse; the writer is always a rewriter, the problem then being how to differentiate and authenticate the rewriting" (1979, 76).

Classical and Renaissance discussions of imitation fall into three basic categories.[8] The first, which is of little interest here, defines imitation as copying or following a model as accurately as possible. A second and much more influential approach describes it as an endeavor not to reproduce a model exactly but to transform that model in a manner suited to the imitator's personality and situation. Seneca is the major classical exponent of this viewpoint, and his *Epistulae Morales* contain several discussions of the concept. In his view, the best ideas are "common property," yet these ideas cannot simply be repeated by one writer after another. "Let there be a difference between yourself and your book," he urges, since "the truth will never be discovered if we rest contented with discoveries already made." The model is a guide or an aid to the imitator—a source of ideas, forms, and images, but not of limits and restrictions: "Men who have made these discoveries before us are not our masters, but our guides. Truth lies open for all" (33.2, 9, 10–11). Seneca's letters are full of organic metaphors—precepts are seeds (38.2); subjects grow (79.6)—and he employs natural imagery to describe the process of imitation as well, comparing it to the creation of honey out of nectar (84.5) and to the digestion of food (84.7). He also argues that the relation between an imitation and its model is analogous to that between a child and parent: "Even if there shall appear in you a likeness of him who, by reason of your admiration, has left a deep impress upon you, I would have you resemble him as a child resembles his father, and not as a picture resembles its original; for a picture is a lifeless thing" (84.8). According to Seneca (and those who echo his views), imitation is a dynamic, living process akin to the workings of nature; mere repetition is unnatural, stultifying, and sterile. Moreover, imitation is implicitly a form of historical thought. It is a concept that simultaneously allows artistic forms and ideas to evolve according to the dictates of context and a writer's own personality and ensures continuity by positing a necessary relation between the new and the old. It both acknowledges and limits change.

The third approach to imitation differed considerably from the stoic philosopher's transformative emphasis; it defined imitation as an endeavor to compete with and surpass a model rather than merely alter it.[9] This view of imitation tends to draw its metaphors from warfare rather than nature, and in Latin it is often associated with the verb *aemulari* rather than *imitari*. Its earliest known proponent is Hesiod, who, in the opening section of *The Works and Days,* describes a beneficent form of strife that "raises a man to work, even though he be inactive. For anyone when idle having looked upon another being rich, he, I say, makes haste to plant, and well to order his house; for neighbour rivals neighbour, when hastening toward riches; but this condition is good for mortals. Both potter is jealous of potter, and craftsman of craftsman; and poor man has a grudge against poor man, and poet against poet" (lines 20–26).

Quintilian, however, was probably the most influential classical advocate of this viewpoint. He argues that imitation must always be competitive, even combative. One attempts not to repeat or transform the model but to overcome it: "And even those who do not aim at supreme excellence, ought to press toward the mark rather than be content to follow in the tracks of others. For the man whose aim is to prove himself better than another, even if he does not surpass him, may hope to equal him. But he can never hope to equal him, if he thinks it his duty to tread in his footsteps: for the mere follower must always lag behind" (*Institutio Oratoria* 10.2.9–10; cf. 10.2.11). Speaking of paraphrase, Quintilian notes that "its duty is . . . to rival and vie with the the original" (10.5.5), and the goal of this rivalry (*certamen* and *aemulatio* are Quintilian's terms for it) is quite simply the displacement of the original model by the imitator's creation, which then becomes a model for other writers to compete with in what seems to be an endless process: "For this glory also shall be theirs, that men shall say of them that while they surpassed their predecessors, they also taught those who came after" (10.2.28). Greatness comes only at the expense (through the defeat) of prior greatness; it can be maintained only by a continuing superiority over all who assert their rival claims. If for Seneca imitation is a process similar to the natural and apparently uneventful passage of characteristics from parent to child, for Quintilian, Hesiod, and others who share their views it is a form of generational conflict. As the author of *On the Sublime* puts it, "Plato would not have reared so many flowers among the precepts of philosophy or so often employed poetic material and language had he not, I tell you, striven with all his heart against Homer for the preeminence, a young antagonist against one who had attained high honors" (Gilbert 1940, 164).

Enthusiasm for this emulative version of imitation was often accompanied, however, by a suspicion that competition is not always beneficial; emulation may easily become—is, in fact, often indistinguishable from—malice and envy.[10] *Aemulatio* is, Cicero notes, a word with two meanings: "For one thing, rivalry [*aemulatio*] is used of the imitation of virtue . . . and rivalry is distress, should another be in possession of the object desired and one has to go without it oneself" (*Tusculan Disputations* 4.8.17). Some sixteen hundred years later Robert Burton was making essentially the same point in his own characteristically jumbled manner. Emulation is, Burton assures us a close relative of hatred, faction, and desire of revenge, not to mention envy; moreover, "every society, corporation, and private family is full of it . . . scarce three in a company but there is siding, faction, emulation betwixt two of them, some *simultas,* jar, private grudge, heart-burning in the midst of them (1932, 1:267)." Similarly, according to Thomas Hobbes, "*Griefe,* for the successe of a Competitor in wealth, honour, or other good, if it be joyned with Endeavor to enforce our own abilities to equall or exceed him, is called EMULATION: But joyned with Endeavour to supplant, or hinder a Competitor, ENVIE (1968, 126)." For others, this was a distinction without a difference, since, as Joseph Webbe wrote to Jonson in 1628, the air too often is infected by "some ill sauouring breath of Mallice, now called emulation" (Herford, Simpson, and Simpson 1925–52, 11:359).

As this brief account suggests, the concept of imitation that Jonson inherited was in fact three or four different concepts, all involving a relationship between an imitator and a model / rival but defining that relationship in ways ranging from complete subservience (attempting to copy the model) to hostility (attempting to overthrow it). Taken together, the various attitudes doubtless point to the ambivalent emotions inherent in any imitative act (any, at least, performed by a mature person) and delineate the complexity of an activity that Jonson and others believed central to human existence.

When we turn to Jonson's own comments about the concept, we find a similar range of attitudes. On one hand, as Richard Peterson (1981) has demonstrated in detail, Jonson repeats with approval the Senecan view of imitation as a method of gathering, digesting, and transforming literary models in ways dictated by the pressures of the imitator's personality and his historical situation. His well-known motto *tamquam explorator* has its source in the writings of the stoic philosopher (*Epistulae Morales* 2.5–6), as does—ultimately—his equally well-known comment, "It is true they [the ancients] open'd the gates, and made the way, that went before us; but as Guides, not Commanders" (*Discoveries,* lines 137–39; cf. *Epistulae Morales* 33.11).

He paraphrases Seneca's comparisons between imitation and the creation of honey and between imitation and digestion (*Discoveries,* lines 2467–80); and although at times Jonson's observations on ancient writers imply an emulative as well as an imitative impulse, in general his relation to classical antiquity seems to have involved a mixture of "respect for authority and vigorous independence," a "process of judicious gathering in and transforming," and a "generous willingness to encounter and assimilate" (Peterson 1981, 5, 21, 30).[11]

Yet Jonson's comments about imitation are more complex than this account implies. Whereas his relation to classical models was a relatively unproblematic one in which cultural and historical differences guaranteed at least some likelihood that his creations would be distinct from those they drew upon, thus preventing the confusions of indentity described in his account of the *theatrum mundi,* his attitude toward writers less distanced in time was considerably different. Jonson was too good a historian—and, I think, too aware of his own impulses—to deny our tendencies to be less critical of the past than of the present and to idealize what no longer exists because, finally, it has little power over us. As he notes in a passage taken from Velleius Paterculus, "Wee *praise* the things wee heare, with much more willingnesse, then those wee see: because wee envy the present, and reverence the past; thinking our selves instructed by the one, and overlaid by the other" (*Discoveries* lines 39–42); and in another passage which has no known source: "*There* is a greater Reverence had of things remote, or strange to us, then of much better, if they bee neerer, and fall under our sense. Men, and almost all sort of creatures, have their reputation by distance" (lines 1489–92). Jonson is capable even of complicating Seneca's procreative metaphor for the relation of imitator and model by moving that metaphor firmly in the direction of Quintilian's generational conflict or Harold Bloom's (1973) "anxiety of influence": "*Greatnesse* of name, in the Father, oft-times helpes not forth, but o'rewhelmes the Sonne: they stand too neere one another. The shadow kils the growth: so much, that wee see the Grand-child come more, and oftner, to be the heire of the *first,* then doth the *second:* He dies betweene, the Possession is the *thirds*" (*Discoveries,* lines 413–18; no known source). The passage reads like an epigraph for the fate of many of Jonson's own literary sons, similarly overwhelmed by their unwillingness or inability to cope with the father's greatness. One can be too close to the model, to the source, and that proximity can be self-destructive.

It can also lead to acts of aggression. Not only does *Discoveries* contain several passages detailing our different responses to things that are distant from or near to us; it also contains others that suggest a close relation between unsuccessful imitation and malice—most notably a long passage drawn from J. J. Scaliger: "It is a barbarous envy, to take from those mens vertues, which because thou canst not arrive at, thou impotently despairest to imitate. Is it a crime in me that I know that, which others had not yet knowne, but from me? or that I am the Author of many things, which never would have come in thy thought, but that I taught them? It is a new, but a foolish way you have found out, that whom you cannot equall, or come neere in doing, you would destroy, or ruine with evill speaking" (lines 261–70). We have here entered the realm of an emulation that has merged—as Cicero and Burton, among others, warn—with hatred and envy. And it is perhaps worth noting that Jonson intensifies the effect of the original passage by referring to those afflicted with this "barbarous envy" in the second rather than the third person (in the first sentence, *nequit* is translated as "thou canst not arrive at," and so on), and by altering the target of this envy from "you" to "me" (*sciat hodie magnum crimene esse te scire* becomes "Is it a crime in me that I know").[12]

According to Jonson, most relationships between contemporaries or near contemporaries who have similar interests are emulative and thus characterized by the ambivalent emotions that often accompany competition. The importance of envy in his work is in part due to this belief: emulation and envy are key components of the Jonsonian world, especially that of the 1616 folio.[13] A brief examination of one additional section in *Discoveries* may help reinforce this point. Discussing in an apparently original passage the effect a virtuous man has on those around him, Jonson notes that "he is growne to active men, an example; to the sloathfull, a spurre; to the envious a Punishment" (lines 1295–97). However one finally chooses to paraphrase this quotation, it seems at first glance to imply that worthy individuals—the "active men"—respond to the virtue of others in a relatively positive and perhaps uncompetitive way. They may imitate or follow the example before them, but they do not envy or rival it. But Jonson also employs these ideas in one of his poems, slightly altering the passage and clarifying its meaning: in active men a virtuous deed

> Doth Emulation stirre;
> To th' dull, a Spur
> It is: to th' envious meant
> A meere upbraiding Griefe, and tort'ring punishment.
> (*Vnder-wood* 75.116–20)

The second and third responses remain essentially unchanged, but the first is redefined in a manner that precludes the possibility of an uncompetitive response on anyone's part. The sequence begins with emulation, not imitation; in doing so, it suggests that contemporary exploits may always produce something of an emulative effect, that the response in the best minds to contemporary greatness is rivalry. One does not imitate one's peers disinterestedly.

Whatever the general validity of these comments, which Jonson gathered together in commonplace-book fashion, they are an accurate assessment of his own literary relationships. If Jonson's relation with the literary past is inclusive, generous, and assimilative, his relations with his contemporaries, even in praise, are exclusive and discriminating. He tends to praise fulsomely only literary figures who are distanced by time and canonized by authority; his attitude toward contemporary poets and dramatists (despite exceptions like his epigrams in praise of Donne and the more ambiguous example of his poem on Shakespeare) is, to put it mildly, much less accepting. As Thomas Hobbes would later state, near midcentury, "Competition of praise, enclineth to a reverence of Antiquity. For men contend with the living, not with the dead; to those ascribing more than due, that they may obscure the glory of the other" (1968, 161). Talking with William Drummond, Jonson thus had no difficulty in finding the time to say a few harsh things about Sidney, Spenser, Shakespeare, Drayton, Silvester, Harington, Donne, Middleton, Ralegh, Petrarch, and

Guarini—not to mention Samuel Daniel. And the English poet and dramatist's extraordinarily complex *imitation* of classical authors—itself a highly dynamic and individual activity—unquestionably served in part an *emulative* function in relation to his contemporaries.

Predictably, Jonson's most effusive expression of indebtedness to a contemporary, his epigram to William Camden (*Epigrammes* 14), is directed to a non-poet: that is, to a "father" whose potential conflict with his "son" is minimized because they are already sufficiently distanced by their interests. The problematic tendency toward the loss of distinctions that Jonson believed inherent in the generally imitative nature of all human endeavor is less pressing in relationships where some degree of difference is already ensured—by different vocations (as with Jonson and Camden), by different eras and cultures (as with Jonson and classical writers). The considerable historical and linguistic distance between the classical age and the Elizabethan and Jacobean periods allowed Jonson to imitate Greek and Latin authors without losing his own voice and so eliminated any real need to compete with those writers in order to assert his own originality. One can praise the past, even follow it to some extent, precisely because it is the past and is obviously other. It is in the contemporary scene that imitative tendencies threaten most seriously to destroy distinctions in the name of custom or use; thus it is there that we most often encounter emulation and envy, as individuals attempt to establish their identities by outdoing or defeating those who are most like them—in Jonson's case, other poets and dramatists. Similarity, not difference, most often leads to competition, and this causal sequence is embedded in the various meanings of *corrival* and *competitor* during the Renaissance. A "corrival" or a "competitor" is at once an equal, an associate, and an opponent,[14] and the intensity of the competition between such figures usually increases the more closely they are linked (hence, for example, Jonson's focus on Marston in the War of the Theaters). As René Girard (1977, 49) has shown, "Order, peace, and fecundity depend on cultural distinctions: it is not these distinctions but the loss of them that gives birth to fierce rivalries."

I have argued above that the literary quarrels of the 1590s were competitions of this kind, and much of Jonson's career as well can be viewed fruitfully from this perspective. The act of emulating is both a recognition of the importance of imitation and an attempt to imitate (compete) in such a way as to create (ultimately) difference rather than similarity, and so to establish hierarchy and order out of the imitative tendency toward equality and (potential) confusion. It is a particularly militant form of comparison whose final goal is contrast. That is why Jonson is so careful to make his opponents known, to define by negatives and by exclusion: witness the scarcely veiled attacks on Anthony Munday, Marston, and Shakespeare in the plays; the polemical prologue to the first comedy in the 1616 folio, *Every Man in His Humour;* the similarly intended opening poem in *The Forrest* ("WHY I WRITE NOT OF LOVE"); and the scornful reference to the epigrams of John Weever and John Davies early in Jonson's own collection of poems in that genre (*Epigrammes* 18). Only by such comparisons, by juxtaposing his art to that of his presumed inferiors and rivals, could he demonstrate his difference from and superiority to them. The emulator demands an opponent; he cannot exist in isolation.[15]

Jonson's awareness of the benefits to be gained by contrasting his art with that of other writers is perhaps most apparent in an epigram entitled *"To a Friend, and Sonne"* (*Vnder-wood* 69). In this poem, as he does so frequently, Jonson deals with friendship, a concern that leads him—not unexpectedly—to a discussion of the difference between true friends and flatterers; he compares it to that between a real dog and a painter's unskillful depiction of one. What both the flatterer and painter dare not do in order to protect their fraud is "come in the comparison" (line 8). The painter, evidently employing a "subtler skill" than that with which he created his picture, hires a boy to drive all real dogs away from his shop (lines 9–13); similarly,

> So doth the flatt'rer with faire cunning strike
> At a Friend's freedome, proves all circling meanes
> To keepe him off; and how-so-e're he gleanes
> Some of his formes, he lets him not come neere

Where he would fixe, for the distinctions feare.
For as at distance, few have facultie
    To judge; so all men comming neere can spie.
    (lines 14–20)

As is often true in Jonson, the cause of this problem is a "cunning"
and duplicitous ("circling") attempt to obscure differences—here between the "formes" the flatterer "gleanes" from the actions of true
friends and the reality those forms mimic, an attempt that can succeed only if the forgery remains isolated from its original. The solution is an act of judgment, but this act is possible only if the imitation and its model are juxtaposed. In this situation, separation
obscures differences; proximity highlights them: "For as at distance,
few have facultie / To judge; so all men comming neere can spie."
Jonson's goal, these lines imply, is to create distance by first overcoming it; he insists upon creating the comparisons lesser authors may
wish to avoid.

In his competitiveness, admittedly, Jonson probably differed little
from some of his more ambitious contemporaries or, for that matter,
from most other authors seeking fame. The desire to surpass one's
peers is hardly unusual. Jonson did differ, however, in the breadth of
expression that he gave to emulation. We find it not only in the relations between his works and those of other writers—that is, where
we expect to find it—but also in the works themselves, in elements
of characterization, theme, and structure. Emulation was not simply
one of Jonson's most notable personal activities; it was also (and often)
his subject, as if he felt compelled to examine as carefully as possible
the dynamics of an endeavor that formed an important part of his life.
This is not surprising: Jonson usually fused artistic concerns with social and personal ones, and emulation is not, of course, central only
to artistic enterprises. Yet the amount of attention he gave to this
activity is remarkable, for it exceeds that of even Horace and Aristophanes, the two classical writers he most resembles in this respect
(see Chapters 3 and 4). The artistic world Jonson created is very much
a replica of the one he believed to be his own. Looking in some detail

at a few of his works that make emulation their subject will develop and clarify these points.

Among his poems, Jonson's most explicit depiction of literary competition is *Epigrammes* 112, entitled "To a Weake Gamster in Poetry":

> With thy small stocke, why art thou ventring still,
>> At this so subtile sport: and play'st so ill?
> Think'st thou it is meere fortune, that can win?
>> Or thy ranke setting? that thou dar'st put in
> Thy all, at all: and what so ere I doe,
>> Art still at that, and think'st to blow me'vp too?
> I cannot for the stage a *Drama* lay,
>> *Tragicke,* or *Comick:* but thou writ'st the play.
> I leaue thee there, and giuing way, entend
>> An *Epick* poeme; thou hast the same end.
> I modestly quit that, and thinke to write,
>> Next morne, an *Ode:* Thou mak'st a song ere night.
> I passe to *Elegies;* Thou meet'st me there:
>> To *Satyres;* and thou dost pursue me. Where,
> Where shall I scape thee? in an *Epigramme?*
>> O, (thou cry'st out) that is thy proper game.
> Troth, if it be, I pitty thy ill lucke;
>> That both for wit, and sense, so oft dost plucke,
> And neuer art encounter'd, I confesse:
>> Nor scarce dost colour for it, which is lesse.
> Pr'y thee, yet saue thy rest; giue ore in time:
>> There's no vexation, that can make thee prime.

Lines 7–16 of the poem are taken largely from Martial (*Epigrams* 12.94). The Roman epigrammatist's account of the annoying attempts of a foolish would-be poet to ape another poet's every move, despite the latter's conciliatory endeavors to give him what he wants, would obviously have been attractive to Jonson. But Jonson alters and expands Martial's account (12.94.6) of this "ambitious man's" attempt to seek the speaker's fame, particularly in his handling of that speaker. Although Martial's persona is sarcastic and contemptuous, he is also completely passive, displaying an almost Horatian forbearance before the onslaught of his foolish adversary, wishing at all costs not "to stand in rivalry" (12.94.2) with Tucca, and finally resigning the field to his opponent, requesting at the conclusion of the poem that Tucca cede him whatever generic scraps the foolish poet has been unable to devour: "If there is anything you don't want Tucca, leave it to me" (12.94.12). In the part of the poem drawn from Martial, Jonson's persona seems somewhat less caustic than his prototype: he "modestly" (line 11) leaves the writing of epics to the gamester, and he is equally desirous not to compete.

Yet this apparent tolerance is coupled with a more assertive stance than that of Martial's speaker. In the lines Jonson adds to his model (1–6, 17–22), he defines poetry as a form of gambling ("ventring"), a "subtle sport" that involves risk and the attainment of power over others. In the process, Martial's implicit references to the less attractive aspects of emulation—Tucca's desire to appropriate the speaker's fame (12.94.10), the suggestions of violence when he "snatch[es]" the speaker's quill (*plectra rapis nobis, ambitiose, nove;* 12.94.6)—are intensified and made explicit. This game is not a harmless one: by being "still at that" which the speaker does, the gamester, Jonson's persona complains (line 6), "think'st to blow me'vp."

Given this somewhat startling clarification of the opponent's intent, Jonson's speaker becomes much less tolerant than Martial's of his adversary's folly. Instead of giving up the field (Jonson omits the last line of Martial's poem), he points to his own superiority by predicting the gamester's defeat, once again making explicit what is only suggested in the Latin model. It is a function of the speaker's stature that he can "pitty" the gamester's "ill lucke," and the description of the fool's ineptness at primero in the following lines is a scarcely veiled account of his intellectual and artistic shortcomings, coupled with advice that he stop playing altogether. Seeking wit and sense, he will, the speaker assures him, never be "encounter'd": that is, never succeed in attaining even a modicum of these attributes and, perhaps as a result, never be able to engage in a serious literary conflict ("encounter") or, rather, one in which he is taken seriously. The gamester is neither able to conceal this failure (one sense of "colour") nor self-aware enough to be embarrassed by it (another sense). The "rest," which the speaker urges the gamester to save, is at once the remainder of the poetaster's wit and the possibility of a peaceful life; the speaker warns, "There's no vexation, that can make thee prime"— that "vexation" referring both to the effect the gamester intends his actions to have on the speaker and what he himself suffers in hopes of drawing a winning hand and establishing his superiority. The final word of the poem, "prime," thus indicates the gamester's goal—one evidently possessed by the speaker and attainable only by wresting it from him, by eliminating all distinctions between the speaker's art and that of his inferior.

Of course, this gamester is, so to speak, small game himself and so not much of a threat. The speaker discourses with complete assurance and authority. There is no real "encounter" in the poem; the opponent is in fact hardly an opponent at all. To see how this "subtle sport" is played by poets more nearly equal in ability, we turn to two more interesting and instructive poems: a verse epistle that Francis Beaumont sent to Jonson in approximately 1613 and Jonson's epigram in reply.

By the time Beaumont wrote his epistle, he was a well-known and highly respected figure in the English literary world, the author of an Ovidian verse narrative, *Salamacis and Hermaphroditus* (1602); a comic masterpiece, *The Knight of the Burning Pestle* (c. 1607); and a tragedy of some distinction, *The Maid's Tragedy* (c. 1610)—as well as a member (with John Fletcher) of the most successful dramatic collaboration of the age. He was also a friend of Jonson's and had written commendatory verses for *Volpone, Epicoene,* and *Catiline.* The verse epistle was evidently composed while Beaumont was away from London and contrasts his present situation with his experiences with Jonson at the Mermaid Tavern. This is how it begins:

> The Sun which doth the greatest comfort bringe
> To absent friends, because the self same thinge
> They know, they see, howe euer absent; is
> here our best Hay-maker (forgiue mee this,
> It is our Country style) In this warme shine

I lye, and Dreame of your full Mermaide wine:
O wee haue water mixt with Claret Lees,
Drinke apt to bringe in dryer heresies
then beere; Good only for a Sonnett straine
with fustian Metaphors to stuff the Braine,
soe mixt, that giuen to the thirstiest one
T'will not proue Almes, unless hee haue the stone:
Tis sould by Puritans, mixt with intent
to make it serue for either Sacrament.
I thinke with one Draught mans Invention fades,
Twoe Cupps had quite marr'd Homers Il{l}iades. [16]
(lines 1–16)

As these lines indicate, the opening section of the poem presents a humorous contrast between the inspiration afforded a poet by London and that afforded by the country, a contrast represented by the different qualities of the beverages available to the would-be poet and suggesting that the speaker's situation is relatively unconducive to art. The point of the comparison is to provide an apology for the blight from which Beaumont is suffering—"our Countrey style"—a blight that has evidently been the direct result of the replacement of Jonson's robust and inspirational Mermaid wine by a watery, thin, and stultifying country brew. The passage is full of mock-religious imagery: the country wine leads only to "dry" (that is sterile) heresies; without the aid of a philosopher's stone it cannot provide "alms" even for the thirsty; Puritans sell it for profit, since its watery quality makes it equally suitable for either baptism or communion—comments implying in one way or another that this wine deadens rather than inspires, despite being used in two instances for what should be life-giving sacraments. Even Homer could not have withstood its deleterious effects.

As the poem continues, however, the thrust of the contrast alters somewhat, and we learn that the country offers one thing London does not—peace:

and yet I thinke
It is a Potion sent vs downe to drinke

By speciall Prouidence, keeps vs from fights,
Makes vs not laugh, when wee make leggs to Knights;
T'is this that keepes our minds fitt for our states,
A Med'cine to obey our Magistrates,
for wee doe live more free, then you; noe hate,
Noe envie of anothers happie state
moves vs, wee are all equall: every whitt
Of land, that God giues men here, is their witt
If wee consider fully; for our best
and Gravest man, will with his Main-house-least
scarce please you; wee want subtilty to doe
the Cittie tricks, Lye, Hate, and fflatter too:
Here are none that can beare a fained showe.
(lines 21–35)

What is important here is Beaumont's suggestion that the same qualities of life and liquor that make invention fade and wit deteriorate are also a source of contentment and harmony. The country is a place characterized by an uncritical acceptance of authority on the one hand, and of equality on the other. The former (however comically) makes satire even of James's new creations (knights) unthinkable (line 24); the latter makes contention nonexistent. The freedom of country life is defined as a freedom from emulation and envy (lines 28–29 probably allude to the passage from Hesiod quoted above), a freedom which in the Mermaid world is in much shorter supply. And although Beaumont's persona is careful to remind us that this peaceful acceptance of equality is also an acceptance of mediocrity—country wit, associated with the land (lines 29–31), is heavy and ponderous, not quick and fiery; the most cherished family jokes ("Main-house" jests) will "scarse please" Jonson—when he adds that individuals in the country also lack the "subtilty" to lie, hate, and cheat in true city fashion, we are once again reminded that the unremarkable mediocrity of Beaumont's new life has its advantages. The ability to "beare a fained showe" is, as Jonson had by this time demonstrated in several of his plays, an art closely related to the more noble version that he and Beaumont presumably practice. What the lines imply, of course, is that a society which allows one kind of artfulness must also allow the other. If the fullness of the Mermaid wine fosters imaginative creations of the highest order, it also fosters discontent, criticism, and deceit—an ambiguity that seems to be inescapable.

As a result, when Beaumont changes ground once more and returns in the remainder of the poem to an emphasis on the beneficial aspects of his experiences at the Mermaid, he does so by employing a simile which by now should be familiar and which keeps the ambivalent, and especially the competitive, aspects of those experiences before us. "Mee thinkes," he tells Jonson,

> the litle witt I had is lost
> Since I saw you; for witt is like a Rest
> Help vpp at Tennis, which men doe best
> with the best Gamsters.
> (lines 42–45)

We are once again back in the realm of competition, of the games poets play against one another in order to hone their skills and prove their inequality, games that must be lost as well as won. And this realm, as the poem points out, is very much Jonson's.

Beaumont's famous account of the Mermaid gatherings follows (lines 45–58), with their "nimble" and "subtill" (now a positive quality) words and wit so extraordinary that it might "iustifie the Towne / for three dayes past." That description, in turn, brings him back to a realization of what he has lost. "When I remember this," he confides, "then I needs must crye" (lines 59, 61). The possibility that he might be "euermore / Bannisht vnto this home" (lines 74–75) is, finally, almost unbearable, and Beaumont concludes by praying that destiny will

> once againe
> Bring mee to thee, who wilt make smooth, & plaine
> The way of knowledge for mee, and then I
> who haue noe good in mee, but simplicitye,
> Knowe that it will my greatest comfort bee
> T'acknowledge all the rest to Come from thee.
> (lines 76–80)

These are perhaps the most beautiful lines in the poem. Having now
been reduced to a "simplicitye" analogous to his surroundings, Beaumont offers himself up to Jonson's careful tutelage in order to gain
understanding. Beaumont will return from the country not only with
its simplicity but also with its humility. He will return not to compete but to learn and to obey his "magistrate" in letters, just as he
and his fellows gladly obey their superiors in the country (lines 25–
26). The mock religious aura of the poem's opening section here returns in what seems to be a more serious guise. Whereas that aura
served earlier to emphasize the spiritual aridity of the country, it now
serves to stress Beaumont's subservience to Jonson, who will become
his guide or (as the last lines suggest) his "Maker," the source of all
that Beaumont will become.

The verse epistle, then, is more than a glorification of the Mermaid
Club, although it certainly is that as well. It presents a fairly complex
picture of the literary environment Jonson inhabited, recognizing that
environment's competitive nature and assessing, quite shrewdly, the
ambivalent effects of that competitiveness. That Beaumont finally felt
the attractions of Jonson's milieu to be more important than its dis-
advantages is not surprising; he was, after all, a considerable poetic
talent who had had more than a little success by the time he composed the poem. What is perhaps more surprising is that Beaumont,
having painted an essentially Jonsonian picture of London literary circles, states an intent to reenter those circles in a totally uncompetitive
way. For Beaumont surely knew (indeed, the wit of his poem proclaims) that he was more than some simple rustic swain seeking guidance. Jonson knew it as well. As his response shows, he found Beaumont's poem much more complex in meaning and intent than I have
as yet implied. Jonson may have believed that William Drummond
"was too good and simple, and that oft a mans modestie, made a fool
of his witt" (*Conversations,* lines 586–87), but such was certainly not
his view of Francis Beaumont.

Jonson's reply to the verse epistle (*Epigrammes* 55) is a remarkable
combination of wit and ambivalent emotion:

> How I doe loue thee BEAVMONT, and thy *Muse,*
> That vnto me dost such religion vse!

How I doe feare my selfe, that am not worth
  The least indulgent thought thy pen drops forth!
At once thou mak'st me happie, and vnmak'st;
  And giuing largely to me, more thou tak'st.
What fate is mine, that so it selfe bereaues?
  What art is thine, that so thy friend deceiues?
When euen there, where most thou praysest mee,
  For writing better, I must enuie thee.

Perhaps the most striking thing about this poem is the relation of its opening and closing words. It begins with an emphatic expression of love; it ends with an admission of the inevitability of envy.[17] How the poem gets from one to the other is arguably the major source of its interest. Jonson begins by recalling the religious overtones at the conclusion of Beaumont's epistle, as if to place the two works within the framework of an imaginary conversation. But Beaumont's "religion" leads not to the exaltation of the speaker here but to its opposite, and in lines 3–4 the relationship between Beaumont and Jonson that the former had defined at the end of his poem begins to shift. Jonson, who was in the epistle Beaumont's guide or "Maker," suddenly is thrust into a subservient position as he questions his worthiness. His friend's extraordinary praise becomes an "indulgent thought"—a phrase that transforms the younger poet into a kind and uncritical father or (in keeping with the religious associations) confessor of an undeserving son or penitent. The fact that these thoughts "drop forth" like manna also continues the religious motif but again reverses the roles of worshiper and divinity. Further, as the speaker's status erodes, he becomes more passive: he loves in line 1, fears in line 3, and then is acted upon by his more powerful friend for the remainder of the poem. Beaumont makes, takes, deceives, praises, while the speaker's fate can only act upon itself. The speaker finally does regain some measure of control in his ability to envy, but even that action is enforced from without: "I *must* enuie thee," he concedes (emphasis added). Beaumont's is the gift that impoverishes because it cannot be repaid. It creates fear, not security; it takes away contentment at the same time that it confers praise. As a result, the speaker is left by line 7 in a position similar to that of the sinner in George Herbert's poem "The Thanksgiving," attempting somehow to respond to a gift that is unmerited and, he fears, unrequitable.

But Beaumont is not, of course, Herbert's God, nor is Jonson a Christian penitent; and the next line of the poem redefines Beaumont's "indulgent thought" in a new and surprising way: "What art is thine," the speaker asks, "that so thy friend deceiues?" The verb "deceiues" is a surprising choice and gives the line added emphasis. On one level it simply indicates that the speaker expected Beaumont's praise to have results other than those that actually occurred, but on another it strongly suggests trickery on Beaumont's part, and that implication gives added weight and richness to the noun "art" with which the line begins. Beaumont's "art" is both his literary skill *and* his duplicity, his ability (in his own words) to "beare a fained showe" and so transform what appears in the epistle to be praise and a complete submission of himself to Jonson's mastery into an expression of his own power and dominance. Far from reentering the world of the Mermaid Tavern with his country-generated docility intact, Beaumont's very expression of his desire not to compete has become a competitive act, an attempt to overgo in the guise of doing the opposite.

It is probably worth noting Jonson's statement elsewhere (*Conversations*, line 154) that Beaumont, in contrast to the Drummond-like persona he adopts in the epistle, "loved too much himself & his own verses." Whatever the accuracy of this typically ungenerous remark, Jonson's epigram does suggest that Beaumont's goal in the epistle is not self-abasement but its opposite; and both the strategy and its results are admirably summed up by the ambiguity of the phrase "for writing better" in line 10. From one perspective its referent is Jonson, whom Beaumont has praised for his wit. But a second and finally dominant reading of the line would assign the phrase to Beaumont, who in his praise of Jonson and disparagement of himself has in fact proved (this time, anyway) his superiority and so has written "better."

The response Beaumont's skill elicits, however, is not praise but envy. Although this reaction is intended in part as a joke—the culminating example of the extraordinary wit both poets display in this exchange—the word "enuie" remains an unsettling one despite the humor, and the suggestion that envy is an unavoidable response— "I must," says the speaker—does nothing to diminish this effect. At other times Jonson tries to distinguish between emulation and its more negative cousin; praising the work of James Nabbes, for instance, he concludes:

> And this
> Faire Æmulation, and no Enuy is;
> When you behold me wish my selfe, the man
> That would haue done, that, which you onely can.
> (*Ungathered Verse* 24.21–24)

Yet here, in a poem addressed to a man whom he for the most part admired and certainly respected, Jonson seems at pains (if only as a joke) to call our attention to the complex motives that accompany even the relations between friends, thus paying tribute to the truth of the balanced account of the Mermaid world that Beaumont had presented in his poem and, at the same time, going Beaumont one better by admitting openly—as Beaumont does not—that he himself is at times driven by some of the less attractive aspects of that world. In doing so, Jonson perhaps regains some of the stature taken from him (so he says) by Beaumont's clever and witty "praise."

I have dwelt at length on this exchange of poems because it exemplifies in particularly subtle ways the central role that emulation played in so many of Jonson's relationships—those with people he admired and those with people he did not—as well as Jonson's careful examination of that role. Additional nondramatic examples of the tendencies I have been describing might be gleaned from a study of Jonson's relations with his literary "sons"; such a study might consider, among other things, how many of his protégés go to extraordinary lengths in their poems to profess their desire not to rival their putative father, and Jonson's complex and sometimes antagonistic attitude toward the one son who did (probably unintentionally), Richard Brome.[18] Jonson's poetic tribute to Shakespeare in the 1623 folio is also an illuminating example of some of the attitudes I have been emphasizing, one whose complexity approaches that of the exchange with Beaumont.[19]

Emulation is an even more important subject in the plays, as I hope to demonstrate in later chapters. The "doubleness" inherent in the very nature of the theater, our awareness that the people onstage are both characters in the play and actors playing those characters, offers a perfect opportunity for variously exploring aspects of imitation in both life and art. For the moment, however, I would like simply to demonstrate how many of the ideas and impulses I have been discussing are molded into the plot structure of one of Jonson's comic masterpieces, *The Alchemist*.

The play begins, as is well known, with a quarrel involving priority—"Why, I pray you, haue I / Beene countenanc'd by you? or you, by me?" (1.1.21–22)—and identity: "Who am I," Face asks Subtle early in the first scene (line 13), only to be told that he would have "had no name" (line 81) without the alchemist's aid, "name" here carrying the twin and typically Jonsonian meanings of eminence and specific identity, with the added irony that Face's "name" as it is given in Jonson's list of "the Persons of the Play" indicates that he lacks a fixed essence. He is a mask, not a stable human being. The quarrel, of course, never reaches a resolution; Doll brings them up short with a threat of violence (lines 118–19), coupled with a reminder that their union is a union of equals. Was not their enterprise, she asks, "begun out of equalitie? / The venter *tripartite?* All things in common? / Without prioritie?" (lines 134–36).

Doll, as I hope is by now evident, could not be more wrong. Her solution is in reality a reaffirmation of the situation that caused the conflict in the first place. As with the literary quarrels at the end of Elizabeth's reign and Jonson's relations with his peers, it is what might be called the threat of equality that here leads to competition and conflict. The prescription for peace within the "venter tripartite" is difference, not similarity; that is why Face and Subtle, even after ostensibly having been reconciled, approach the day's business competitively—"'Slid, proue to day, who shall sharke best" (line 160)—

and, in their last words before the entry of their first victim, emphasize individual rather than communal concerns. Praising the wisdom of Doll's actions, Face tells her:

> thou shalt sit in triumph,
> And not be stil'd DOL Common, but DOL Proper,
> DOL Singular: the longest cut, at night,
> Shall draw thee for his DOL Particular.
> (lines 176–79)

Their united campaign then begins, only to dissolve into additional quarrels that eventually destroy their commonwealth altogether.[20]

A satisfactory resolution of the knaves' competitive energies does not (cannot) occur within the boundaries of the "venter tripartite," because that union lacks a mechanism for allowing the victory of one competitor over another without disrupting the basis of its framework: equality. The "articles" of this commonwealth, given the emulative urges of at least two of its members, prevent its being able to survive by allowing a readjustment of the relationship between those members, with one having priority over the other. Here again, Hobbes provides a useful gloss: the situation at the beginning of *The Alchemist* is in many ways a comic version of what he calls the state of nature, in which a widespread desire within a group for eminence and power, together with the inability of any particular individual in that group to assert his or her will over the others with some degree of finality, leads to endless warfare: "During the time men live without a common Power to keep them all in awe, they are in that condition which is called Warre; and such a warre, as is of every man against every man" (1968, 185).[21] Difference does not exist, "nothing can be Unjust," and "there be no Propriety, no Dominion, no *Mine* and *Thine* distinct; but onely that to be every mans that he can get; and for so long, as he can keep it" (p. 188). Only by creating a sovereign absolute power outside this competitive jungle—in other words, by creating an absolute principle of difference—can conflict be averted, individuals' emulative desires channeled and limited, and hierarchical relationships established. The invention of a sovereign power establishes the essential distinction upon which all other social distinctions are predicated: just and unjust, mine and thine, and so on (p. 202). As Hobbes puts it, "The question who is the better man, has no place in the condition of meere Nature; where . . . all men are equall"—but at war with one another. "The inequallity" and thus the order "that now is, has been introduced by the Lawes civill" (p. 211).

So too in *The Alchemist* a resolution of the rivalry between Face and Subtle comes not from within the world of the competitors—where no one is willing to acknowledge priority or able to attain it—but from without, from a *superior* who grants approval to one rival and not the other. That superior, of course, is Lovewit. Yet Lovewit, unlike Hobbes's sovereign, does not remain completely detached from the rivalries that swirl about him. When he becomes involved in the machinations of his butler, he becomes a competitor as well (for Dame Pliant), thereby blurring somewhat his distinctiveness and, as a result, his authority. Lovewit's realization near the end of the comedy that this is so (see 5.5.146–56) underlies his admission of subservience to his butler. If *The Alchemist* ends with a union between a young sharker and a not very strict master, just as it began with a volatile alliance of three tricksters, the later partnership differs from the earlier in one very significant respect: it is not a union of equals. "I will be rul'd by thee in any thing, IEREMIE" (5.5.143), Lovewit pledges, his words almost seeming to answer Subtle's much earlier accusation that Face "had no name" before the bogus alchemist came to his aid (1.1.81). Face has now gained a name, and in both the senses implicit in Subtle's statement: he is preeminent among the characters in the play; he has been given the kind of personal designation, Jeremy, that none of his actual or potential rivals has. And although both aspects of Face's accomplishment are, certainly, flawed (his eminence lies in trickery, and his name, Jeremy Butler, is hardly the epitome of individuality and specificity), he has a Christian name, nevertheless—something that Subtle, Doll, and Lovewit lack. That is why Face (now become Jeremy) asks for and receives, however problematically and ambiguously, our approval at the conclusion of the comedy. As Edward Partridge (1973, 190–95) points out while discussing Jonson's epigrams, in the world of this artist we name those we praise and praise those we name.[22]

The complex of emotions and actions variously designated by the terms *imitation, emulation,* and *envy* plays, then, a large and important role both in Jonson's career and in the works he created. It is central to his relations with other writers; it often forms the subject and / or underlying structural pattern of his poems and dramas. To those who applauded his strategies Jonson's career became a symbol of, in John Oldham's words, the victory of "Proportion, Order, Harmony"—that is, difference—over "a wretched Anarchy of Wit: / Unform'd, and void" like "the old *Chaos,* e're the birth of Light, and Day" (Herford, Simpson and Simpson 1925–52, 11:538–45; cf. 11:314, 335–36). To those less sympathetic, Jonson's endeavors seemed the destructive and malicious result of his own personal inadequacies, most notably the self-love and envy that dominate Drummond's description of him and that are so prominent in one of our last glimpses of the aging poet. "I was invited yesternight to a solemne supper by *B. J.,*" writes James Howell. "There was good company, excellent chear, choice wines, and joviall welcome; one thing interven'd which almost spoyld the relish of the rest, that *B.* began to engross all the discourse, to vapour extreamely of himselfe, and by vilifying others to magnify his owne *muse.*"[23]

Moreover, some of Jonson's more astute contemporaries recognized very early the problems inherent in the career that he had defined. Samuel Daniel may have been one of them. Thomas Dekker was another, not only capable of sizing up his opponent's goals and parodying them but also aware that Jonson's pursuit of difference led him to destroy the very thing he sought. The Horace of Dekker's *Satiromastix* strikes out in all directions—at friends and at foes, at the virtuous as well as the corrupt—tearing down indiscriminately in order to exalt himself. It is a point that Jonson understood only some ten years later, when he wrote *Catiline.*

But the importance of the praise or blame Jonson elicited from other writers was, finally, overshadowed by the importance of the responses of a much larger if less talented group: as Jonson knew very well, the successful completion of the career he envisioned was dependent in large part upon the power invested in the readers and spectators to whom he presented his works. A poet can (must, in Jonson's view) juxtapose his work to that of a rival for purposes of comparison, but a third party is needed to evaluate the works, note the differences, and state a preference. (Lovewit performs this function in *The Alchemist,* Justice Clement in *Every Man in His Humour.*) Jonson's audience, in short, ultimately had the power to grant the victory—the distinction—he sought. The English playwright's relations with his peers thus became inextricably linked to his relations with readers and spectators, relations that proved equally complex.

2

AUTHOR AND AUDIENCE

The setting is the Piazza del San Marco. The most important onstage spectators are apparently only two in number: Peregrine, a skeptical, intelligent English youth; and Sir Politic Would-be, a man who takes great pride in his ability "to note, and to obserue" (*Volpone*, 2.1.101), Peregrine's foolish, self-appointed guide to the subtleties of Italian life. The object of their attention is Scoto of Mantua, a famous mountebank, who has set up his shop before them and is about to peddle his miraculous elixir at a bargain price. The man they see is not, of course, Scoto at all, but Volpone, exuberantly playing yet another role as he attempts to gain the favor of Celia, Corvino's beautiful wife. Her regard—that is, both her gaze and with it her affirmation of his merit—will signal the success of his impersonation and provide further testimony to the cleverness and wit of this Venetian *magnifico*. Standing by her window, Celia, much more than Peregrine or Sir Pol, has the power to give him the recognition he wants; and Volpone, like all performers, is at the mercy of his audience as his performance comes to an end. He seeks, Volpone/Scoto tells his onlookers, *"only, a pledge of your loues, to carry something from amongst you, to shew, I am not contemn'd by you"* (2.2.213–14). Much later, Volpone will make the same plea (this time on Jonson's behalf and to us, not Celia) in the concluding lines of the play.

Volpone's performance in front of Celia's window might itself be described as a commentary on the importance of audience. He begins by noting the unusual setting he has selected, a location far from his normal place near the more important and public part of the piazza (2.2.33–38). He has come to this *"obscure nooke,"* Volpone/Scoto explains, because *"I cannot indure, to see the rabble of these ground* Ciarlitani, *that spread their clokes on the pauement, as if they meant to do feates of actiuitie, and then come in, lamely, with their mouldy tales out of* BOCCACIO, *like stale* TABARINE, *the Fabulist"* (2.2.48–52). In his role as Scoto, Volpone fears that his "art" will be contaminated by that of his inferiors. He is in search of distinction, of difference; he must distance himself from the *"very many* [who] *haue assay'd, like apes in imitation of that, which is really and essentially in mee, to make of this oyle"* (2.2.149–50). And since there are no practitioners of his trade so foolish as to lack *"their fauourers"* on the more public part of the piazza, he has set up his bench far *"remou'd from the clamours of the* canaglia" (2.2.64, 70–71) in order to find a more attentive and judicious audience, one that will be able to distinguish his careful and learned art—*"For, whil'st others haue beene at the* balloo, *I haue beene at my booke"* (2.2.167–68), Volpone says—from the inferior versions of his fellow mountebanks. By separating himself physically from the *"ground* Ciarlitani"—he is now both above and apart from them—Volpone/Scoto emphasizes what he believes to be the enormous gap between his skills and those of apparent rivals. He will speak, as Jonson had earlier promised to do, "safe from the wolues black iaw, and the dull asses hoofe" ("Apologetical Dialogue," line 239).

Volpone's entire speech, obviously, is a hoax: he is not Scoto; he is not attempting to distinguish his wares from those of other mountebanks. Yet Volpone's impersonation of Scoto is closely related to his own interests in at least one important way: like the character he is playing, Volpone is genuinely concerned with audience, and not simply because he wants to gain Celia for himself. Although Celia's response, like those of the other characters whom he wishes to trick, is essential to his success—she is a spectator he must please as well as dupe—her importance is only momentary. Once this particular plot has been completed, Volpone will move on to another victim. It is not the practical success of his schemes but his belief that he is unique and gains "no common way" (1.1.33) that is truly important to Volpone. Like the "Scoto" he creates, he must distinguish himself from others who seem most like him: that is, from other Venetians who prey upon the innocent and the foolish. That distinction is fundamental to Volpone's sense of identity, and it cannot be gained merely by a victory over (the acquiesence of) an audience composed of Celias, Corvinos, Corbaccios, and Voltores, because these individuals lack the judgment and subtlety necessary to appreciate the cleverness and originality of his endeavors to gull them. They can provide him (unwillingly) with money and pleasure but not stature.

In *Volpone* there is only one character capable of this kind of appreciation: Mosca. He is the "rare friend" who can understand and praise Volpone's "rare" plots. He is essential both for the aid he provides and for his ability to respond to and so support Volpone's need to feel unique, his ability to grant the distinction so important to his master. Volpone and Mosca could not exist apart from one another: each is a necessary component of the other's identity; each is the mirror by which the other sees himself. Thus, when Volpone is beaten by Corvino after Celia throws down her handerchief, he assuages his disappointment by recalling with Mosca the skill of his disguise. "I did it well" (2.4.31), he says, and Mosca quickly supplies the response Volpone needs (although with some irony): "So well, would I could follow you in mine, / With half the happiness," he answers, "and, yet, I would / Escape your *epilogue*" (2.4.32–34). Quickly reversing roles, Mosca then turns to his own imminent plot, telling his master, "Wee'll part / And, as I prosper, so applaud my art" (2.4.37–38). Although Mosca is flattering Volpone (the phrase "wee'll part" also anticipates their later rivalry), at this point both men recognize their dependence upon each other's approval, and rightly so. As Volpone explains in the final speech of the drama, "The seasoning of a play is the applause."

In these scenes Volpone and Mosca replay—as at times do so many of Jonson's dramatic characters—aspects of Jonson's own situation, despite the marked difference between their "art" and that of the man who created them. Much of what Volpone says in the mountebank scenes echoes, as has often been noted,[1] the material in the letter to Oxford and Cambridge Universities that precedes the published versions of the play. What is of particular interest for my purposes is that the letter acknowledges in its very first sentence the same reliance upon audience that I have been discussing above: *"Neuer (most equall* SISTERS*),"* Jonson states, *"had any man a wit so presently excellent, as that it could raise it selfe; but there must come both matter, occasion, commenders, and fauourers to it"* (lines 1–4).

The admission was not an easy one for Jonson to make; he could not have been comfortable with a situation that gave so much power and authority to his audience, even if that audience were composed of some of the most learned members of his society.[2] Jonson understood only too well that an audience's power to praise is necessarily accompanied by the power to condemn. If Donne's approval of a single poem has the authority to confer the title of poet on Jonson— "Reade all I send," Jonson urges his great contemporary, "and, if I find but one / Mark'd by thy hand . . . My title's seal'd" (*Epigrammes* 96.7–9) —Jonson's decision to open his work to Donne's judgment is an act of daring (lines 1–2). Like all readers or spectators, Donne can "dis-auow" as well as "allow" (lines 5–6), destroy as well as create reputations.

As a result, Jonson often expresses a stoic indifference to the responses of others, coupled with an absolute assurance of his own worth. In *Discoveries* (lines 1984–87) he expands with apparent approval a statement by Vives that enunciates a somewhat condescending acceptance of the faults of readers: "If the obscurity [of a work] happen through the Hearers, or Readers want of understanding, I am not to answer for them; no more then for their not listning or marking; I must neither find them eares, nor mind." In a poem addressed to Alphonso Ferrabosco (*Epigrammes* 131.1–4), he acknowledges that, once published, a poem is no longer controlled by its author:

> When we doe giue, ALPHONSO, to the light,
>   A worke of ours, we part with our owne right;
> For, then, all mouthes will iudge, and their owne way:
>   The learn'd haue no more priuiledge, then the lay.

Similarly, in the quarto edition of *Catiline,* Jonson's address "TO THE READER IN ORDINAIRIE" predicts, calmly if scornfully, that the play will inevitably be mishandled by those who are incapable of understanding it: *"The Muses forbid, that I should restrayne your medling, whom I see alreadie busie with the Title, and tricking ouer the leaues: It is your owne. I departed with my right, when I let it first abroad. . . . I leaue you to your exercise. Beginne"* (lines 1–4, 23–24).

But such moments of indifference were, for the most part, feigned. Jonson was dependent in too many ways on the responses of others to ignore their actions for very long. On the most basic level, he was dependent upon those responses for his livelihood. Without the approval of playgoers or, at the very least, a rich patron, his career as a poet would necessarily come to an end. In addition, Jonson's preference for comic rather than tragic forms of drama increased his reliance upon audience rather than diminished it. Humor is inherently social: it cannot exist without an audience; its success or failure is signaled by the response of that audience. As Northrop Frye (1957, 164) has taught us, "The resolution of comedy comes . . . from the audience's side of the stage." In his discussion of jokes, Freud (1960, 143, 156) is equally insistent that "no one can be content with having made a joke for himself alone," because "telling my joke to another person would seem . . . to give me objective certainty that the joke-work has been successful . . . [and] to complete my own pleasure by a reaction by the other person upon myself"—a point Plutarch makes with considerably less enthusiasm: "Whoever laughs at the remark [the joke] and takes pleasure in it is in the position of one who confirms the slander," he argues (*Moralia, Table-Talk* 631). Finally, the responses of readers and spectators were crucial, as I have suggested in Chapter 1, to the successful completion of Jonson's career. The distinction he sought could be granted only by their approval.

That is why understanding became for Jonson an activity involving not only intelligence, but also support. As both Volpone and Mosca evidently know so well, "to understand" in a Jonsonian sense is at once to comprehend and to assist or prop up,[3] and that assistance can be gained only if the writer is willing to "submit" himself and his work to the judgment of others. This last sentence is a paraphrase of Jonson's "To the Reader extraordinary," a three-line companion to the address to faulty readers in the quarto edition of *Catiline*, and his dedicatory epistle to William, Earl of Pembroke, makes essentially the same point. Jonson craves *"leaue to stand neere"* the Earl's *"light: and, by that, to bee read"* (lines 2–3)—the judgment of this noble reader presumably protecting both the poet and his poem by providing a guide for the judgments of others.[4] Indeed, I suspect that Jonson's preference in the titles of his poems for the preposition *to* rather than *on* is a further indication of the importance he gave to readers and spectators: the preposition calls our attention to audience, as well as to content, by establishing a particular reader or type of reader as the primary receiver of the work and encourages us (as we overhear) to laugh at that reader (if the poem is satiric and its addressee foolish) or to concur with both Jonson's description of that reader and his or her presumed response to that description (if the person being addressed is idealized). In the passage he translated from John of Salisbury (*Discoveries,* lines 1100–1109), the role of spectator is virtually synonomous with virtue (see Chapter 1), and the careful and judicious comments of intelligent observers often have a corrective function in his plays, limiting eccentricity by inhibiting our tendencies to live in worlds of our own making, worlds whose tenuous existence is possible only in the absence of audience and where we act, in Crites' words, "As if we practiz'd in a paste-board case, / And no one saw the motion, but the motion" (*Cynthia's Revels* 1.5.63–64).

Power in the Jonsonian world is not wielded solely by observers or readers, however. Surprisingly, the role of spectator is in fact a somewhat ambivalent one. In order to exercise its considerable authority over the works submitted to it, an audience must first submit itself to those works. Before it can judge, it must follow. "Things, wrote with labour, deserue to be so read" (*Discoveries,* lines 2465–66), Jonson says, and that labor involves in part a loss of freedom and control. It involves, in other words, a degree of subservience to what is being (in this instance) read, because that work has become the focus of the reader's attention. If to understand a poem is both to comprehend and to support that poem, understanding also requires that one first stand below (submit to) the poem; if observers judge and bestow merit, they also show the respect and deference of servants.[5]

Mosca is Volpone's "obseruer" in both senses (1.1.63); and, although the parasite usually attempts to deflect credit for his own plots onto his master—"I but doe, as I am taught; / Follow your graue instructions," he states early in the comedy (1.4.139–40)—Volpone fulfills the same role, and more frequently, for his supposed inferior. Moreover, neither character is totally comfortable with the role of audience because that role is in their opinion secondary; each would be the object of the other's regard and the focus of attention; neither is really content to be a passive onlooker for long. For Volpone and Mosca, to be a spectator is at best to be a voyeur, at worst to be a victim.[6] Each would rather receive than give applause.

Among Jonson's works, *Every Man out of His Humour* contains perhaps the most instructive account of these issues. As Jackson Cope (1973, 226–36) has shown, it is a play composed of spectators: the audience in the theater, the grex onstage, and various characters (especially Macilente and Buffone) who take turns watching and commenting upon the actions of others. The role of observer is an especially powerful one here: Cordatus comments on the action with unchallenged authority, and "Macilente," writes Cope, "is that dominant spectator who is also Mazzoni's ideal poet of the ideal poem; he is a *visionary* in the creative sense Mazzoni gave the metaphor: one who both sees and creates the poem." Yet for many of the characters the role of spectator is not an attractive one; they prefer to command the regard of others, to be seen rather than to see.

Nowhere is this inclination more pronounced than in a series of scenes (3.1–3.6) that take place in the aisles of Paul's—scenes that are, I suggest, Jonson's version of the "paper warres" described by Iudicio in *The Return from Parnassus*. Shift establishes the tenor of the entire episode when he enters complaining about his inability to find any takers for the skills he has advertised: "This is rare, I haue set vp my bills, without discouery" (3.1.1), he comments, and "discouery" is very much what these scenes are about. Far from coming to Paul's "to spit in priuate" (3.1.6), the characters assemble there to engage in activities of a very different sort: to be observed and to attract the attention of others. That is why Clove and Orange, two gallants who have apparently wandered onstage from somewhere in the audience—"mere strangers to the whole scope of our play" (3.1.17–18), according to Cordatus—are displeased that the scene is not yet filled: "I wonder, there are no more store of gallants here!" (3.1.14–15), Clove laments, thereby adding to Shift's his own expression of disappointment at not being discovered.

More and more characters gradually enter, forming several groups that move about before us in an elaborate ritual that "approaches the quality of an abstract ballet in which the pattern is supreme" (Enck 1957, 51). By act 3, scene 4, there are three different groups in addition to the grex onstage: Puntarvolo, Sogliardo, and Buffone; Clove and Orange; Deliro, Briske, and Macilente—the first absorbed in the absurdities of Shift's bills, and the second attempting to command the attention of the third. "Monsieur ORANGE," Clove whispers, "yond' gallants obserue vs; pr'y thee let's talke fustian a little, and gull 'hem: make 'hem beleeue we are great schollers" (3.4.6–8). Unfortunately, their ruse is a failure; Macilente proves to be a scornful audience—"O, here be a couple of fine tame parrats" (3.4.19–20)— and Deliro and Briske are an unattentive one. "They marke vs not," Clove complains, and the two fools return to their "former discourse" (3.4.39–40). Briske, meanwhile, has sufficiently overcome his own self-absorption to notice the presence of Puntarvolo and his group, but Deliro is not willing to give the knight and his companions the benefit of his regard even for a moment: "Let 'hem alone," he urges, "obserue 'hem not" (45).

The three groups of characters continue to move about the stage (watched by Cordatus and Mitis). Each is apparently self-contained and for the most part oblivious to the others, because to take notice—to become, in other words, spectators—would be to grant another group the primacy each one seeks for itself. Even when Puntarvolo emerges from discussing with Carlo and Sogliardo the latter's new coat of arms and greets Briske—"Saue you, good monsieur FAS-TIDIVS"—the contact is only momentary—"Silence, good knight: on, on," Buffone commands (3.4.72–74), and Puntarvolo turns inward once more, no longer attentive to the activities going on around him.

Then, as if a signal has been given, the groups dissolve and recompose, this time forming four separate groups onstage which in turn recombine to form three when Carlo exits. Fungoso enters with his tailor to create yet another group, while Briske, discoursing on his self-sufficiency and indifference to audience—"I pursue my humour still, in contempt of this censorious age" (3.5.9–10)—indicates just the opposite: that his sense of self is totally dependent upon the responses of others. In this, of course, he is no different from most of his companions.

The strange ballet finally comes to a climax when Buffone reenters, promising that he will "vsher [in] the most strange peece of militarie profession, that euer was discouer'd in *Insula Paulina*," but at the same time urging this audience to retain its power by pretending to ignore what it is about to see: "Here he comes; nay, walke, walke, be not seene to note him, and we shall haue excellent sport" (3.5.31–32, 39–40). Buffone has manufactured a quintessentially Jonsonian scene. A varied group of onlookers gathers to judge the actions of a foolish actor. They will respond with scorn rather than approval; their comments will expose Shift's silliness; they will laugh at rather than with him—actions that will make their superiority to him at once obvious and unquestionable. However, the dominance and authority of these spectators is shaky at best. Although his actions are totally absurd, Shift accomplishes what no other character in this episode has been able to accomplish: he melds the onstage rival groups into a single audience; his antics become the focal point toward which all eyes are directed. An episode that begins with the knave's complaint that no one is paying attention to his bills of advertisement, then develops as an elaborate dance of individuals intent both on being observed and on denying that goal to others, ends with the "discovery" that Shift has been seeking: "Sir, if I should denie the manuscripts, I were worthie to be banisht the middle I'le, for euer" (3.6.130–31). Even though this "strange peece of militarie profession" has been scorned and mocked, he has also been watched by all. Shift is both subservient and superior to his onstage audience, both loser and winner at once. He may be a fool, but he is certainly a very instructive one.

The ambiguity of Shift's situation is an ambiguity that Jonson thought inherent in all relations between actors or authors and their respective audiences. He found in his own contemporaries the same unwillingness to follow and the same resistance to paying attention to others that he describes in the scenes just discussed. Elizabethan spectators were, Jonson believed, all too ready to claim an audience's authority to judge and condemn without acknowledging the complementary and prior responsibility to accept a role secondary to what they were watching or reading. Thus, in *Every Man out of His Humour,* Asper urges Mitis and Cordatus to watch the audience offstage in order to discover anyone who might use

> his wryed lookes
> (In nature of a vice) to wrest, and turne
> The good aspect of those that shall sit neere him,
> From what they doe behold!
> (Induction, 181–84)

In *The Devil Is an Ass,* Fitzdottrel is a caricature of just such a spectator; he goes to the theater not to attend to the play at hand but to be regarded by others:

> To day, I goe to the *Black-fryers Play-house,*
> Sit i' the view, salute all my acquaintance,
> Rise vp between the *Acts,* let fall my cloake,
> Publish a handsome man, and a rich suite
> (As that's a speciall end, why we goe thither,
> All that pretend, to stand for't o' the *Stage)*
> The Ladies aske who's that? (For, they doe come
> To see vs, *Loue,* as wee doe to see them).
> (1.6.31–38)

Fitzdottrel, of course, lives in a world all his own, the kind of "pasteboord case" that Crites describes in *Cynthia's Revels;* as the passage indicates, he would be both actor/author and audience at once. But in doing so, he also seeks a position suspiciously like the one enjoyed by a monarch at a court entertainment, where, Stephen Orgel (1975, 9) argues, "what the rest of the spectators watched was not a play but the queen at a play, and their response would have been not simply to the drama, but to the relationship between the drama and its primary audience, the royal spectator."[7] At court, the work and its author were, in other words, peripheral to more important concerns; the audience's attention was often directed elsewhere. Jonson's quarrel with Inigo Jones was in part an attempt to keep his authority from being eroded even further at such entertainments. It is one thing to be pushed off center stage by a queen or king, another to be upstaged by the wonderful creations of an architect.

Furthermore, a situation that Jonson apparently accepted (or was forced to accept) as a necessary feature of a masque at court—one representing the dominance of the monarchy in all things, its absolute centrality—must not, he felt, be translated into the public and private theaters, which was exactly what the actions of a Fitzdottrel threatened to do. In a playhouse the play and poet, so Jonson thought, should be the focus of attention, and it is perhaps indicative of the lengths to which he went to ensure this that Dekker accused him of precisely the sort of theatrics that Jonson found so indefensible among the members of his theater audience. Arraigning Horace/Jonson at the end of Dekker's *Satiromastix* (5.2.298–307), Sir Rees ap Vaughan commands:

> Moreouer, you shall not sit in a Gallery, when your Comedies and Enterludes haue entred their Actions, and there make vile and bad faces at euerie lyne, to make Sentlemen haue an eye to you, and to make Players afraide to take your part. . . . Besides, you must forsweare to venter on the stage, when your Play is ended, and to exchange curtezies, and complements with Gallents in the Lordes roomes, to make all the house rise vp in Armes, and to cry that's *Horace,* that's he, that's he, that's he, that pennes and purges Humours and diseases.

Fitzdottrel, Dekker suggests, was something of a self-portrait.[8]

Dekker unquestionably had a great deal to gain by making Jonson look absurd, and we have no way of knowing whether or not this description is an accurate one. I suspect that it is not. But Dekker was certainly correct to point out that Jonson wanted to make his art the object of its audience's undivided attention; knowing that he must submit his works to the judgment of others in order to gain distinction, Jonson demanded that they first submit themselves to the works. In part, the problem he faced was "one of vying theatricality" (Carlson 1977, 453); Jonson's audience was, he believed, simply unwilling or unable to focus its attention upon anything other than itself; it was a more serious and, to him, dangerous version of the isolated groups that move about the stage in the third act of *Every Man out of His Humor*. Bluntly stated, most of the spectators in the theater had in his opinion only one goal: to "possesse the Stage, against the Play. To dislike all, but marke nothing."[9]

By themselves, such rival theatrics do not form an insoluble problem. As annoying as the activities of a Fabian Fitzdottrel may be in the theater, they can be eliminated by the simple expedient of publication. Readers do not have the possibilities for display that are available to spectators in a playhouse.[10] But publication does not dispel, and may even strengthen, another more powerful and finally inescapable threat to an author's control over the works he or she pens. As numerous contemporary theorists have argued, and as Jonson himself frequently lamented, the act of interpretation can (and may always) be an act of aggression, an assertion of dominance—in Jonson's terminology, a claim of possession. And this claim can be made as easily in the study as in the theater.

One of Jonson's most detailed accounts of the kind of interpretive aggression he feared occurs in the Induction and choric sections of *The Magnetic Lady*, the last drama he completed before his death. Although the comedy is one of his least successful works,[11] it is remarkable nevertheless for the extraordinary sense of closure that pervades the play, as Jonson surveys his entire literary career from a vantage point near its conclusion and returns, in Herford's words, "frankly, even ostentatiously, to the methods and devices by which his earlier comedies had first won fame" (Herford, Simpson, and Simpson 1925–52 2:204). For my purposes, the most important aspect of this retrospective quality is the play's depiction of the problematic and often antagonistic relation between author and audience. There are, to be sure, moments in *The Magnetic Lady* when Jonson, perhaps remembering past frustrations, seems ready to end what might be called his quarrel with audience—when the Boy explains to his onstage spectators that the author has chosen not to supply a prologue because "he has lost too much that way already, hee sayes"; or when he later states that it is not his function to comment on the action of the comedy: "I have heard the Poet affirme, that to be the most unlucky *Scene* in a *Play,* which needs an Interpreter; especially, when the *Auditory* are awake" (Induction, lines 120–21, 145–47). But the hesitancy is illusory: the Boy, in effect, provides the prologue that the author ostensibly denies, while the very scenes in which he appears patently attempt to control our responses and guide our understanding, despite his (and the author's) disclaimer. By 1632 all scenes must have seemed "most unlucky" to Jonson because they were subject, he believed, to the whims and ignorance of spectators who, left to themselves, would distort what they were watching beyond recognition. When the Boy comments that, the author being absent, "I have dominion of the Shop, for this time, under him," his statement anticipates a conflict for "dominion" that will be the subject not only of the remainder of the Induction but also of the choric scenes after each of the first four acts, a conflict that is already implicit in the presence of spectators—"sent unto you, indeed, from the people"—in the "Shop" itself: that is, onstage (Induction, lines 14–15, 27).

For two of the characters who take part in these scenes, the Boy and Mr. Probee, there is little question about which claim in this disagreement is the superior one: both associate meaning with intention and condemn any attempt to interfere with the orderly unfolding of the poet's art. The Boy implies that the gentlemen's presence (and its potential threat to authorial control) is allowed only because it will serve ultimately to affirm that control rather than deny it. His description of the relation between play and audience both emphasizes the fragile delicacy and complexity of the drama and points out that this fragility requires, in turn, skillful and patient handling by the audience:

> For, I must tell you, (not out of mine owne *Dictamen,* but the *Authors,*) A good *Play,* is like a skeene of silke: which, if you

take by the right end, you may wind off, at pleasure, on the bottome, or card of your discourse, in a tale, or so; how you will: But if you light on the wrong end, you will pull all into a knot, or elf-lock; which nothing but the sheers, or a candle will undoe, or separate. [12]

(Induction, lines 135–41; cf. 4.8.51; 5.10.81]

The Boy presents only two alternatives: one either carefully unravels the complexity of the drama in order to discover an authorially controlled meaning, or one ignores intention, tangling everything up and ultimately cutting the play to pieces or destroying it completely. Misinterpretation is, the Boy suggests, a form of violence.

However, one of the onstage gallants, named—not surprisingly—Damplay, does not see things in quite this way. Unwilling to allow any poet to "give me the Law" (Chorus 3.23), Damplay asserts both in word and action that authorial intention is of little importance, given the audience's competing and antithetical need for total freedom of response. For Damplay, meaning is preeminently the property and creation of the reader or spectator, not of the author. And while he is a relatively restrained spectator during the Induction and the Chorus following act 1, he suddenly announces after act 2 what he will later call his "priviledge" and "prerogative," his "*Magna Charta* of reprehension" (Chorus 3.21, 24–25).

From Jonson's point of view, Damplay's initial misstep occurs when he unhesitatingly assumes, without attempting to determine whether the work itself supports his assumption, that the characters in the play he is watching are veiled portraits of his contemporaries. Probee, who has a much different sense of interpretive procedures, immediately urges Damplay to rethink what he is doing: "It is an insidious Question, Brother *Damplay*," Probee says. "It is picking the Lock of the Scene; not opening it the faire way with a Key" (Chorus 2.10–12; cf. Induction to *Bartholomew Fair,* lines 135–45). Probee suggests that without warrant from the author his friend's attempt to discover actual individuals behind dramatic characters is akin to stealing; it is the surreptitious appropriation by the reader of the meaning of the play, a meaning which belongs to the author and can "legally" be revealed only by employing the key provided by the play itself—and the playwright. The fundamental issue for Probee (and Jonson) is not whether the play refers to contemporary events and persons; it is whether the author has intended such references. In this instance, so Probee says, he has not. [13]

Damplay, however, is unconvinced by such arguments. Although he no longer claims that the characters in the drama actually represent historical figures, he nevertheless affirms his right to create such connections: "Why, I can phant'sie a person to my selfe *Boy*, who shall hinder me?" Echoing the second prologue to *Epicoene* (lines 11–14), the Boy replies that to do so amounts to a usurpation of the "*Authors* words" for Damplay's "owne ill meaning," making a "Libell of his *Comoedy*" in the process; and Probee, no longer content simply to equate such nonsense with lawlessness, now adds that it is a kind of sickness as well: "It is an unjust way of hearing, and beholding *Playes* . . . to appeare malignantly witty in anothers *Worke*" (Chorus 2.24–25, 27–29, 44–47; cf. *Poetaster* 5.3.145–47; and Jonson's letter to Salisbury in Herford, Simpson, and Simpson 1925–52 1:195). Furthermore, this unjustified domination over and appropriation of another's text can be accomplished, Probee states, only by distorting and twisting that text—that is, by doing violence to it: "It is the solemne vice of interpretation, that deformes the figure of many a faire *Scene*, by drawing it awry; and indeed is the civill murder of most good *Plays*" (Chorus 2.34–36).

To Damplay, all of this is beside the point. What seems to the Boy and Probee an act of distortion and robbery is to him an expression of freedom, of the spectator's liberty to understand in whatever way he or she pleases, without restraint and without the interference of the author. To do otherwise is to give the writer an intolerable and unprecedented authority: "Why, *Boy?* This were a strange Empire, or rather a Tyrannie, you would entitle your Poet to, over Gentlemen, that they should come to heare, and see *Playes*, and say nothing for their money." When the Boy tries to explain that Damplay may say what he wishes "so it be to purpose, and in place," Damplay rejects immediately the emphasis on a careful examination of context and intention implicit in the Boy's words: "Can any thing be out of purpose at a *Play?*" he sneers. The question is obviously rhetorical.

It denies the legitimacy of *any* limitation on audience response; it suggests that understanding is a form of self-expression rather than a careful unveiling of an authorially intended meaning. "Who," Damplay asks a few lines later, "should teach us the right, or wrong at a *Play?*" If the answer is, as Damplay surely intimates, "no one," then there can be no wrong responses, no comments "out of purpose," and above all, no "Tyrannie" of the author. Indeed, the gallant's statement is at once so extreme and self-assured that the Boy is momentarily speechless. Such ideas are, he finally sputters, the result of "a popular ignorance . . . not onely fit to be scorn'd, but to be triumph'd ore" in a struggle between author and audience that will finally determine whether ignorance will continue to destroy the fragile fabric of drama after drama, committing, in Probee's memorable phrase, "the civill murder of most good *Playes*" (Chorus 2.53–59, 68, 72–76). [14]

By the end of *The Magnetic Lady* this struggle has been resolved in the author's favor. Damplay does not manage to ruin the play of which he is part. His silence during the final scenes of the comedy represents his grudging acquiesence to the arguments of Probee and the Boy. Momentarily, at least, he has been defeated. Damplay's seventeenth-century counterparts, however, could not be dismissed so easily. As foolish as the gallant's ideas may seem, they had in fact a long and distinguished heritage. Stripped of their more excessive and self-indulgent elements, his statements reflect an attitude toward interpretation that had dominated Western thought since the beginning of the Christian era and that remained a powerful influence until nearly a century after Jonson's death. And that was precisely Jonson's problem. He faced an audience accustomed to an interpretive methodology that not only had endured for some two thousand years but also threatened, in his opinion, his authority over his own works.

For many of Jonson's contemporaries, the accepted manner of interpreting literature was allegorical; that is, they tended to look beyond or behind the surface of a text in order to uncover its relation to certain eternal truths in a process of discovery limited only by the skill and ingenuity of the reader. [15] The practice of allegorical interpretation was not uniform during the sixteenth and seventeenth centuries, just as the exegetical habits of medieval commentators who worked within this tradition varied one from another, but for my purposes a few general characteristics can be isolated.

First, allegorical interpreters were often uninterested in historical context; the typical commentator tended to overlook the particularity of event or utterance in the hope of elucidating a more important eternal truth lying beneath (or beyond) the surface details. For both Philo and Origen, allegory afforded a means of overcoming the limitations of history and a fallen world; and Erasmus, despite his formidable store of historical knowledge, never really retreated during his life from a commitment, first announced in his tremendously popular *Enchiridion,* to uncover "the hidden meaning concealed in the literal sense" of the gospels (1963, 49), a hidden significance that a modern scholar has called "the copious Christ: the grammar of many meanings" (Boyle 1977, 127). In one of his more enthusiastic moments, Erasmus even argued: "From the interpretations of divine Scripture choose those which go as far as possible beyond the literal meaning" (1963, 53).[16]

In addition, an allegorical interpreter was not, for the most part, concerned with authorial intention. If one believes that truth is unchanging and eternal, then all things, all events, and all texts must, if read correctly, exemplify that truth, whatever an author's or participant's circumstances or desires. Just as no historical event can have a completely unique meaning, so no humanly authored text can claim a significance peculiar to itself. The author, whatever Jonson's Probee may think, does not hold the "key" to the meaning of what he or she has written.

The tendency to minimize the importance of historical context and authorial intention had as its corollary an equally strong tendency to allow the reader as much freedom as possible. The limit on the meaning of a work was neither the work itself nor the author's intention but truth as it was generally defined, together with the reader's ability to relate the work to that truth. In James Preus's words (1969, 164), "What matters . . . is not what the text clearly says or intends but how it is 'handled' (*tractatur*) by the interpreter"; in Marion

Trousdale's (1982, 146), "What such a technique leads to is not 'What did Shakespeare mean in *Hamlet?*' or even 'What does *Hamlet* mean?' but 'How much is there to be discovered from what I am seeing on the stage?'"—an attitude which is not, it seems to me, much different from Damplay's. As long as the accepted system of belief was not violated, the reader (whether an Augustine, an Erasmus, or a Harington) might make over the work in any way that reader wished—fragmenting, distorting, or ignoring the text whenever necessary and replacing whatever unity or coherence it might have with a meaning or meanings that presumably superseded that unity. Furthermore, despite the allegorical interpreter's fondness for multiple meanings—"Those {fables} being the best that admit of most senses," George Sandys assured his audience—those meanings were, in effect, always the same: they simply echoed a belief or beliefs that the reader already understood and accepted. Such readers did not attempt to discover or create new truths; they confirmed old ones.

As practiced by many medieval exegetes and Renaissance commentators, allegorical interpretation was in essence a method of accommodating, appropriating, and dominating an alien text or tradition (the Old Testament, the writings of classical antiquity), a way of domesticating the unfamiliar or objectionable and fitting it into categories of thought already socially sanctioned. And it succeeded, at least in part, by overcoming the resistance of the text, by doing violence to it. Witness Jacob Batt, an ardent defender of classical learning, commenting in Erasmus's *Antibarbarians* on the meaning of John 12:32. Batt begins by quoting the passage itself—"I, if I be lifted up from the earth, will draw all unto me"—and then proceeds to moralize it in a manner that makes explicit the power (and the potential violence) inherent in the interpretive tradition to which he belongs: "Here it seems to me that he most aptly uses the word *traho*, 'I draw,' so that one may understand that all things, whether hostile or heathen or in any other way far removed from him, must be drawn, even if they do not follow, even against their will, to the service of Christ" (1978, 59). Batt, to be sure, was a learned man involved in what is from our viewpoint an essentially praiseworthy attempt to protect the writings of classical antiquity from those who would dismiss them. Nevertheless, it is only a short step from his endeavor to remake the world in Christ's image to Damplay's assertion in *The Magnetic Lady* of his own independence from authorial control. Unless we understand that proximity, we cannot appreciate fully the difficulty of Jonson's position.

Admittedly, all interpretations (including this one) are in a very basic sense allegorical. All readings distort the text in some manner; all reflect the assumptions and values of the interpreter; all may be viewed as an expression of will to power. Nor is it my intention to examine or "expose" the inadequacies of this particular interpretive tradition, if they are in fact inadequacies. It is important to grasp the assumptions of allegorical exegesis, however, if we are to understand both the causes and substance of Jonson's quarrel with audience and the relation between that quarrel and the controversies which at present characterize literary studies. Whereas in recent decades we have become increasingly sensitive to the ways in which readers construct rather than simply discover significance, as well as more aware of how all texts to some extent escape the control of the author who created them, Jonson stands at the beginning of developments that—perhaps for the first time—pushed the reader into the background and created, to paraphrase Damplay, the authorial "Tyrannie" that has lately been questioned so insistently.

"The author," in Michel Foucault's words (1979, 159), "is the principle of thrift in the proliferation of meaning," a principle that "allows a limitation of the cancerous and dangerous proliferation of significations within a world where one is thrifty not only with one's resources and riches, but also with one's discourses and their significations." The imagery of disease in this passage echoes, in a manner I find especially instructive, some of Probee's most striking images in *The Magnetic Lady*, for Foucault's point is also Jonson's, however much the two men may differ on the benefits of this limitation. Similarly, when Jacques Derrida (1974, 158), speaking of the "effaced and respectful doubling of commentary" that attempts to reproduce "the conscious, voluntary, intentional relationship that the writer institutes in his exchanges with the history to which he belongs," concludes that "this indespensable guardrail [against saying almost anything about a text] has always only *protected*, it has never *opened*, a reading," his argument (if not his manner of expressing it) is one that Jonson would certainly have affirmed, though without Derrida's professed desire to move in his own readings beyond that "guardrail."

I have dealt with these issues in some detail because Jonson was the first English author to assert at length his control over the meaning of his own works. More vocally than any English writer who preceded him (and many who have followed), he argued that the "author" should function as the very principle of limitation and authority that Foucault describes. Of course, all writers—past and present—have probably made at some time or another a claim similar to Jonson's; most authors, I suspect, are unwilling to give to others complete authority over the significance of what they have written. But there is no question that both the intensity and duration of Jonson's quarrel with audience were, for an English poet or dramatist, as unprecedented as they were inevitable, given the artistic career he mapped out for himself. Jonson's desire to dominate the English stage was threatened as much by readers and spectators as by other playwrights.

Yet Jonson's views on the relation between author and audience were not created in a "paste-board case" of his own making; they were reinforced, perhaps in part conditioned, by attitudes that had become an important part of contemporary discussions of philology, law, and history by the time he began writing. If Jonson was the first English *poet* to emphasize to any great extent the ideas I have been discussing, the basic issues he raised were nevertheless part of a much larger controversy. On these matters, Jonson positioned himself with the intellectual vanguard of his day; his ideas paralleled (may, in fact, have had their origin in) attitudes accompanying the early beginnings of historicism. During his lifetime the methods by which individuals understood nature, the past, and written texts were slowly undergoing a fundamental alteration in which the methods of interpretation associated with allegorical exegesis were gradually being replaced by attempts to associate meaning with intention and context. It was a development, need I add, that Jonson must have welcomed.

Indeed, not everyone in the Renaissance had been willing to admit that the activities of a Jacob Batt were always valid, however laudable his overall goals might be. Turning his attention to poetry in *The Advancement of Learning,* Francis Bacon, for instance, suspected that in many cases "the fable was first, and the exposition devised, [rather] than that the moral was first, and thereupon the fable framed" (1863, 3:345). Both Petrarch and Boccaccio at times doubted the validity of allegorical exegesis, [17] while Rabaelais (in the Prologue to Book 1 of *Gargantua and Pantagruel*) and Montaigne (in the "Apology for Raymond Sebond") took this skepticism one step further and mocked allegorizers of Homer. Giordano Bruno, defending his use of allegory in *The Heroic Frenzies*, admitted (although perhaps somewhat disingenuously) that it was possible to remake any fable "by virtue of metaphor and allegorical disguise in such a way as to signify all that pleases him who is skillful at tugging at the sense, and is thus adept at making everything of everything" (1966, 63). And John Donne—sounding very much like the Jonson who predicted that Donne's work would perish "for not being understood" (*Conversations,* line 196)—told Henry Goodyear that he was hesitant to publish his poems, because "I shall suffer . . . many interpretations" (1967, 144).

Although the reasons for this growing distrust of the methods and results of allegorical interpretation were complex, a few can, I think, be identified. One cause was the new science and its concern for descriptive accuracy. The Reformation was another, bringing with it a strong interest in the literal and historical aspects of the Bible and a general tendency to minimize the use of allegorical exegesis. As Martin Luther, speaking for many of his fellow reformers, put it: "Scripture had become like a broken net and no one would be restrained by it, but everyone made a hole in it wherever it pleased him to poke his snout, and followed his own opinions, interpreting and twisting Scripture any way he pleased" (1955–76, 38:14). [18] We might recall in the Induction to *The Magnetic Lady* the Boy's similar comparison between the meaning of a play and a skein of silk.

A third—and, for Jonson, more important—impetus behind this increasing desire to restrain the interpretive freedom of the reader was the gradual strengthening of what might be called historicist modes of thought, of "that cast of mind," as Donald Kelley (1970, 4–5) has argued, "which consciously or not . . . emphasizes the variety rather than the uniformity of human nature; which is interested less in similarities than in differences; and which is impressed not with permanence but with change." That "cast of mind" was also Jonson's, and its development in northern Europe variously coincided with, reinforced, and was reinforced by some of the main currents of Protestantism. While it was an important aspect of Renaissance thought from the inception of the period, its full influence was not felt in northern Europe until midway through the sixteenth century.[19]

Allegorical interpretation dismantles and fragments the object in order to demonstrate the essential unity of truth and the permanence that lies beneath apparent change. Such a procedure is valid so long as meaning is believed not to be a product of the text or of its author but to preexist both. One of the basic tenets of historicism, however, is that texts and events can be understood only by relating them both to their original context and to the intentions and desires of the persons who created them, because the meaning of any utterance or document is unique to the extent that the utterance or document is part of the historical process and conditioned by that process. Understanding is therefore no longer a matter of how one "handles" a text in order to relate it to as many truths as possible; it requires a careful reconstruction of what was said, by whom, to whom, and for what purpose. It requires, in other words, a historical method of interpretation.

Jonson had ample opportunity to see these new procedures put into practice, for through much of his life he was closely associated with scholars who made substantial contributions to the development of historical understanding in England.[20] Two, in particular, are worth noting: William Camden and John Selden. The former was, as is well known, his teacher—"to whom I owe," Jonson states (in *Epigrammes* 14.1–2), "all that I am in arts, all that I know." That "all" included, among other things, Camden's commitment to descriptive accuracy in his historical writings, his ability to discriminate truth from falsehood, the actual from the legendary: "What name, what skill, what faith hast thou in things! / What sight in searching the most antique springs!" (lines 7–8). The first major English representative of what

F. Smith Fussner (1962) has called "the historical revolution," Camden was, as the lines imply, an ideal spectator in the Jonsonian sense. Or perhaps it may be more accurate to say that the Jonsonian observer owes a great deal to the models provided by men like William Camden. In Foucault's words (1970, 130), "Though it is true that the historian, for the Greeks, was indeed the individual who *sees* and who recounts from the starting-point of his sight, it has not always been so in our culture. Indeed, it was at a relatively late date, on the threshold of the Classical age, that he assumed—or resumed—this role."[21]

Camden's variation on this theme can be found in the preface to his history of Elizabeth I. Emphasizing his commitment throughout to reveal the facts about his subject, Camden vows that "to take [truth] from History, is nothing else but, as it were, to pluck out the Eyes of the beautifullest Creature in the World" (1970, 4). If history is not a clear and accurate vision of the past, he argues, it is nothing. Detached and painstaking, the historian carefully views and evaluates those who take their places on the world-stage and does so as objectively as possible. Indeed, Camden was so wary of somehow distorting the facts in his accounts that he sometimes, as in this preface, seems eager to avoid interpretation and conjecture altogether: "Scarcely have I anywhere interposed mine own [opinion]," he assures his readers, "no not by the Bye, since it is a Question whether an Historian may lawfully doe it" (1970, 6).

According to Jonson, the "weight" and "authoritie" of Camden's judgments originate largely in the historian's willingness to do precisely what Damplay and his seventeenth-century counterparts would not: Camden submits himself to the facts and documents that are his subject. He does not compete with those documents; he does not impose himself upon them (or so Camden and Jonson thought). It is Camden's "modestie / Which conquers all" (*Epigrammes* 14.9, 11–12). In this, he was as different from most of the medieval and Tudor historians who preceded him (see Levy 1967; and Fussner 1962) as he was from those readers and playgoers whom Jonson believed to be his primary antagonists. And perhaps because of the marked differences between his historical writings and those of earlier English historians, William Camden, like the poet whom he taught so well, felt threatened by "Envy, the attendant on living writers" (1806, 1:xxv). When he predicts that his masterwork *Brittania* "shall be beset on every side by judgments, prejudices, censures, calumnies, reproofs" (1806, 1:xxxv), his words anticipate Jonson's similar complaints in the "Apologetical Dialogue" or the prefatory letter to *Volpone*. This sense of embattlement was also Camden's legacy to his famous pupil, part of the "all" that Jonson received from the "reuerend head" (line 1) who was, the epigram implies, the poet's creator, and so the object of the heartfelt "pietie" (line 14) that is the poem itself.

John Selden was not Jonson's teacher but his friend. They lent books to each other and evidently discussed subjects as abstruse as the Mosaic prohibition against one sex wearing the clothes of the other (Selden 1726, 2:1690–96). When Jonson was released from imprisonment for his part in writing *Eastward Ho!,* he banqueted Camden and Selden, together with some other friends (*Conversations,* lines 273–78); when Selden's *History of Tithes* (1618) aroused the anger of the king, Jonson intervened on his behalf (Herford, Simpson, and Simpson 1925–52, 1:87). Jonson thought his friend "the Law book of ye Judges of England, the bravest man jn all Languages" (*Conversations,* lines 604–5); Selden wrote a long prefatory poem for the 1616 folio and judged Jonson *"poetarum ille facile princeps"* (Herford, Simpson, and Simpson 1925–52, 1:87n).

We can sense something of the close relationship between the two men from the remarkable opening of the epistle Jonson wrote for his friend's first major work, *Titles of Honor* (1614): "I know to whom I write," Jonson announces. "Here, I am sure, / Though I am short, I cannot be obscure" (*Vnder-wood* 14.1–2). Both the assured tone and the assumption of a common purpose and outlook anticipate Jonson's later statement that Hayward and Selden are "two Names that so much understand" (lines 81–82)—understanding here involving, as it usually does in Jonson, both comprehension and support. If Selden has "trusted" much to ask Jonson's judgment (lines 5–7), just as Jonson "dar'd" to send his epigrams to Donne, that trust has been well placed. The stature and knowledge of a Donne are required to grant Jonson the title of poet (*Epigrammes* 96); likewise, the similarity between Jonson's interests and abilities and Selden's makes the poet at once a knowledgeable and understanding judge of the historian's merits. It is Jonson's role to illuminate Selden's virtues—"Stand forth my Object" (*Vnder-wood* 14.29), he commands—by turning an ever "sharper eye" (line 23)—that is, one capable of making ever finer distinctions—upon himself and the man who is his "Object." Furthermore, such distinctions have been, the poem states, Selden's concern as well. In the same way that Jonson's art presumably represents an improvement over and a purification of the less distinguished versions of most of his contemporaries, so the function of Selden's researches is often a corrective one:

> What fables have you vext! what truth redeem'd!
> Antiquities search'd! Opinions dis-esteem'd!
> Impostures branded! and Authorities urg'd!
> What blots and errours, have you watch'd and purg'd
> Records, and Authors of! how rectified
> Times, manners, customes! Innovations spide!
> (lines 39–44)

Judgment for this man, as for Jonson, is very much a matter of separating one from another things that may appear to be identical but in fact are not. His work is a tissue of careful and finely wrought distinctions.[22] Even his words of praise have a Jonsonian ring to them: "*So generous, so ingenuous, so proportioned to good, such fosterers of virtue, so industrious, of such mould are the* few: *so inhuman, so blind, so dissembling, so vain, so justly nothing, but what's ill disposition, are the* most," Selden explains (1726, 3:87), as he describes in the dedication to *Titles of Honor* the virtues of Edward Hayward.

Some of Selden's comments on interpretation similarly provide a useful gloss on Jonson's. Because he "took his stand on the principle that history was not 'whatever had actually happened in the past,' but rather what could be proved with evidence," Selden attempted to make his historical method as "scientific" as possible (Fussner 1962, 276, 290). And whatever the desirability or possibility of this undertaking, his comments on historical interpretation provide a glimpse into a mind that doubtless had much in common with Jonson's. He was, for instance, totally opposed to any interpretive procedure that began with certain accepted truths and then used those truths to explain the matter at hand. Thus, when James Sempil attacked the *History of Tithes* because Selden did not follow the precepts of Christianity in coming to his conclusions, Selden dismissed his opponent's argument with a contempt worthy of his literary friend: "What logick is this? It should *have been* so, *ergo* it *was*. I could so prove, that sir *James* hath not written the greatest part of his *appendix*" (1726, 3:1351). Poor Sempil, of course, was only doing what many others had done before him—creating, like Damplay, the connections he believed it his prerogative to create. But such activities were, according to Selden (and Jonson), no longer worthy of respect.

Not surprisingly, Selden also distrusted allegorizing—"Make no more allegories in scripture than needs must. The fathers were too frequent in them"—partly because that approach tends to fragment a work rather than grasp it in its entirety: "We pick out a text here, and there, to make it serve our turn; whereas, if we take it all together, and considered what went before, and what followed after, we should find it meant no such thing" (1726, 3:2010). We recall that in *The Magnetic Lady* the Boy makes essentially the same point when he compares understanding a play with unraveling a skein of silk. One of Jonson's accounts of the strategies of his enemies provides an even closer parallel: "Nay, they would offer to urge mine owne Writings against me; but by pieces, (which was an excellent way of malice) as if any mans Context, might not seeme dangerous, and offensive, if that which was knit, to what went before, were defrauded of his beginning" (*Discoveries* 1351–56).

Furthermore, Selden's reservations about allegorical exegesis, like Jonson's, went beyond its tendency to deal with parts rather than wholes. For him as for Jonson, the "keys" to the meaning of any text are intention and context, and those are the very areas to which, as I have noted, allegorical interpretation is often inattentive. In Selden's opinion (1726, 3:2059), even the Bible should be approached as a work whose meanings are circumscribed in part by human desires and historical pressures: "Nothing is text but what was spoken of in the bible, and meant there for person and place, the rest is application, which a discreet man may do well; but 'tis his scripture, not the Holy Ghost." Allegorical interpretation (what Selden calls application) no longer has, he argues, any claim to truth. It is an interesting, perhaps a somewhat useful, exercise but nothing more. In the eyes of this careful spectator, as in Jonson's, the relative importance of author and reader had taken a decisive shift in favor of the former.

The influence of William Camden and John Selden was compounded by that of other men in Jonson's circle of friends who held similar views. Among them were Sir Robert Bruce Cotton, the man whose invaluable library made possible the researches of so many English historians and antiquaries; and Sir Kenelm Digby, the probable editor of the 1640 folio.[23] Taken together, these men had, I believe, a considerable effect on Jonson, one that is apparent not only in his attitude toward interpretation but also in his own ventures into historical writing and in the historical perspective that runs through his comments on decorum, literary conventions, and imitation (see Manley 1980, 189–95). Jonson's infamous reputation as "a meere Empyrick, one that getts what he hath by obseruation" (Leishman 1949, 2 Return from Parnassus 1.2.294–95) probably had its origin in his close association with these historians, as did his emphasis upon artistic verisimilitude. The playwright who told Drummond that "he had ane jntention to haue made a play like Plaut' Amphitrio but left it of, for that he could never find two so like others that he could persuade the spectators they were one" (Conversations, lines 420–23), was obviously a man accustomed to the standards of accuracy typical of his historian friends. We might note as well that when Jonson revised Every Man in His Humour for publication in the 1616 folio, changing the setting to London and greatly increasing the descriptive detail of that setting, he added both a dedication to William Camden and a prologue, which at once attacks the lack of verisimilitude typical of so many of the plays of his contemporaries (lines 7–20) and proclaims the superiority of the comedy which follows, because it contains "deedes, and language, such as men doe vse" (line 21). As is presumably the case with Camden's historical writings, the value of Jonson's play becomes in part a function of its accuracy, and in making this assertion Jonson moves his art in a direction charted by the new kind of history that his former teacher and others were gradually creating. His comedy was to be as faithful in its own way to the human situation as were the writings of the historians with whom he spent so much of his time.

Jonson's emphasis upon verisimilitude might thus be characterized as a critique of Elizabethan literary theory analogous to Selden's contemptuous dismissal of James Sempil for basing his arguments on belief rather than on certain knowledge. It was an emphasis that required "a kind of narrative not envisaged by Sidney and the Renaissance defenders of fiction, for the matter is not what may be and should be (whether or not it has been) but what has indeed been" (Nelson 1973, 112–13); as such, it formed an important corollary to his views on literary interpretation and meaning.[24] Jonson's demand for a new way of reading demanded a new way of writing as well, one that stressed the creation of a unified, probable, and verisimilar plot. Meaning and coherence had now to be located in the text; as the products of the author, not the reader, both had to be discovered (unwoven) by that reader rather than imposed from without. Only by apprehending an author's intentional and careful selection and organization of the elements of a poem or play could a reader or spectator uncover its truth. The author's "accurate" mimesis was, in essence, a model for the reader's judicious and accurate handling of the work itself—a connection that Jonson stresses in *Sejanus* (see Chapter 3). Both activities were necessarily limited and controlled by their subject matter; both were, as much as anything else, forms of repetition.

Yet Jonson recognized that the values he espoused did not entail, as they might seem to at first glance, simply the replacement of the old domination of the reader over the author by its antithesis. That possibility undoubtedly was an attractive one to Jonson, as it would be to any poet. Moreover, like allegorical exegesis, it had a long tradition, one that depicted the poet as a kind of orator, cajoling, berating, and transforming his audience according to his desires and often against theirs. Predictably, the imagery associated with this power was often military and sometimes violent. The poet/orator "entraps" the audience or takes them prisoner; he "ravishes" their ears and "pierces" their hearts; he enjoys absolute command.[25] Jonson himself translated with apparent approval one such passage in Quintilian (*Institutio Oratoria* 2.5.8) that praises how the artist "doth raigne in mens affections; how invade, and breake in upon them; and makes their minds like the thing he writes" (*Discoveries*, lines 791–93).

Despite the obvious advantages of the power described in this quotation, however, the reduction of the members of an audience to the level of unthinking puppets was unacceptable to Jonson, primarily because it smacked of fraud and deception. The Jonsonian knave— a Mosca, a Face, a Meercraft—is in part an artist who controls his audience (the various gulls) with the assurance of a puppeteer, providing that audience with a false semblance of their desires in order to fulfill the knave's own purposes. Peniboy Junior perhaps best sums up this attitude toward spectators when he discusses the Staple of News with its proprietors:

> Why, me thinkes Sir, if the honest common people
> Will be abus'd, why should not they ha' their pleasure,
> In the belieuing Lyes, are made for them;
> As you i'th' *Office*, making them your selues?
> (1.5.42–45)

Although this "abuse" is usually relatively harmless in Jonson's plays—his fools simply get the treatment they deserve—it can lead to situations that are more than a little distasteful (Corvino's treatment of Celia in *Volpone*, for instance) or even murderous (Tiberius's manipulation of the Roman populace in *Sejanus*, a subject discussed further in Chapter 3). The same is true even of the efforts of less compromised characters: Truewit's plot to punish Morose in *Epicoene*, or Macilente's almost vicious treatment of the humour characters in *Every Man out of His Humour*.

As Douglas Duncan (1979) has shown at length, Jonson attempts to combat this kind of authorial dominance, just as he attempts to undermine a similar but opposing claim on the part of the spectator or reader. His fit readers must be detached and patient, receptive yet critical, willing to unravel the author's threadlike argument from the correct end, but unwilling to cede complete authority to that author or anyone else.[26] "Nothing is more ridiculous," Jonson argues, "then to make an Author a *Dictator*. . . . For to many things a man should owe but a temporary beliefe, and a suspension of his owne Judgement, not an absolute resignation of himselfe, or a perpetual captivity" (*Discoveries,* lines 2095–2100). Like Francis Bacon, whom Jonson paraphrases in this passage and praises in another for detailing "all defects of Learning, whatsoever" (lines 935–36), he sought "a sort of suspension of the judgement" among his readers and spectators (*New Organon* 1.126). Only by waiting and observing can one avoid becoming another version of Bacon's "jesting Pilate," who asked the right question—*"What is Truth?"*—but foolishly "would not stay for an answer" ("Of Truth").[27]

Jonson's art is thus balanced uneasily between competing and perhaps mutually exclusive demands. He feared the audience upon whose responses he depended. He had somehow to control that audience in order to prevent it from overwhelming his plays and poems, but by doing so he threatened the detachment required of his readers and spectators if their judgment was to be both accurate and meaningful. As in his relations with other writers, his goals in this instance were, I suspect, unattainable. Indeed, Jonson's problems with his audience proved even more intractable than did his difficulties with his fellow playwrights and poets. Chapter 3 investigates the effects of both concerns on *Poetaster* and *Sejanus,* two plays written during the period of Jonson's career when he insisted most strongly upon the differences between himself and other artists and so was involved most vocally in educating his audience about "the right, or wrong at a Play."

3

CHALLENGING ALL COMERS

If I am correct that the Elizabethan War of the Theaters was only the most notable of several (not always conscious) attempts to create an orderly hierarchy of writers within English letters, Jonson's desire to be recognized as a writer significantly different from his peers made his participation virtually inevitable. That his literary battles with John Marston and, later, Thomas Dekker may have been triggered by the former's clumsy attempt to compliment him in *Histriomastix* (Hoy 1980, 1:182–83; Ingram 1978, 43–47) is hardly surprising if one views the situation from Jonson's position. For Marston's compliments, whatever Marston's actual intentions, implied what would have been for Jonson an annoying similarity between Marston and himself, and he seems always to have felt obliged to correct confusions of this sort. The Ben Jonson who *"made himselfe beleeue,"* in Dekker's words, *"that his* Burgonian wit *might desperately challenge all commers, and that none durst take vp the foyles against him,"*[1] may even have welcomed the opportunity for controversy, perhaps viewing the War of the Theaters as a version of the Athenian competitions in which Aristophanes, one of his most important models, had triumphed so often (see Chapter 4). Only through such a duel did Jonson feel that he could demonstrate conclusively his artistic superiority: hence the ostentatious and aggressive assertions of worth and distinction that characterize *Every Man out of His Humour* and *Cynthia's Revels;* hence, too, Jonson's use of a Roman setting in *Poetaster*—a play more intimately connected with the War of the Theaters than any other he wrote. I "chose AVGVSTVS CAESARS times," Jonson explains in the "Apologetical Dialogue" appended to the play,

> When wit, and artes were at their height in *Rome*,
> To shew that VIRGIL, HORACE, and the rest
> Of those great master-spirits did not want
> Detractors, then, or practisers against them:
> And by this line (although no *paralel*)
> I hop'd at last they [his adversaries] would
>   sit downe, and blush.
> (lines 101–7)

Here, as George Parfitt (1976, 115) has argued, Jonson's use of the classical past reflects his "determination to give his fictions maximum authority" and, I would add, to criticize the present. It also provides a precedent for his own much anticipated victory over his adversaries. Just as the very existence of *Poetaster* fulfills a prediction by one of its own characters that the enemies of Latin literature will be judged harshly by later generations (Ovid, at 1.1.81–82), so the misguided fools who dog Jonson's heels presumably will be overcome by the greater justice of a future in which England will be a nation as hospitable to true poets as is the Rome of Augustus that Jonson places before us.

But Jonson's interest in Augustan Rome was based on more than its artistic achievements and its landscape of extraordinary writers, supported and protected by a beneficent and wise ruler. The literary world of the early empire was also highly competitive (Williams 1978, 193–271), a characteristic Jonson would have recognized without difficulty. One source of this knowledge might have been the Roman historian Velleius Paterculus, a man whom Jonson found interesting enough to quote in *Discoveries* (see Chapter 1) and who considers the causes of artistic greatness in a manner that would have been particularly intriguing to the English writer. Attempting to explain why "pre-eminence in each phase of art is confined within the narrowest limits of time" (1.17.4–6), Velleius suggests that "genius is fostered by emulation, and it is now envy, now admiration, which enkindles imitation, and, in the nature of things, that which is cultivated with the highest zeal advances to the highest perfection; but it is difficult to continue at the point of perfection, and naturally that which cannot advance must recede." The attitude expressed here is, one might say, Jonsonian; the association of emulation, admiration, and envy might well have provided Jonson with an indication of a vital link between the classical past and the Elizabethan present.

That does not mean, certainly, that *Poetaster* establishes exact correspondences between the two eras. Jonson was influenced too strongly by the historical precepts of Camden and his circle to ignore the important and undeniable differences between the reigns of Augustus and Elizabeth. Indeed, it is precisely those differences that permitted him to use the classical past in the first place, enabling him to echo it to some extent without creating the blurred boundaries that he believed inimical to the existence of virtue and order and that he was attempting to combat in *Poetaster* itself. There is, Jonson tells us, "no paralel"; his situation is not an exact counterpart to the one he portrays onstage; his stature is not equal to that of the poets he praises. Yet the experiences of a Virgil or a Horace in Augustan Rome were, from Jonson's viewpoint, analogous to his own in important ways; because of this similarity their presentation onstage might be instructive, if only as a way of shaming his detractors. *Poetaster* is in this sense an attempt to illuminate the present by recalling a past that, despite obvious differences, shared a common ground with contemporary society: the presence of poets vying with one another for artistic supremacy. Velleius Paterculus suggested as much, and if Jonson missed the Roman historian's comments on competition and envy, he would have encountered a similar but much more complex and extensive handling of these issues in the works of Horace, the poet Jonson chose as his chief spokesman in a drama that he hoped would guarantee his victory in the War of the Theaters and so settle, once and for all, the question of his superiority to at least some other playwrights.

Jonson had several reasons for making Horace the central character in *Poetaster*. The most obvious is his general admiration for the Roman poet, an admiration that is everywhere apparent. He translated the *Ars Poetica* and several odes; his works are full of Horation echoes. Horace's moral stance and satiric exposure of the follies of his society must have been particularly congenial to the English poet; his ideal of careful craftsmanship was also Jonson's, and Horace's relationship with Maecenas probably represented for Jonson the ideal relationship between poet and patron.[2] In addition, there was, Herford has shown, a historical analogy: "The Horace of the first book of the *Satires,* in particular, who was then about the same age as Jonson at the date of *Poetaster,* had suffered something from the persecutions, the importunities, or the defamations of various persons of the literary and artistic world" (Herford, Simpson, and Simpson 1925–52, 1:418). And this, as we have seen, is Jonson's own explanation in the "Apologetical Dialogue" (lines 101–7) for his use of Roman materials.

Despite these parallels, however, Jonson's choice of a spokesman has seldom been judged a particularly apt one. In Herford's words (1:420), "It was . . . only in the number and bitterness of his literary assailants that Jonson's situation bore any striking resemblance to that of Horace at the time of his early satires." Three centuries earlier Thomas Dekker was less kind: "Thou hast no part of *Horace* in thee but's name, and his damnable vices," a character in *Satiromastix* sneers at the caricature of Jonson standing before him (5.2.249–50).

To some extent, both Herford and Dekker are right: there are important differences between the English dramatist and his Roman predecessor. But although Jonson was certainly unable to adopt the witty and urbane persona usually associated with his classical model, his choice was not as arbitrary as it seems at first glance. Jonson did not misread Horace; rather, he found in the Roman poet a set of attitudes that both anticipated and helped to shape his own. Horace displayed throughout his career a fascination with literary relationships, with imitation and rivalry, not unlike Jonson's. As detached and sophisticated as Horace often seems, he was also, in Eduard Fraenkel's words (1957, 125), "by temperament a fighter" whose desire for fame led him to attack those who opposed "the new and noble type of poetry which he and his friends were endeavoring to bring about." Together with Aristophanes, he provided Jonson with classical precedents that encouraged and helped legitimize the English writer's own attempts to stand apart from his peers.

Horace's concern with rivalry is perhaps most apparent in the satires that deal with Lucilius (*Satires* 1.4, 1.10, 2.1). This series of poems reveals a great deal about the young poet's sense of his relation both to the most important Roman satirist who preceded him and to his own contemporaries as well, since many of Horace's comments must be understood within the context of more general debates between a conservative literary party opposing the Hellenization of Roman literature and "a poetical advance guard" of which Horace was a member (Witke 1970, 56; cf. Fiske 1920, 123, 279–80, 336–49; Knoche 1975, 80). Because Lucilius was championed by the conservative party he was a formidable rival for Horace, despite the fact that Lucilius was no longer alive. Indeed, it was his proximity to Horace—an effect both of the deceased poet's contemporary popularity and their similarity of style and subject matter—that from Horace's point of view made their relationship problematic and more competitive than it might otherwise have been.[3]

Satires 1.4 begins, as C. O. Brink has noted (1963, 158), by creating a tradition for Roman satire and then partially dissociating Lucilius from that tradition. The tradition is that of Old Comedy— "Eupolis and Cratinus and Aristophanes"—and its fearless attacks upon vice: "It is on these that Lucilius wholly hangs," the satirist says. "These he has followed, changing only metre and rhythm" (1.4.1, 6–7). The evaluation is hardly a generous one: the speaker first implies that Lucilius is a relatively unoriginal artist (the verb *sequi* in line 6 is usually associated with slavish imitation); then, after allowing him only three words of praise (*facetus, emunctae naris,* lines 7–8), he follows with more than five lines describing the inadequacies of the older satirist's style. The opening praise given to the Greek dramatists thus provides a background against which to measure Lucilius's shortcomings; Horace's poems presumably represent a return to a more ideal form of satire that flourished in another era and culture. Like Jonson, Horace apparently felt himself instructed by the (distant) past and burdened by the (near) present. Jonson, doubtless, would not have missed the similarity.

This threat to Lucilius's dominant position among Roman satirists is made even more explicit by the sudden entry of an apparent advocate for the older poet, one Crispinus, who, the speaker comments, "challenges me at long odds" to see who can write the most (lines 13–14). The speaker declines, but his refusal is somewhat disingenuous: he has in fact been competing since the beginning of the satire, and his refusal is itself part of the rivalry I have been tracing, an assertion of superiority similar to Jonson's profession of his own unwillingness to compete with the "vile Ibides" he scorns in the "Apologetical Dialogue" (line 219). Lucilius may be an opponent who cannot be ignored, but Crispinus hardly falls within that category.

Satires 1.10 is in part a reply to criticisms of Horace's criticism; there he amplifies and explains the judgments he had made in the earlier poem, argues that Lucilius's own attacks on other poets provide justification for negative comments about Lucilius himself, and makes one other important addition that reveals more clearly the reasons for his concern with the earlier satirist and his unwillingness to ignore others' reactions to *Satires* 1.4. Approximately halfway through *Satires* 1.10 the speaker supplies a catalogue of several literary genres and the poets who are the acknowledged masters of each: Fundanus for comedy, Pollio for tragedy, Varius for epic, Virgil for the eclogue. He then turns to satire: "This satire, which Varro of the Atax and some others had vainly tried, was what I could write with more success, though falling short of the inventor; nor would I dare to wrest from him the crown that clings to his brow with so much glory" (1.10.46–49). On the one hand, the passage is an admission that an imitator can never attain the same status as an inventor of a literary form—and Lucilius was, for Horace and his contemporaries, the inventor of Roman satire. On the other hand, this praise is placed in a somewhat ambiguous context by the implication that the speaker's right to compose satire is predicated largely on the relatively imperfect state of the genre (cf. Fiske 1920, 41). Only because Roman satire lacks a giant like Virgil or Varius, because others have "vainly tried" their hands at it can the speaker compose his versions of this form. Being able to write better than previous practitioners of the genre is his justification for writing; and, given the numerous criticisms of Lucilius's style in both *Satires* 1.4 and 1.10, that "better" also includes a judgment about the qualitative relationship between Horace's poems and those of Lucilius, although the latter's fame as inventor of the genre can never be denied.

Horace's involvement in literary controversy, then, was not merely based upon a commitment to a particular style or literary program, as important as that commitment may have been; his involvement (like Jonson's, some sixteen centuries later) was also a matter of justifying his own act of writing satire and creating a poetic identity, which could be defined only by clarifying the differences between his own poetic voice and those of other Roman satirists, Lucilius preeminent among them. Without such distinctions—without, implicitly, Horace's ability to surpass his models/rivals—Horace the satirist would be indistinguishable from other Roman poets.

Once that identity had been established, however, Lucilius was no longer a potential competitor. When Horace, now a relatively famous and successful writer, again comments some five years later on his predecessor, his remarks are both deferential and laudatory (see *Satires* 2.1.16–17, 28–34, 62–79). Lucilius's poems now provide a defense of and justification for the speaker. Similarity is stressed rather than difference because Horace knows, and expects his readers to know as well, that the poet he now accepts as a model is one he has in some ways surpassed.

With a prominent place in Latin letters finally secured, however, Horace paradoxically found himself in the precarious position Lucilius had occupied: having displaced the earlier satirist, he then became a model to be displaced by others, a situation whose ironies Horace seems to have overlooked. This predicament is described most fully in *Epistles* 1.19, a work that Fraenkel has called "the only thoroughly bitter document that we have from Horace's pen" (1957, 350). Apparently written in response to the unenthusiastic reception of the first three books of his odes, the letter, which is addressed to Maecenas, both asserts Horace's own power and originality (in his odes and epodes) and attacks those who would undermine that authority by imitating or emulating them. Without displaying the least awareness of the contradiction, Horace, who had found it necessary to compete with other satirists in order to establish his own poetic identity within the genre, attempts to deny that possibility to others. As René Girard observes, "The model" (and Horace is here very much a model), "even when he has openly encouraged imitation, is surprised to find himself engaged in competition. He concludes that the disciple has betrayed his confidence by following in his footsteps" (1977, 146). The situation anticipates Jonson's stormy relationship with John Marston and, much later, with one of the most talented of his "sons," Richard Brome.

Horace's epistle begins, like *Satires* 1.4 and 1.10, by invoking the origin of what might be called a literary tradition: Cratinus's comments on the relation of wine to inspiration. Homer and Ennius are also mentioned, and the speaker quickly turns to a comment he has made on the subject. The comment is unremarkable enough—"To the sober I shall assign the Forum and Libo's Well; the stern I shall debar from song" (*Epistles* 1.19.8–9); less so is his description of its effect: "Ever since I put forth this edict," he explains, "poets have never ceased to vie in wine-drinking by night, to reek of it by day" (lines 10–11). Although the tone of these lines is witty and ironic, they introduce two issues that will be developed with much more seriousness in the remainder of the poem: the speaker's stature and power (the use of the verb *edicere* in line 10 is not accidental), and the many connections among imitation, competition, and violence. Thus, the description of wine-drinking poets is followed first by a scornful reference to those who might attempt to gain Cato's reputation by aping his appearance (lines 12–14) and then by an account of an endeavor to emulate, which ended in self-destruction: "In coping [*aemula*] with Timagenes, his tongue brought ruin to [*rupit*—literally "burst asunder"] Iarbitas; so keen was his aim and effort to be deemed a man of wit and eloquence" (lines 15–16). The speaker then returns to his own plight. Apparently victimized by the adulation of foolish poets, he complains: "O you mimics [*imitatores*], you slavish herd! How often your pother has stirred my spleen, how often my mirth" (lines 19–20).

That his reaction in this case has more in common with the former than the latter is demonstrated by what follows. In response to the potential threat (or annoyance) represented by this servile group, the speaker asserts his authority even more strongly by declaring in the most emphatic terms his difference from ordinary writers: "I was the first to plant free footsteps on a virgin soil; I walked not where others trod. Who trusts himself will lead and rule the swarm" (lines 21–23). Authority here rests in beginnings, and those who create beginnings are those who follow their own inclinations, not the ways of others; for authority is also a function of difference, of the distance between the "I" that plants free footsteps on a virgin soil and a faceless "swarm" of beelike poets. One could only wish that these "bees" did not, like their Senecan or Elizabethan counterparts, have a habit of imitating.

The speaker continues to detail his accomplishments in the next twelve lines and then turns to a subject more closely related to the apparent cause of the letter: the unpopularity of some of Horace's odes. The focus shifts from what he has done to what he has not—"I am not one to hunt for the votes of a fickle public"; "I am not one who . . . deign[s] to court the bribes of lecturing professors" (lines 37–40)—but the intent of the rhetoric is the same: to distinguish him from other writers, just as Jonson employs negatives to define more accurately the virtues of those he praises (including himself). The poem does not end with such distinctions, however; rather, it concludes with a sobering recognition of the difficulty of attaining peace by withdrawing from a world shot through with imitative and competitive impulses. We recognize, if the speaker does not, that his very desire to stand apart, withdraw, and discourage imitation invites emulation and envy from others. Thus, his refusal to recite his "worthless writing" in public is recognized (and rightly so) as a sign of arrogance (lines 42, 44–45); and the poem concludes with the speaker, fearful that further argument might lead to a vicious gladiatorial contest between himself and other poets, pleading for peace: "'The place you choose suits me not,' I cry, and call for a truce in the sports. For such sport begets tumultuous strife and wrath, and wrath begets fierce quarrels, and war to the death" (lines 47–49). Like the earlier description of inebriated poets, this passage exemplifies the clever wit for which Horace is so often praised. But in this case the humor scarcely conceals the intensely serious concerns that lie beneath it. By the time he wrote this epistle Horace had discovered two things of which he seemed unaware in the earlier satires: the potential destructiveness of emulative endeavors and, equally important, their tendency to proliferate.

Unless it is contained within some well-defined structure, competition is difficult to control; a poet who commits himself to a literary world where emulation is a powerful force chances committing himself to a career of endless rivalry, since rarely is a universally accepted mechanism available to declare a victor or to signal the completion of the competition. As Quintilian understood and as Horace learned to his displeasure, "victory" over a model or rival only makes a poet more likely to be emulated by others, and although that emulation is an indication of stature, it can also be a source of difficulty. There is seldom a possibility of withdrawing from the competition, just as there is little possibility of a final victory. Yet without competing, Horace would not in his own view have been able to become a satirist at all. Emulation is a perfect Catch-22: one competes in order to establish an identity, order, and difference, but success in this endeavor often leads others to imitate and rival that success, thereby destroying (potentially) the very differences it was intended to create.

Horace, then, had much to tell Jonson about the relations between poets; his attitudes toward both Lucilius and Lucilius's followers provided Jonson with a possible guide or model for the English writer's own attitude toward his contemporaries. The same complex of emotions I have attempted to trace in Horace—his competitiveness, his very different attitudes toward near and distant models, his desire for distinction coupled with scorn for the responses that distinction aroused in others, his futile desire to withdraw from a competitive world which gradually came to seem cruel and destructive—are present in Jonson as well and played a large part in attracting the Englishman to this particular Roman author.

If at the time he wrote *Poetaster* Jonson was unable, or unwilling, to confront the more pessimistic implications of Horace's message, he understood the satirist's combativeness and involvement in literary rivalry very well indeed. That understanding can be seen most readily by looking carefully at the first of *Poetaster's* two major borrowings from Horace: the use of *Satires* 1.9 as the basis for act 3, scenes 1–3. Although Jonson's handling of his predecessor's poem is an adaptation that alters Horace's material according to Jonson's own purposes, it is an adaptation that moves the poem in the direction I have been charting, a direction sanctioned by Horace's own concerns with his rivals, concerns that anticipated Jonson's. The ideas Jonson stresses in this episode are present—in less developed and perhaps less complex form—in the original. Jonson simply placed the Roman poet's description of an encounter with an exasperating boor within a context that highlights those ideas, and then made alterations in that description which emphasized them even further. Jonson knew his model better, and differently, than has sometimes been supposed.

By the time Jonson's boor meets his Horace on the Via Sacra, we already know a great deal about Crispinus. By virtue of his name, Crispinus has, in O. J. Campbell's words (1938, 120), "a kind of hereditary right to arrive at pseudo poetry by way of pseudo gallantry." It is not enough that he is an inferior poet who seeks inspiration from an equally inferior source—Cloe (see 2.2.75–79); he is also, despite a singular lack of courage, a man drawn to self-display and competition with his apparent superiors. In the scene immediately preceding his encounter with Horace, Crispinus scurries about the outskirts of the remarkable group of men and women who have gathered at Albius's house, secretly asking Cloe to "intreat the ladies, to intreat me to sing" (line 135) and—when he is exposed by her simpleminded inability to remain silent about the ruse—suddenly (and nervously) vowing that he does not wish to rival Hermogenes in any way. "Not I, sir, I'le challenge no man" (line 149), he protests, until he is coaxed into performing a single stanza of "the dittie" (line 160) he has mastered—a ditty written, appropriately enough, by Hermogenes himself. Meanwhile, Hermogenes, after initially affecting a Jonsonian (and Horatian) aloofness from the entire business—"Sir, all this doth not yet make mee enuie you: for I know I sing better then you" (lines 176–77)—suddenly loses his self-control, sings the second verse of the song, and then prepares to sing another and, one suspects, another after that, until he is dissuaded by Ovid, who proposes to "end this difference within" (lines 199–200). The incident is almost a microcosm of the War of the Theaters: a mixture of envy, hostility, and feigned indifference to rivalry, a "difference" whose purpose is simultaneously the preservation of already established distinctions (Hermogenes' goal) and the destruction of those distinctions in the hope of creating new ones (Crispinus's intent). Ironically, neither party is particularly successful in getting what he wants, but Crispinus remains undaunted, vowing to become a poet and announcing that he will outdo Albius for the affections of his wife: "Ile presently goe and enghle some broker, for a *Poets* gowne, and bespeake a garland: and then ieweller, looke to you best iewell yfaith" (lines 224–26).

Act 2 concludes with these words. Act 3 begins with Jonson's adaptation of Horace's *Satires* 1.9, while the impression of Crispinus's folly and ambition is still planted firmly in our minds. In the Latin original the speaker encounters "a man I knew only by name" on the Via Sacra, suffers through the apparently interminable attempts by this boor to ingratiate himself with the satirist, pleads unsuccessfully with his friend Aristus Fuscus for help, and is finally rescued only when his tormentor is taken off to court. Jonson presents the same sequence of events with a single exception: it is his Horace who leaves the scene rather than his antagonist—a change suggesting that in Jonson's Rome pretension and folly may be harder to dislodge than in the Rome of Horace. Crispinus is not an annoying anomaly but a representative of a growing and potentially threatening group of poetasters who cannot be ignored. As a result, Jonson's Horace is much more embattled than his classical model.

Jonson also alters the sequence of several speeches present in the Latin poem, expanding some of them and adding others. Two additions early in the episode are of particular interest. In one of these, Jonson lets us inside the mind of Crispinus *before* he actually addresses Horace: "'Slid, yonder's HORACE! they say hee's an excellent *Poet:* MECOENAS loues him. Ile fall into his acquaintance, if I can; I thinke he be composing, as he goes i' the street! ha? 't is a good humour, and he be: Ile compose too" (3.1.3–7). In the second, after Crispinus proclaims, like his Roman counterpart, that he is a scholar (line 20; cf. *Satires* 1.9.7), he adds (rather, Jonson adds): "Nay, we are new turn'd *Poet* too, which is more; and a *Satyrist* too, which is more than that: I write iust in thy vaine, I. I am for your *odes* or your *sermons,* or any thing indeed" (lines 23–26).

The additions place the entire encounter within a framework of artistic imitation, which is only one of several concerns in the satire. Crispinus is a man on the make; Jonson's Horace, a man who presumably has made it. The former's goal is to appropriate in some fashion Horace's stature and authority by mimicking his behavior as closely as he can—in other words, by overcoming if possible the distinctions between them. Although this intent seems innocuous enough, given Crispinus's folly—he is hardly a candidate for literary greatness—as the episode progresses and Crispinus gains confidence that he is not, in fact, much inferior to his model, the same impulses that lead him to mimic Horace also lead to rivalry and an endeavor to displace Horace's most honored friends: "I protest to thee, HOR-ACE (doe but taste mee once) if I doe know my selfe, and mine owne vertues truely, thou wilt not make that esteeme of VARIVS, or VIRGIL, or TIBVLLVS, or any of 'hem indeed, as now in thy ignorance thou dost; which I am content to forgiue" (lines 161–65). Crispinus goes on to announce his superiority, based on his speed in composing and skill in singing (lines 165–67, 179–81).

With Horace's poet friends having presumably been put in their places, Crispinus then turns his attention to Horace's patron. In *Satires* 1.9.45–48 the boor, after questioning the satirist about Maecenas, offers himself as a possible ally in securing more firmly the patrician's support: "You might have a strong backer, who could be your understudy, if you would introduce your humble servant. Hang me, if you wouldn't find that you had cleared the field." Jonson's version of the same speech is as follows: "Thou should'st find a good sure assistant of mee," Crispinus pledges, "one, that would speake all good of thee in thy absence, and be content with the next place, not enuying thy reputation with thy patron. Let me not liue, but I thinke thou and I (in a small time) should lift them all out of fauour, both VIRGIL, VARIVS, and the best of them; and enioy him wholy to our selues" (lines 239–46). In addition to detailing just what is involved in "clearing the field [*summosses omnis*]" and making explicit the purpose of such an activity—enjoying Maecenas "wholy to our selues" —Jonson's version makes one other important addition to the original: it brings into the open the possibility of rivalry between Horace and his apparent ally. By stating that he would be content with "the next place, not enuying thy reputation with thy patron," Crispinus in fact suggests just the opposite: that he will *not* be content and will attempt to "lift" Horace out of favor—just as he hopes he and Horace will replace Virgil and Varius—leaving Maecenas no longer wholly to "our selues" but to himself alone. An episode that began with Crispinus attempting to mimic Horace's every move ends by implying that the goal of this mimicry is the displacement of Horace by Crispinus. And that is just what the poetaster tries to achieve in the remainder of the play.[4]

Crispinus's ambivalent response to Horace once again replays in comic fashion the general issues of the War of the Theaters, at least as Jonson understood them. The poetaster's desire to eliminate the very real and, according to Jonson, necessary distance between his poems and those of Horace is a humorous and exaggerated version of the willful disregard for distinctions among poets and the complex mixture of servility and hostility that Jonson seems to have found in Crispinus's flesh-and-blood model, John Marston—attitudes that in Jonson's eyes threatened to equate Marston's (and, somewhat later, Thomas Dekker's) literary talent, however inferior, with his own. Even the "Apologetical Dialogue" appended to *Poetaster* was in large part a response to this threat; its sole purpose, Jonson tells us, was to ensure *"that Posteritie may make a difference, betweene their manners that prouok'd me then, and mine that neglected them euer"* ("To the Reader," lines 7–9); and in the "Dialogue" itself the Author suggests that one reason for his difficulty in composing more than a single drama each year is his fear that his plays will somehow be contaminated by those of his inferiors, a fear so powerful that at one point (lines 195–98) he implies regret at writing anything at all:

> I would, they could not say that I did that,
> There's all the ioy that I take i' their trade,
> Vnlesse such Scribes as they might be proscrib'd
> Th' abused theaters.

But Jonson knew well enough that a prohibition of this sort was not likely, and he was left to detail, as best he could, how the inability to discriminate might lead to an entire gallery of evils, conflict among them. The encounter between Crispinus and Horace is perhaps the most obvious portrayal of these concerns in *Poetaster* but not by any means the only one. In fact, the initial indication of this problem comes from a somewhat surprising source: Pantilius Tucca. The braggart's opening speech is an outraged response to what he believes to be an indefensible violation of hierarchy and decorum, Luscus's statement that Ovid Senior's advice to the old man's wayward son merely echoes what Luscus had said "afore-hand" (1.2.21): "How now, good man slaue? what, *rowle powle?* all riualls, rascall? why my master of worship, do'st heare? Are these thy best proiects? is this thy desseignes and thy discipline, to suffer knaues to bee competitors with commanders and gent'men? are we *paralells,* rascall? are we *paralells?*" (lines 24–29).

Luscus's claim that he has spoken similarly is here described as a competitive and potentially subversive act, and the close association between equality and conflict is indicated by three key words in Tucca's speech: *riualls, competitors,* and *parallels.* The first carries with it the meanings of its Latin original, as well as its more obvious English significance. A *rivalis* is an individual who uses the same stream as another; he is also a man who enjoys the same mistress as another, and so competes with that other in love. Likewise, a *competitor* is at once a partner or associate and an opponent; and a *parallel* is something of equal worth or value.[5] Taken together all three words intimate a causal relationship between equality and rivalry (we might recall that in the "Apologetical Dialogue" Jonson carefully states that his situation is no "paralel" to that of Virgil and Horace): we compete most often with (relative) equals, because only in such relationships is difference obscured and status unsure. That this insight comes from one of the most foolish characters in the play—one who does as much as anyone else in the drama to tear down distinctions by both action and style of speech[6]—surely is ironic, but the irony does not undermine the validity of Tucca's point. Despite his posturing and extravagant language, Tucca makes more sense than he may know.

Luscus's perhaps inadvertent flattening of distinctions anticipates the actions of Crispinus and Demetrius, who would measure all things according to their own meager abilities (5.3.355–58), as well as the cheapening of ideals inherent in the mock banquet arranged by Ovid and his fellow poets.[7] The passage Virgil reads from the *Aeneid* describes a similar activity: Fame's attempt to *"scale* IOVES *court"* (5.2.83). All of these characters threaten in one way or another the careful system of hierarchical relationships that is, according to Jonson, essential to order and to the protection—even the existence—of virtue. That is why Caesar's reaction to the apparently harmless games of Ovid and his companions is so harsh and unyielding. In his view the banquet is a form of imitation that debases the original, bringing the gods down to the level of a frivolous humanity (4.6.34–38), rather than moving that humanity toward the divine, and Caesar responds to this travesty by reasserting the reality both of hierarchical relationships within Roman society and of his own power and authority: "If you thinke gods but fain'd, and vertue painted," he tells the revellers, "Know, we sustaine an actuall residence," one whose distance both apart from and above the localities frequented by his subjects defines Caesar's "imperiall power" (lines 48–49, 51). Situated at the pinnacle of a system of differences that constitutes the order of the Roman state, his duty is to preserve and protect the distinctions that provide the basis for that order, no matter how minor a particular threat to that system may seem.

It is perfectly in keeping with Caesar's commitment to this goal that he later pardons Gallus and Tibullus, because they are gentlemen (5.1.1–7), and, somewhat more ambitiously, attempts to transform the disorderly and unpredictable gifts of fortune into a consistent pattern based on "worth and iudgement" (line 61)—that is, on his ability to distinguish. Caesar goes far beyond "the vast rude swinge of generall confluence" that "is, in particular ends, exempt from sense" (5.2.41–42) when he elevates Virgil to a position appropriate to the poet's character and accomplishments—an action that not only separates Virgil from other poets but also demonstrates that Caesar is "a man, distinct by it, / From those, whom custome rapteth in her preasse" (lines 44–45). Like Jonson's, the emperor's ideal is "responsible hierarchy" (Parfitt 1976, 144; cf. Beaurline 1978, 134–37). The same is true of Jonson's Horace. In response to Crispinus's suggestion that Rome's most famous poets must inevitably rival one another, Jonson's satirist—echoing and expanding the material in the English dramatist's source—describes Maecenas's circle as an environment characterized by the untroubled acceptance of virtue and difference:

> Sir, your silknesse
> Clearly mistakes MECOENAS, and his house;
> To thinke, there breathes a spirit beneath his roofe,
> Subiect vnto those poore affections
> Of vnder-mining enuie, and detraction . . . .
> . . . .
> . . . each man hath his place,
> And to his merit, his reward of grace:
> Which with a mutuall loue they all embrace.
> (3.1.248–59)

Order, peace, and the recognition and acceptance of one's "place" in a carefully determined hierarchical system of differences go hand in hand in the world of this "comicall satyre."

The imitative tendencies of poetasters are not, however, the only threat depicted in the drama to virtue and art. *Poetaster* presents a series of enemies to poetry; the mercantile mentality of Ovid Senior, the foolishness of Demetrius and Crispinus (poets of little or no talent), and the misguided values of Ovid and his companions (poets who misuse their extraordinary gifts) hardly exhaust the list, for the problems described also involve the activities of readers and spectators. As I argued in Chapter 2, this additional concern was for Jonson very nearly unavoidable: only his audience finally had the power to grant the distinction he sought. In fact, Jonson's desire to emphasize in *Poetaster* both the importance and the vexed nature of relations between authors and audiences seems to have encouraged him to include in the folio version of the play a second major borrowing from Horace: a translation of *Satires* 2.1, which becomes act 3, scene 5, of Jonson's comedy. Horace's encounter with Crispinus details the dynamics of literary rivalry; the second borrowing, a conversation between Horace and Trebatius, deals with the reception of Horace's poems and the dangers he faces. The later scene's rhymed couplets give a ceremonial quality to the episode, as Horace and his friend return to the issues of the play's opening debate between Ovid and his father—both sides having gained stature and the poet, this time, triumphant. Horace must overcome the folly of inferior readers, as well as that of untalented writers, if his name is to survive.[8]

The materials with which Jonson prefaced the comedy make basically the same point. The entry of Envy at the opening of the Induction signals unmistakably that we are entering a world in which emulation has merged with its more sinister relative, a world characterized by frequent attempts to darken all that is light, to obscure that which stands out. The tactics that Envy catalogues are, in essence, a handbook of misinterpretation, a description of violent appropriations of a text by those who have no real interest in understanding it:

> wrestings, comments, applications,
> Spie-like suggestions, priuie whisperings,
> And a thousand such promooting sleights as these.
> (lines 24–26)

The target of all this mayhem is the author as well as his poem: the audience must "hisse, sting, and teare / His worke, and him" (lines 52–53), the sequence of verbs tracing a movement from a negative response to an act of destruction. Given this situation, it is no wonder that the Prologue appears armed "against the coniuring meanes / Of base detractors, and illiterate apes" and takes the time to explain the *"allegorie* and hid sence" of his strange costume in order to prevent the very sort of misunderstanding he is complaining about (lines 8–9, 12). At the same time, the Prologue attempts to differentiate between the author's reaction to the activities of his enemies and the attitudes of those enemies. "Their moods he rather pitties, then enuies," we are told. "His mind is aboue their iniuries" (lines 27–28).

The calumnies of bad readers are also linked with the attempts of a Crispinus or a Demetrius to equate himself with his superiors, when Envy, fearing that the purity of Rome will defeat its evil purposes, seeks aid from "poet-apes" who can "wrest, / Peruert, and poyson all they heare, or see, / With senselesse glosses, and allusions" (lines 35, 38–40). Bad poets are dependent upon bad readers for their success, are at times indistinguishable from those readers. Poetry cannot be divorced from its social context. A Virgil cannot exist without a Caesar to applaud him and protect him from abuse, whether that abuse stems from slavish imitators or from an ignorant and hostile audience.

Thus, the two hopelessly inferior poets in this play are also less than ideal spectators. Both Crispinus and Demetrius are fond of standing apart from the action around them, affecting the kind of detachment that enables Crites to understand and judge his contemporaries, pretending to be observers amid a world of feverish actors. Yet a stance that is often in Jonson a sign of stature and wisdom is, for these characters, just the opposite. Or perhaps it might be said that their success at observing matches their success at poetry. In both instances they corrupt the model they would imitate; here they reduce what should be a position of power and insight into a showcase for their own foolishness.

Demetrius, for example, first slinks into the play in act 3, scene 4, apparently trailing after the player Histrio and standing off to the side while Tucca's pages perform at their master's command. All we hear from this shabbily clad figure are two expressions of approval, spoken in concert with Histrio (3.4.227, 243), in response to lines of verse that are hardly the stuff of greatness. His appearance is so curious that Tucca, having finally noticed the poetaster some three hundred lines into the scene, is amazed by the puppetlike figure before him. "What's he, with the halfe-armes there, that salutes vs out of his cloke, like a *motion?* ha?" (lines 318–19), he asks, anticipating our own questions. Only somewhat later (4.3.104–5) do we realize that Demetrius's strange behavior probably represents an attempt to mimic Horace's own famous detachment; his complaint that the satirist is "nothing but humours, and obseruation" scarcely conceals his own desire to play a similar part, though without the content, authority, and poetic talent that should accompany it.

Crispinus likewise enters the play as a man highly skilled, by his own account, at watching others. This is the role he adopts on Chloe's behalf, anticipating Demetrius's description of Horace and implying that he is "for" this activity, just as he will be "for" all that Horace does when they meet on the Via Sacra: "I warrant you, sweet ladie; let mee alone to obserue, till I turne my selfe to nothing but obseruation" (2.1.165–66). Unfortunately, Crispinus, like his fellow, only deflates the role he so assiduously assumes. He sees without insight, observes without understanding. At Ovid's banquet in act 4, scene 5, his inane responses to the jests around him lead Hermogenes to accuse him of being hired by the authors of the witticisms to voice his applause; and when plaguing Horace in act 3, scenes 1 and 2, he proves himself singularly adept at ignoring or misreading the satirist's increasingly clear indications of displeasure—to Horace's discomfort and our laughter.

The most misguided interpreter in *Poetaster,* however, is neither of the two foolish would-be poets. That award belongs to Asinius Lupus, a man even less capable of judging correctly than they are. Like Savolina in *Every Man out of His Humour,* Politic Would-Be in *Volpone,* and Overdo in *Bartholomew Fair,* Lupus believes himself to be an individual of enormous insight, capable of seeing beneath the surface of things to discover hidden truths that others are unable to apprehend. His faith in his ability to decipher a world full of obscure and ambiguous meanings leads him to ignore the obvious in favor of his own constructs. "IVPITER, I thanke thee, that thou hast yet made me so much of a politician" (4.4.30–31), he exults, but the central attribute of this politician is a blind and obsessive paranoia rather than

subtlety or wisdom. Just as in *The Magnetic Lady* Damplay over-
whelms the intended sense of the drama he is watching in order to
assert his prerogative to discover whatever meanings he desires, so
Lupus insists on imposing his own silly order on the society around
him. He thus proves himself a fit companion to Envy, skilled in all
of the "promooting sleights" (line 26) which that figure lists so en-
thusiastically in the opening speech of the play.

Lupus shatters with ease the harmonious setting in which Virgil
begins his recitation of the *Aeneid* when the tribune bursts into Caesar's palace shouting his discovery of treason and libel beneath the
apparently innocuous surface of one of Horace's poems. A concrete
example of the evil forces Virgil has just been describing, Lupus dis-
places the author of the work before him and makes it, as Horace
ironically notes, his own: "If you will needes take it," the poet assures
the tribune, "I cannot with modestie giue it from you" (5.3.99–100).
Reading is for Lupus, as Jonson believed it was for too many of his
contemporaries, an act of appropriation, an assertion of the reader's
own will over that of the author, who no longer controls the sense of
his words and who is thus vulnerable to the whims of anyone who
(mis)reads him. A comic yet threatening practitioner of what Jonson
undoubtedly felt to be the worst excesses of allegorical interpretation,
Lupus finds his truths in all things, but to do so, this "malicious,
ignorant, and base / Interpreter" must, Virgil explains, "distort, and
straine / The generall scope and purpose of an authour, / To his particular, and priuate spleene" (lines 141–44).

Lupus, of course, is easily put in his place; his defeat parallels that
of Crispinus and Demetrius later in the scene. His exposure, like that
of the poetasters, ends a major threat to the artistic health of Augustan Rome, since misguided readers constitute a danger to poetry
equal to if not greater than that posed by inferior writers. Neither
group has a place within the idealized society with which *Poetaster*
concludes—a society in which the most powerful individual, Caesar,
is also a model reader.

Yet even within this setting the status of poetry is somewhat precarious. Although Lupus is defeated, Virgil cannot continue reading
his epic after the interruption. "Our eare is now too much prophan'd
(graue MARO) / With these distastes, to take thy sacred lines" (lines

165–66), Caesar laments, admitting that even in defeat the enemies of art have gained a kind of victory, ruining at least for the present the ceremonial atmosphere with which the fifth act began. While Caesar can protect poetry from its enemies, that endeavor necessarily delays the enshrinement of Virgil and his poem, an outcome whose implications are not entirely hopeful.[9]

This precariousness explains in part the sense of desperation that pervades the final scene of this comedy. Despite its optimistic veneer, the conclusion reveals in its uneasiness more than its creator's fervent desire to translate Horace's onstage victory into the artistic world of Elizabethan England; it reveals as well Jonson's fear that there was not even the faintest "paralel" between the events depicted in the play and the artistic direction of his own society. And he was right. *Poetaster* did not transform the literary landscape of Elizabethan England; it did not establish once and for all something like the hierarchy of poets that Jonson believed existed in Augustan Rome; it did not, finally, disentangle Jonson's art from that of the supposed poetasters. Just as Ovid, near the beginning of the comedy, is able to return to his poetry only after the noisy interruptions of Luscus come to an end (1.1.40–42), so too the Author in the "Apologetical Dialogue," after wearily reciting once more a litany of abuses to which true art is subjected and finding his own ability to compose virtually paralyzed by the ignorance of the audience he faces (lines 205–15), regains his power to create only by withdrawing from the society he normally inhabits. Struck by what is apparently a flash of inspiration, he turns to his friends and commands:

> Leaue me. There's something come into my thought,
> That must, and shall be sung, high, and aloofe,
> Safe from the wolues black iaw, and the dull asses hoofe.
> (lines 237–39)

Momentarily, Jonson had given up attempting to instruct and control his audience. His career had not progressed as he had hoped; the stage was not yet his. One senses, moreover, that for the first time he suspected that it might never be.

But Jonson's attempt to secure a privileged place in English letters did not end, obviously, with *Poetaster,* whatever disappointment he felt about the outcome of the War of the Theaters. The "Apologetical Dialogue" announces as much, promising "fresh straines" that shall "Giue cause to some of wonder, some despight, / And vnto more, despaire, to imitate their sound" (lines 229–32). Those "fresh straines" are the verses of *Sejanus,* a play that was evidently intended both to encourage imitation and to make it impossible. According to the anonymous author of one of the prefatory poems in the quarto edition (see Herford, Simpson, and Simpson 1925–52, 11:314), the play was to have been two tragedies in one: a depiction of Sejanus's fall from power and the cause of a similar fate among Jonson's fellow writers:

> And as *Seianus,* in thy *Tragedie,*
> > Falleth from *Caesars* grace; euen so the Crew
> > Of common *Play-wrights,* whom Opinion blew
> Big with false greatnesse, are disgrac'd by thee.
> > Thus, in one *Tragedie,* thou makest twaine.

(We might be reminded of Jonson's gamester or Iarbitas's fate in Horace's *Epistles* 1.19.) The polemical role that this drama was to play in the development of Jonson's career explains his decision to delete the contributions of a "second Pen" ("To the Readers," line 45) from the published versions of the play. Far from stemming merely from his unwillingness "to defraud so happy a *Genius* of his right, by . . . lothed vsurpation" (lines 47–48), the change was, more importantly, the result of his endeavor to make the play (and so its triumph) wholly his own and thus to prevent the complications—and with them the blurring of distinctions and authority—that would have accompanied the presence of another's work in the tragedy.

Unfortunately, "the spoile of conquest" to quote one of the play's defenders (Herford, Simpson, and Simpson 1925–52, 11:317), was not, as is well known, awarded to Jonson. The tragedy remained double, but the victims were not Sejanus and Jonson's rivals; rather, the tragedy became Jonson's own, a rather distressing turn of events that he himself notes in the dedicatory letter to Lord Aubigny: *"It is a poem, that (if I well remember) in your Lo. sight, suffer'd no less violence from our people here, then the subiect of it did from the rage of the people of*

ROME." (lines 9–12). Although one facet of this violence involved the play's unpopularity, *Sejanus* also was mistreated, according to its author, in another and potentially more damaging way. Jonson told Drummond that he "was called befor ye Councell for his Sejanus & accused both of popperie and treason" by Northampton (*Conversations,* lines 326–27), a man whom he seems to have thought as skilled as Lupus at ignoring intention and as unwilling to unravel patiently the meaning of the entire work. These were the faults Jonson found, we recall, in many of his enemies: "Nay they would offer to urge mine owne Writings against me; but by pieces, (which was an excellent way of malice) as if any mans Context, might not seeme dangerous, and offensive, if that which was knit, to what went before, were defrauded of his beginning" (*Discoveries,* lines 1351–56).

That Jonson intended *Sejanus* to speak at some level to the political concerns of its day is certainly true enough, and there have been several instructive analyses of the possible political implications of the tragedy.[10] Whether or not it contains (or contained) the sort of topical references that might justifiably have aroused Northampton's suspicion is much more difficult to determine. The ease with which Jonson apparently was cleared of the charges, together with the fact that he was evidently still proclaiming his innocence some fifteen years after the initial production, suggest to me that it did not. But whatever allusions the original production may or may not have made to contemporary events, for my purposes the tragedy's major interest lies elsewhere: in its various ways of dealing with the very interpretive issues with which Jonson himself was concerned throughout his career, and in the somewhat ironic although not totally unpredictable relation between its depiction of those issues and the mistreatment about which Jonson complained to Drummond.

The first indication that *Sejanus* is concerned with interpretive matters is Jonson's own comments about his careful use of historical materials as the basis for the drama. Although at one level his extraordinary emphasis on historical accuracy—an emphasis advertised by the marginal notations in the quarto edition of the play—"probably marks the most complete attempt ever made to follow the dictates of Italian Renaissance critics, who had judged history to be the only proper basis for a tragedy" (Barish 1965, 3),[11] at another it is an endeavor to prevent misreading by "those common Torturers, that bring all wit to the Rack: whose Noses are euer like Swine spoyling, and rooting up the *Muses* Gardens" ("To the Readers" lines 29–31).

Annabel Patterson has demonstrated that in Renaissance texts such an emphasis was often at once defensive and deliberately provocative: the use of historical materials "allowed an author to limit his authorial responsibility for the text . . . and, paradoxically, provided an interpretive mechanism" by inviting the reader to consider, among other things, "the implications of the model, and the methods of selection, transmission, and adaptation" (1984, 53–57). In the case of *Sejanus,* she finds Jonson's dependence upon Tacitus especially fraught with complexity and ambiguity. But the most important interpretive lesson that a reader is to learn from Jonson's handling of his sources in this instance is not, finally, encouragement to absolve the English dramatist of responsibility for whatever political implications may be discovered in the tragedy. In fact, in the prefatory letter Jonson is affirming his authority over the text rather than denying it, and the defense provided by his use of historical materials lies not in the mere existence of the materials themselves, or in their origins apart from Jonson and his time, but in the model established by his handling of those materials.

Jonson's careful reconstruction of a key moment in the reign of Tiberius once again announces his adherence to principles of historical accuracy that he would have associated with a William Camden or a John Selden; as I have already argued in Chapter 2, that adherence, like his more general commitment to verisimilitude, had important implications for the way in which he wanted his works to be read. In effect, Jonson afforded himself as little flexibility in dealing with history as he expected his readers or viewers to employ in dealing with his own drama. Both activities would necessarily involve an accurate restatement, a careful imitation, or perhaps a faithful translation of a preexistent work or works. The marginal citations are proof enough of Jonson's "integrity in the *Story,*" and they challenge readers to follow the author's example when they approach the play itself.

There is a thematic challenge as well. As noted above, Jonson's letter to Aubigny draws a parallel between the violent fate of his play and that of its central figure; his prefatory letter "To the Reader" links misinterpretation with torture and the subversion of virtue, in addition to explaining his decision to delete the work of another poet in order not to "defraud" that poet. Destruction, fraud, usurpation—all are activities Jonson associated with ignorant audiences. That they are also concerns within the tragedy itself is not accidental, for the prefatory materials point toward an equation between misinterpretation and political tyranny that is one of the major themes of the drama. Not content only to provide a model of interpretive restraint in his handling of history, Jonson wove his concern with audience into the fabric of the play.

Approached from this perspective, *Sejanus* becomes as much a concluding moment within the overall scheme of Jonson's career as it is an anticipation of what is to come. If the relationship between Sejanus and Tiberius is in some ways the model for the relationships between the major characters of his later comic masterpieces, the tragedy's focus on issues vitally related to the behavior of spectators and authors provides a forceful conclusion to the period in Jonson's development when he was most openly concerned with standing apart from his contemporaries and, as a result, most vocally involved with the inadequacies of his audience. Although *Sejanus* does not, certainly, mark the end of Jonson's quarrel with audience—that quarrel continues throughout his career—it does mark the end of what was perhaps the quarrel's most intense phase, taking up some of the issues with which *Poetaster* and the other "comicall satyres" had already dealt but doing so in a more subtle manner. *Sejanus* is very much a parable about interpretation and authorial control; as such, the play predicts—ironically, and with more accuracy than Jonson could have known when he wrote it—its own fate.

To move from the Augustan Rome of *Poetaster* to the Tiberian Rome of *Sejanus* is to journey from an idealized environment that nurtures and protects art to one that will scarcely tolerate it. When in the later play the historian Cremutius Cordus defends his writing by citing Augustus as an example of a sovereign whose response to and understanding of literature are exemplary (3.414–18), we cannot help but be reminded of Horace's similar difficulties in the comedy and Augustus's role in solving them. But in *Sejanus* the outcome of the complaints against Cordus is far different: his books are burned; he will commit suicide shortly afterward. Everywhere there are signs of a decline so precipitous that whatever the historian's intentions, praise of the past inevitably becomes a condemnation of the present, a situation clearly understood by those in power (2.303–12).

The tragedy begins with an elaborate series of contrasts suggesting that Cordus may be right when he argues that "*Braue* CASSIVS *was the last of all that race*" of true Roman patriots, or that Arruntius is exaggerating only slightly when he laments, "There's nothing *Romane* in vs; nothing good, / Gallant, or great" (1.102–4). The opening lines are dominated by negatives. The Germanicans are "no good inginers"; they "want the fine arts, & their thriuing vse"; they have "no shift of faces, no cleft tongues"; they are "no guilty men, and then no great"; they have "nor place in court, office in state" that they "owe" to their crimes (lines 4–20)—a catalogue which reaches a climax when Silius turns and looks at the other group onstage: Satrius and Natta. "But yonder leane / A paire that doe" (lines 20–21), he sneers, that "but" establishing with great force the distance between virtuous Romans and the flatterers who threaten to overwhelm them. This contrast metamorphoses into one between past and present— the former associated with virtue and freedom, the latter with corruption and slavery (lines 56–70)—a distinction that soon gives way to others: Sabinus's heated insistence on the superiority of Germanicus to Alexander, and Arruntius's comments on Germanicus's differences from even the most virtuous Romans now alive: "I am sure / He was too great for vs," Arruntius explains, "and that they knew / Who did remoue him hence" (lines 143–59). These contrasts, in turn, anticipate the final one in the series, one between this quintessential Roman and the monster who now dominates the city. "Here comes SEIANUS" (line 175), Cordus warns, and the group stands aside to watch this new colossus's followers grovel at his feet.

The progression of the drama's opening lines is reminiscent of the movement of Jonson's poem to Lucy Bedford (see Chapter 1). As in the epigram, Jonson seems intent upon establishing ever finer distinctions, in this case all pointing to the dwindling stature of the Roman state. In such a society even eloquence has little, if any, power. Whereas in *Every Man out of His Humour* language had the ability to dissolve a foolish world, here it is helpless before the tyranny of a Tiberius or a Sejanus. Power is now a function of silence, not speech; Arruntius, the character in the play who most resembles Crites, is weak precisely because he continually, and eloquently, utters what he believes. In Sejanus's contemptuous phrase, Arruntius "only talkes" (2.299), and later Satrius notes that this virtuous man's loquaciousness makes him essentially harmless: "Tut, hee's not yet / Look'd after, there are others more desir'd, / That are more silent" (lines 407–9).

Arruntius's powerlessness erodes (even further than does the idiocy of Crispinus and Demetrius in *Poetaster*) the credibility usually associated with observers in Jonson's works. Certainly not a fool like the poetasters or Lupus, Arruntius nevertheless lacks the authority of Cordatus in *Every Man out of His Humour* and Crites in *Cynthia's Revels*. As John Sweeney has pointed out, all the Germanicans are impotent versions of Jonson's earlier satiric commentators; in *Sejanus*, "to be an audience is to be a victim" (1981, 69, 80; cf. Vawter 1973, 49). The only "informers" in this play are not spokespersons for the author; they are spies, men who pander to the whims of those in power, supplying whatever information those rulers require but paying no attention to criteria of truth and accuracy as they do so. Together with the men they serve, they are remarkably similar to the ignorant and malicious audience Jonson envisioned all around him. They are, in effect, readers whose violence is actual rather than metaphorical. George Parfitt has argued that it is "almost possible to see *Sejanus* as a desperate attempt by Jonson to make his audience see themselves in the roles of those who, in the play, ignore or seek to destroy virtue" (1976, 67). I would omit the qualification. Whatever else it involves, Jonson's first tragedy is a play intimately concerned with the respective roles of those who speak or write and those who should attempt to understand them.

One clue to this interest occurs during the discussion of Germanicus and Alexander, noted above. Arruntius praises his recently deceased countryman, stating that he embodied all that was noble in Rome. Cremutius Cordus agrees and confides:

> I thought once
> Considering their formes, age, manner of deaths,
> The neernesse of the places, where they fell,
> T'haue paralell'd him with great ALEXANDER.
> (1.136–39)

The comparison is in Tacitus (*Annals* 2.73), although there it is not made by Cordus. Tacitus presents it without comment and includes a suggestion that Germanicus was morally superior to Alexander and might have surpassed the latter's military achievements had he lived longer. In *Sejanus,* however, the comparison is angrily rejected: Sabinus suddenly turns to Cordus and dismisses the idea as pernicious nonsense.

> I know not, for his death, how you might wrest it:
> But, for his life, it did as much disdaine
> Comparison, with that voluptuous, rash,
> Giddy, and drunken *Macedon's,* as mine
> Doth with my bond-mans.
> (lines 143–47)

Cordus is not an evil man, nor is he a foolish one. His comparison is an example of a technique frequently employed by both classical and Renaissance historians, who often stress the similarities between apparently disparate figures in order to demonstrate the essential unity of human existence. Sabinus, in contrast, chooses to emphasize the uniqueness of Germanicus: "All the good in him . . . he made his," Sabinus argues, although Germanicus did have "touches of late *Romanes*, / That more did speak him" (lines 147–50). In Sabinus's opinion, Cordus's parallel is a distortion because it denies difference; it is a misinterpretation that violently twists the truth rather than an accurate description of that truth (the verb "wrest" means—among other things—to twist, tear away, usurp, take by force, pervert, deflect from its proper purpose, and misinterpret). As such, Cordus's statement must be rejected.

But there is a reason more important than its inaccuracy for Sabinus's angry response to Cordus's admittedly harmless comparison. His reaction can be more satisfactorily understood once we realize that misinterpretation is one of the central tools of Sejanus's and Tiberius's tyranny. The ability to deny Romans the intended meanings of their words and actions, to destroy the importance of context and of difference in order to impose a preordained (and usually malicious) significance on what is said and done, is what makes Sejanus and Tiberius so powerful and destructive. In the imperial Rome of Jonson's play, to be able to control the meaning of one's words is to be free, and it is that control which the play's evil characters would deny. As in *Poetaster* and *The Magnetic Lady,* the issue is dominion, power. In Silius's words, "Euery ministring spie / That will accuse, and sweare, is lord of you, / Of me, of all, our fortunes, and our liues" (lines 64–66). And later in the play Sabinus, about to become another of Sejanus's victims, laments that "our writings are . . . made to speake / What they will haue, to fit their tyrranous wreake" (4.132–39). As Agrippina cynically assures her friends, what Sejanus and Tiberius "can contriue, / They will make good" (4.39–40).

Perhaps the most powerful depiction of these ideas is the meeting of the Roman senate during act 3. This episode involves interpretation in two ways: first, the attempts of Arruntius and his companions to see beneath the apparent intentions of Tiberius and Sejanus and apprehend their true ones; second, and of more interest here, the willful and murderous misrepresentation of the words and deeds of Silius and Cordus. The former is the more important victim. Brought forward without warning and caught in a net of false accusations, he defiantly labels Tiberius's fraud "worse then violence" (3.209) and, replying to Afer's suggestion that he wants more than justice, adds:

No, my well-spoken man, I would no more;
Nor lesse: might I inioy it naturall,
Not taught to speake vnto your present ends,
Free from thine, his, and all your vnkind handling,
Furious enforcing, most vniust presuming,
Malicious, and manifold applying,
Foule wresting, and impossible construction.
(lines 223–29)

The speech requires little explication. The endeavor to turn words and actions to an already chosen significance (lines 295–97) is at once, Silius asserts, unnatural, unjust, and destructive. It is tyranny—the tyranny of audience, not (as Damplay feared in *The Magnetic Lady*) of author. The potential triumph of Lupus's imagination over authorial intent in *Poetaster* is only a less fearful version of that of Sejanus's "impossible construction" over the true nature of the Roman's words and deeds; and the victory of that "construction" fails here to culminate in murder only because Silius, unwilling to subject himself further to the power of this audience, regains some control over his life by taking it.

The trial of Cordus, which follows, is in some ways anticlimactic. By juxtaposing the two trials (in Tacitus they are separate), Jonson of course emphasizes the relation between the "furious enforcing" of words and actions in the political realm and the misreading of literature, and he provides Cordus with a noble and moving defense of art, borrowed from Tacitus (*Annals* 4.34–35). Equally important, although Cordus's defense seems more successful initially than Silius's, he also will finally succumb to the power of the men he so eloquently opposes. As Jonson undoubtedly expected the more learned members of his audience to know, Cordus leaves the senate only to starve himself to death shortly thereafter (*Annals* 4.35). The outcome can scarcely be otherwise in a Rome where distinctions no longer exist except at the whim of those in power, where anything can be made to mean anything as citizens' words and actions are forced into conformity with a predetermined significance, and where the result of this process is always destructive. "Nothing hath priuiledge 'gainst the violent eare," Arruntius laments late in the tragedy. "All matter, / Nay all occasion pleaseth" (4.311, 314–15). He continues:

> Nor is now th'euent
> Of any person, or for any crime,
> To be expected; for 'tis alwayes one:
> Death, with some little difference of place
> Or time.
> (lines 318–22)

Two passages in Tacitus that may have influenced Jonson's handling of this theme make essentially the same point: "I present a series of savage mandates, of perpetual accusations, of traitorous friendships, of ruined innocents, of various cases and identical results—everywhere monotony of subject, and satiety. . . . Nor could any distinction be traced between alien and relative, between friend and stranger, between the events of to-day and those of the dim past. Alike in the Forum or at a dinner-party, to speak of any subject was to be accused" (4.33; 6.7). Jonson could not have helped identifying with this situation, which ironically predicted the fate of his own play, victimized by a careless and malicious audience whose only goal (so he thought) was to accuse and condemn its author.

Remarkably, *Sejanus* has more to tell us about the relations between authors and interpreters than even this. The climax of the play's depiction of a tyranny of misinterpretation occurs at the speech by Arruntius quoted above, a speech whose accuracy is affirmed by the entry of Nero under guard immediately upon its conclusion. When the first of Tiberius's confusing letters arrives, less than a hundred lines later, the drama begins to move in a new direction. As I argued in Chapter 2, Jonson understood very well that the cure for a destructive domination of reader over author is not simply the reversal of that relationship; his depiction of Macilente, not to mention that of Mosca or Face, shows as much. Jonson's uneasiness with a situation in which an author rather than an audience is totally dominant is perhaps most clearly indicated, however, by his portrayal in this play of Tiberius, whose power over the Roman populace brings *Sejanus* to a brutal and chilling end. A tyranny based upon the cynical misreading of words and actions metamorphoses in act 4 into a tyranny of authorial control.[12]

Tiberius is at once the most withdrawn and inscrutable author-figure in the Jonson canon. "Nearly invisible when seen, Tiberius remains as unseen as possible, retired even when present" (Goldberg 1983, 182). Because "Tiberivs heart / Lyes a thought farder, then another mans" (3.97–98), his words and actions create a veil that must be carefully pierced by a cunning observer if his true intent is to be grasped, yet the difficulties involved are considerable. "Rare poemes aske rare friends," Jonson wrote to the Countess of Bedford, implying that readers must somehow share a common stature with the text they confront if they are to understand and support it (cf. Fish 1984). As *Poetaster* shows, a Virgil requires an Augustus Caesar; the greatness of the former can be recognized and preserved only by the greatness of the latter. But Tiberius has no equals, no rivals; there is no fit audience for this author and, as a result, no totally comprehending one— or so Tiberius would like us to believe. Praising Sejanus in the first act, he concludes that no one should "ask the causes of our praise," because

> Princes haue still their grounds rear'd with themselues,
> Aboue the poor low flats of common men,
> And, who will search the reasons of their acts,
> Must stand on equall bases.
> (1.536–40)

Open only to his peers, Tiberius is in effect open to no one at all.

His riddling letters, then, simply represent one more example of the opacity that is his chief characteristic. Their purpose is to create a climate of uncertainty that will make his audience all the more eager to assume whatever stance he desires.[13] Tiberius is, one might say, the author of Sejanus's fate, and he accomplishes his goal by making the minds of uncomprehending Romans "like the thing he writes" (*Discoveries,* line 793). Only the characters who are able to remain relatively detached, critical, and skeptical escape taking part in the drama's concluding orgy of destruction, because understanding here, as always in Jonson, is a matter of waiting and carefully sorting out a complex scheme of intention. "Stay," Lepidus urges Arruntius, "Note," "Obserue" (4.493, 494, 504)—the verbs urging a Baconian resistance to reaching a (probably wrong) conclusion before all the relevant materials have been examined. However, like the Pilate of the scientist's first essay, most of the Romans in the play lack the patience to wait for an answer. Lepidus, stoically removed from the situation, first glimpses the actual import of Tiberius's plot; Arruntius, emotionally more involved and partially blinded by his own cynicism, grasps it somewhat later. But the majority of Romans, confused and desperate for certainty, give up their detachment and self-possession; caught up in an art they do not understand, they turn on a man they once worshiped and feared and tear him apart.

The intimations of ritual sacrifice that surround Sejanus's death (5.886–87) create the final and perhaps most bitter irony in the play. There is no renewal for the Rome that we see, only decline. If Sejanus is to be reborn, it will be in the form of Macro, a creature even more monstrous than the man he replaces. Similarly, Tiberius's cruelties will soon pale in comparison with the perversions of Caligula. Nor does the Rome of the play deserve any better. Far more than being, as its last lines imply, a chronicle of the evil effects of pride (5.898–903), *Sejanus* is a depiction of an uncomprehending and vacillating populace that totally lacks the capacity to make judgments. The Romans' susceptibility to Tiberius's art is a perfect complement to their willingness to acquiesce to the tyrannical disregard of meaning that provided Sejanus with so much power. As a result, the only action of which they are capable is destruction—without understanding, driven by rumor and the whims of fortune, controlled by forces of which they are unaware.

"Who," Lepidus asks, "would depend vpon the popular ayre, / Or voyce of men, that haue to day beheld . . . SEIANVS fall?" (5.705–8). Although the answer, obviously, is "no one," it is an answer that Jonson himself apparently had difficulty in accepting—hence the tacked-on moral with which the tragedy concludes. The only sensible response to the destructive powers of both an ignorant multitude and those whom that multitude blindly and capriciously supports is to withdraw as much as possible from the society terrorized by such powers, and Lepidus says as much, earlier in the play. He has survived, he tells Arruntius, by "the plaine, and passiue fortitude, / To suffer, and be silent," by the ability to "liue at home, / With my owne thoughts, and innocence about me, / Not tempting the wolues iawes" (4.294–98). That the last line of this speech recalls the Author's desire, in the "Apologetical Dialogue" (line 249) to sing "Safe from the wolues black iaw" only reinforces the pessimism of the play's message. Jonson certainly knew after the disastrous reception of *Se-*

janus, if he had not known before, that to sing—indeed, to speak in any form—is to be unsafe. Only through silence can one hope to escape from the power of ignorant, uncomprehending, and malicious interpreters. But Jonson, fortunately, could never bring himself to stop talking.

4

THAT SUBTLE SPORT

By the time the quarto edition of *Sejanus* appeared in 1605, Jonson must have felt that his career was at a standstill. The War of the Theaters had ended unsatisfactorily; his first tragedy had for the most part failed to elicit from its audience and other poets the wonder and despair predicted with such assurance in the "Apologetical Dialogue." Yet as disappointing as Jonson's situation may have seemed to him, it had in fact some extraordinarily positive effects. On a personal level, his disillusionment undoubtedly encouraged both his reconciliation with John Marston at about the time *Sejanus* was hissed off the stage and his willingness some two years later to restrain his competitiveness long enough to collaborate with Marston and John Chapman in writing *Eastward Ho!* And on an artistic one, Jonson's frustrations provided the basis—indeed, the impetus—for the most successful years of his dramatic career, a period in which he created three comic masterpieces—*Volpone, Epicoene,* and *The Alchemist*—as well as a tragedy, *Catiline,* of considerable interest, if not merit.

Although there were, certainly, several reasons for and aspects to his new found success, this chapter concentrates on one that I find especially significant: Jonson's ability to internalize his competitive impulses more completely and subtly within these plays than he had been able (or wished) to do in his earlier works. Rivalry and audience remain important concerns, especially the former, but they are handled more indirectly and insightfully.[1] In essence, Jonson presents a more complex and ambiguous landscape in these later dramas; we no longer find the vivid contrasts between virtue and evil, wisdom and folly that typify the societies of the "comicall satyres" and, to a somewhat lesser extent, *Sejanus*.

The men and women who inhabit the worlds of *Every Man out of His Humour*, *Cynthia's Revels*, and *Poetaster* (to return to those plays for a moment) attempt to establish their authority and superiority in two different but related ways. They may attempt to control the world-stage by becoming the focal point of attention and involving others in their skillful performances (Shift, Amorphus, Tucca), or they may seek dominance by standing apart and censuring the activities they see around them (Macilente, Crites, Horace). In general, the less admirable characters choose the former method; the more virtuous ones usually prefer the latter, unwilling for the most part to compete with their inferiors (though of course a fool like Crispinus may also endeavor to adopt this latter stance). However, as I have argued, attempts to withdraw from a world driven by competition are never, in Jonson's works, totally successful. Even a vow not to engage in rivalry tends to become a competitive act. That may have been so for the Horace of *Epistles* 1. 19, and it certainly was for the Jonson of the materials appended to the published versions of *Poetaster*. Like Francis Beaumont and some of his own creations, Jonson is often most competitive when he speaks of not competing at all.

This rather misleading and perhaps even dishonest association of virtue (both his own and that of his characters) with a disinclination toward rivalry is not present in the three great comedies of the 1616 folio. That pretense—and for Jonson, at least, it was a pretense—disappears, as does the somewhat facile contrast between foolish, competitive role players and virtuous, ostensibly uncompetitive spectators. No longer do we encounter sharp oppositions between good and bad poets (Horace and Crispinus), virtue and its detractors (Crites and the courtiers); no longer does Jonson identify himself directly with one figure or another. Elements of his former aggressiveness remain (most notably in the prefatory letter to *Volpone*), and Jonson is as determined as ever to surpass his peers, but these aspects of his art are

muted somewhat. Less overtly concerned with justifying the superiority of his works and less obviously intent on instructing his audience about the correct method of responding to his dramas—in
part because that audience had proved itself incapable (he thought)
of being instructed—Jonson began instead to focus his energies upon
creating a dramatic structure capable of revealing the complex dynamics of rivalry itself. And in developing this investigation of an
activity that was central to the artistic career he had outlined for himself, Jonson was influenced by a second classical writer, who, like
Horace, had a great deal to tell him both about the relations between
poets and, more important, about how to incorporate his interest in
those relations into his own plays. That writer was Aristophanes.[2]

In the history of Western literature, Aristophanes is something of an
anomaly. Both praised and condemned in antiquity and the Renaissance, his work remained largely unimitated. Unlike Menander, he
did not bequeath to later dramatists an easily reproducible plot structure and cast of characters; the wide range of elements that fill his
plays evidently proved extremely difficult to repeat. If, in the case of
Horace, Jonson was drawing upon a well-known, highly respected,
and frequently imitated author, in that of the Greek playwright he
was using a writer whose reputation and influence were considerably
less formidable. With the exception of Jonson himself the only English Renaissance dramatist who made significant use of Old Comedy
was Thomas Randolph, and Randolph was one of the most respectful
of the "sons of Ben"; his interest in the Greek playwright was probably encouraged, perhaps even suggested, by his literary father.[3]
     The reasons for Aristophanes' lack of influence are not difficult to
discover. As is well known, comic theory in the Renaissance was based
on a Terentian model, and a theory that often had little room for
Plautus was not likely to be particularly hospitable to Old Comedy
(Herrick 1964, 57). Aristophanes' sixteenth-century editors (presumably admirers of his work) sometimes attempted to make his plays
conform to a Terentian five-act structure (Baldwin 1947, 303), and
the popularity of *Plutus* during the period was due largely both to its
deviations from Old Comedy conventions (deviations recognized by

Renaissance critics) and to the fact that the play is both less ribald and more obviously moral than the remainder of Aristophanes' works. On the whole, however, the Greek playwright's dramas were at once too difficult, too heterogeneous, too distinct from Roman comedy, and, for some, too raucous and tasteless to be widely influential.

Yet it was precisely this enigmatic figure whom Jonson chose to invoke in the Induction to a play that he certainly hoped would secure his place as an English dramatist of the first rank and, perhaps, alter the course of English comedy. *Every Man out of His Humour* is, Cordatus explains to Mitis, "strange, and of a particular kind by it selfe, somewhat like *Vetus Commoedia*" (Induction, lines 231–32). Admittedly, Cordatus posits not an identity between Jonson's drama and Attic comedy but a relation involving both similarity and difference. Furthermore, Cordatus's reference to *Vetus Commoedia* occurs within a discussion in which he both argues that comedy is a continually developing form, rather than a fixed and immutable one, and emphasizes the right of all dramatists to alter the literary forms they inherit according to their own needs and the pressures of their particular historical situations. "I see not then," Cordatus tells his friend, "but we should enioy the same licence, or free power, to illustrate and heighten our inuention as they [the ancient writers] did; and not bee tyed to those strict and regular formes, which the niceness of a few (who are nothing but forme) would thrust vpon us" (lines 266–70).

Nevertheless, Jonson did go to the trouble to establish a generic context for his play; even if *Every Man out of His Humour* is only "somewhat like" Old Comedy, he does ask us to read the play against a background provided by that genre, to see it in relation to a classical form that the more educated members of a Renaissance audience might be expected to recognize. And while one function of Cordatus's comparison is to call attention to the play's didactic purpose—Asper's attempt to "strip the ragged follies of the time, / Naked, as at their birth" (lines 17–18) with a ferocity that Renaissance readers probably would have associated with Aristophanes (Campbell 1938, 1–14)— there is more to Jonson's allusion to Old Comedy than a mutual interest in satirizing contemporary society, important as that interest was. Within the context of English drama at the end of the sixteenth century, the phrase "somewhat like Vetus Commoedia" was an assertion of difference and, as Jonson's enemies readily understood, superiority. That assertion had been implicit and sometimes explicit in Jonson's earlier dramas, especially *Every Man in His Humour,* which stresses the need to distinguish between good and bad poets. However, *Every Man in His Humour* was not itself a new or revolutionary type of play. Despite its superiority to the vast majority of Elizabethan comedies that preceded it, it was not structurally different from most of them in any significant way. *Every Man in* draws heavily upon New Comedy conventions and in doing so it undermines to some extent its own claim to uniqueness and, ultimately, the careful distinctions it urges its audience to draw between true poets and the "seruile imitating spirit[s]" that Asper would later castigate in the Induction (line 67) to *Every Man out.* What Jonson needed to discover, clearly, was a dramatic tradition radically different from the one that formed the primary basis for English Renaissance comedy, and he found it in Aristophanes. By aligning his work with that of the Greek playwright, Jonson not only placed himself outside the mainstream of English drama but did so in a particularly emphatic manner, given the scarcity of English imitations of Aristophanes during the sixteenth century. Jonson, doubtless, would not have had matters any other way.

Equally important, Jonson encountered in Aristophanes an author whose attitude toward audience and his fellow playwrights was as combative as Jonson's own and who, moreover, was able to embody that combativeness within the fictions he created. The Greek festivals were, after all, literary competitions, and Judith Engle has demonstrated that the metatheatrical elements of Aristophanes' plays often "stage—by implication if not overtly—the unremitting in-fighting that marks the dramatic genres and that serves comedy as a poetics of sorts, a way in which the practitioners of the art stake out their artistic territory" (1983, 115; cf. Whitman 1964, 57–58).

The element of Aristophanes' comedies that most emphatically conveys his intention to separate his art from that of his contemporaries is the *parabasis,* for the Aristophanic *parabasis* is as much an instrument of self-praise as of moral instruction. He employs it to explain his intentions (*The Wasps*), to call attention to the good he has done for Athens (*The Acharnians*), and to complain about the inadequacies of his audience (*The Knights; The Clouds*). Most important, Aristophanes employs the *parabasis* to proclaim his artistic superiority and attack his rivals. In *The Clouds*, defending the modesty and originality of his own muse, the playwright (in the person of the chorus leader) labels Eupolis a "stinking thief, who bashed / Hyperbolus in *Marcias*, which was my *Knights* rehashed"; he is equally hostile toward Hermippus and other unnamed poets who "plagiarized *my* joke about the eels" (p. 136).[4] This assertion of superiority is echoed a little less stridently at first in the *parabasis* of *Peace*:

> If it is meet and right and fitting and due
> To honour him who is the most renowned
> And best of all the comic tribe, our poet
> Asserts that he alone deserves such honour.
> (Pp. 122–23)

But the claim that "our poet" has booted out the "rubbish" that previously cluttered the comic stage leads once again to the denigration of his competitors—this time Melanthius and Morsimus—in order to ensure that there will be no place for any other poet in the concluding revels:

> Spit good and hard on that vile bard
>   And on his viler brother,
> And then at least we'll spend the feast
>   Alone with one another.
>   (P. 125]

Success, evidently, cannot be shared.

Aristophanes' expressions of his desire to outdo his rivals are not confined to his *parabases*, moreover; the *agones* of his comic protagonists sometimes become associated with his own (see Engle 1983; Ehrenberg 1943, 23–24). The most obvious example of this fusion between artistic and plot competitions is the debate between Euripides and Aeschylus that concludes *The Frogs*. The Hell of this comedy, like the Athens of its author, is a place characterized by rivalries of all kinds; only the most skillful member of each profession is allowed to feast in the Great Hall, and it is surely not accidental that Dionysus can bring only a single dramatist back to Athens. Nor is it surprising that Aristophanes begins the play by contrasting his comedy with less worthy examples of the form. Xanthius, weighed down by an enormous load of luggage, complains about Dionysus's unwillingness to let him play a comic porter scene and attempts to change his master's mind: "It's the regular thing, I tell you. Phrynichus, Lysis, Ameipsias, all the popular writers do it." To his dismay, Dionysus—and, by extension, the audience—remains unimpressed, for in the god's view the boredom caused by these scenes has a somewhat destructive effect upon the life expectancy of those who watch them: "Every time I go to a show and have to sit through one of these scintillating comic routines, I come away more than a year older" (pp. 156–57).

In *The Knights* Aristophanes seems deliberately to have created a connection between his own situation and that of the Sausage Seller, a cheeky comic hero who is attempting to wrest power from a demagogic opponent called the Paphlagonian. Like his protagonist, Aristophanes is, the play suggests, a challenger—not only an artistic talent who will eclipse the lesser dramatists around him but also a champion whose battles against the tyrannical and politically powerful Cleon evidently are already famous (Engle 1983, 112–13). The comic battle for leadership between this suspiciously Aristophanic Sausage-Seller and the spectacularly unsuccessful Paphlagonian thus appropriately leads to a *parabasis* in which a mocking description of the comic playwright Cratinus's former might—"uprooting every tree, / Oak, plane, competitor" (p. 56)—links Aristophanes' most formidable dramatic rival to the now hapless Paphlagonian by echoing the imagery of the just concluded battle scene.

Similarly, in *The Acharnians* an elaborate contrast between Dikaiopolis's preparations for a festival and Lamachus's for war metamorphoses into an attack on Antimachus, a poet and former choregus for Aristophanes (p. 101). At the end of the play, Dikaiopolis's victory in the drinking contest on Pitcher Day merges almost completely with Aristophanes' eagerly anticipated, but as yet only imagined, victory in the dramatic competition in which the play was being staged—"Where are you judges? Where's the King? I've come to claim my prize," he shouts (p. 104)—an association reinforced by Dikaiopolis's striking likeness to his creator: he refers to former troubles with Cleon; he is something of a comic poet; and he may have worn a mask that resembled the dramatist.

This combativeness did not go unnoticed by classical and Renaissance commentators.[5] Jonson recognized it, as well—with important results for his own work. Together with Horace's comments on his rivals, the precedent provided by Aristophanes encouraged, I believe, Jonson's attempts to separate himself from his fellow dramatists. Jonson's attacks, in his plays, on other writers and his decision to put his enemies onstage (in *Poetaster,* certainly, and perhaps other dramas) owe a great deal to his Greek predecessor, and his inductions and choric interludes are in essence adaptations of the Aristophanic *parabasis*; they fulfill the same combative and competitive function.[6] The Elizabethan War of the Theaters might even be described as a less structured version of the literary *agon* of the Greek festivals. Its function, from Jonson's point of view, was the creation of a hierarchy of poets like that in *Poetaster;* its failure, again from Jonson's perspective, was its lack of finality, the absence of a mechanism that guaranteed the emergence of a clearly acknowledged victor (as in the Greek festivals).

Although Aristophanes' final legacy to Jonson is less obvious, it is in some ways more significant, certainly for the plays considered in this chapter. Given the English dramatist's desire to surpass his contemporaries, it was quite probable that this desire would find its way into his plays in forms other than direct assertion, personal attack, and literary parody. And it did—in a manner suggested or at least encouraged by Aristophanes' tendency to associate his own artistic *agon* with that of his protagonists. As we have seen, emulation very early became an important motivating force for the characters in Jonsonian drama. In *Every Man out of His Humor,* for instance, we glimpse this tendency in the relationship between Briske and Fungoso, Macilente and Buffone; in *Poetaster* it is a major emphasis in the encounter between Crispinus and Horace. Likewise, in all three "comicall satyres," Jonson—like the Aristophanes of *The Acharnians* and *The Knights*—displays a fondness for creating characters who bear a remarkable resemblance to their creator and whose victories in the course of the action mirror that creator's fervent hopes.

Jonson's most subtle and profound embodiment of the emulative impulse, however, and by extension his most important adaptation of the Aristophanic model, occurs in the four plays that follow the ambiguous resolution of the War of the Theaters and the disastrous reception of *Sejanus*. In each of these plays, competition of an implicitly artistic nature forms the mainspring of the plot. Jonson's key discovery—encouraged at least in part by his reading of Aristophanes—was the realization that increasing the number of intriguers usually present in comedy would enable him to displace the typical comic conflict between wit and gull by a much more interesting and complex conflict or competition between the wits themselves: Mosca and Volpone; Truewit, Clerimont, and Dauphine; Face, Subtle, and (perhaps) Surly. The conventional plot of comic intrigue most often pits youth against age, intelligence against folly, and so on; Jonson's version pits art against art. Furthermore, the goal of this new conflict is no longer marriage or sexual satisfaction or, even, money; it is supremacy, the creation of a new hierarchical relationship out of an apparent democracy of equals, the elevation of one wit above the others. The resolution of *Volpone* may seem less conclusive than those of *Epicoene* and *The Alchemist* precisely because in that comedy, as in the War of the Theaters, there is no apparent victor: the inability of either Mosca or Volpone to defeat the other leads to the downfall of both. In these plays, equality is inherently unstable.

Moreover, Jonson's overall attitude toward emulation in these comedies and in *Catiline*—which, despite its obvious flaws, provides a fitting capstone to this period of his career—is also somewhat ambivalent, the result of the unsatisfactory resolution of his earlier attempts to surpass his contemporaries and the beginning of a recognition, like Horace's, that emulation is an unending and potentially destructive process. Using Aristophanes as a guide, Jonson had found a dramatic structure capable of embodying the complexities of his own artistic situation: his desires, his fears, his animosities, his failures. *Epicoene* and *Catiline* in particular demonstrate just how thorough and instructive Jonson's analysis of the "subtle sport" he describes in *Epigrammes* 112 (see Chapter 1) could become.

Like the two comedies that immediately precede and follow it, *Epicoene* contains a scene in which almost all of the characters unite to vent their fury on an individual or individuals whom they perceive as a threat to their collective well-being. In *Volpone* the targets are Celia and Bonario; in *The Alchemist* the opponent is Surly. In *Epicoene* the comic victim of communal violence is Morose, who is driven mercilessly offstage at the end of act 3 with almost the entire cast in noisy pursuit. As Ian Donaldson has observed (1970, 36–42), the unanimity displayed by Morose's tormentors gives the episode a ceremonial quality, as if members of a community have united to expel and mock an antisocial force: a person who, in Calvin Thayer's words (1963, 81), is a "comic symbol of the absolute negation of what holds society together—the negation of rational discourse, indeed *any* discourse."

Morose's momentary escape to a precarious perch on the topmost rafters of his house thus becomes an ironic representation of the isolation and ascendancy he wishes to claim for himself. The other characters recognize in Morose more than an antisocial force; they recognize as well—and reject and punish—his desire for power and his unwillingness to share authority. They perceive, as we must, that Morose's obsessive emphasis on silence is his way of dominating others by filling the world he inhabits with the sound of his voice only, by eliminating all discourse but his own. With the exception of Truewit, Morose speaks at greater length than any other character in the comedy (Hallahan 1977, 127); his first speech is 41 lines long. There is only one relatively silent character in *Epicoene,* and he, ironically, is the very person Morose wishes to ruin.

Yet the nearly unanimous punishment of Morose at the end of act 3 no more indicates the existence of a unified human community in this comedy than do the momentary unions of gulls against a common foe in *Volpone* and *The Alchemist*. Neither is it an indication of a fundamental difference between the old man and the other characters. Morose is punished not so much because he seeks power and wishes to monopolize all discourse for himself as because he does both too openly and in ways too extreme for this society to tolerate. Nearly all of the characters in *Epicoene* seek in one way or another what Morose seeks: authority and recognition. Many of them would like to fill society with the sound of their own voices and no others, making their contemporaries silent and thus secondary. They are all virtually incapable of carrying on a successful conversation, since a conversation demands a degree of mutual respect and attention that is either beyond their abilities or contrary to their desires. "How these swabbers talke!" (4.4.167), Truewit complains at one point, providing, and not without irony, what might be an epigraph for the entire drama. In this society, to speak is to perform, preferably nonstop and at length, monopolizing attention and preventing anyone else from interrupting and marring the spectacle.

As a result, the unity the characters display in tormenting Morose is short-lived, no more than a momentary lull in the competitive impulses they normally direct at one another. Their superiority to this strange antagonist established, they are again free to expend their energies on more familiar rivalries—which involve, for the most part, those they most resemble. Daw and LaFoole are ready-made victims for Truewit's plotting, not only because they are fools (and they certainly are that) but also because their similarity makes "aemulation betwixt" them very likely (3.3.93). Truewit plays upon tendencies that the gulls' cowardice will not permit them openly to acknowledge. Likewise, the Collegiates' special sorority, itself an attempt to symbolize its members' collective uniqueness, is quickly undermined by their competition for Dauphine, a competition which in Haughty's words will serve to correct those who see an "equality of ranke, or societie" among them (5.2.12) but which, because of the repetitive nature of their actions and their common desire for Dauphine, does just the opposite, emphasizing a basic equivalence that each one would deny.

The gallants also seek to establish differences and, at first glance, do so more successfully. If they join with the other characters in tormenting Morose, they also spend much of the play reinforcing their

sense of difference from, and superiority to, their sometime allies—
a distinction that is essential to their own collective sense of identity.[7]
To the question, "What is a gallant?" they can accordingly answer,
"Not a Morose, still less a John Daw or Amorous LaFoole." This form
of negative definition is, as we have seen, extremely congenial to Jonson, and the three young protagonists in *Epicoene* are quite adept at
defining what they are by demonstrating what they are not. In this
endeavor the gallants' preferred role, as is the case with the virtuous
characters in the "comicall satyres," is that of audience. Unlike Crites
and Horace, however, Truewit and his friends do not suffer the folly
of others with some discomfort or attempt to withdraw from the
company of their inferiors. On the contrary, the gallants seek out the
gulls—not because they want to reform or punish them (like Macilente) or even to bilk them of their money (like Volpone), but because the young men are in a crucial way dependent upon their inferiors' ability to provide a source of amusement that will both
demonstrate and reaffirm the gallants' own worth.

That is why, to cite only a single example, Truewit introduces
Tom Otter to his companions by pointing out that Otter is a potential source of mirth "equall with your Daw, or La-Foole, if not transcendent" (2.6.52–53) and follows this statement with a catalogue
of Otter's absurdities so extensive that Clerimont is nearly speechless—"For gods loue! we should misse this, if we should not goe"—
and Dauphine, having heard more than enough to justify his interest, becomes critical of further delay: "No more of him. Let's goe see
him, I petition you" (lines 68–69, 73–74). Otter's function, in other
words, is to provide a spectacle for these "judging spectators"; like
the other fools, he is in their eyes something less than human—an
"excellent animal" Truewit says (line 52)—a dark background against
which their sparkling wit can effectively be displayed.

The gallants' need to maintain and highlight this contrast also explains their uncharacteristic anger toward Daw and LaFoole when the
two fools presume to criticize Dauphine before the Collegiates. Despite the unimportance of this particular audience and the harmless-
ness of the statements, the young men are unwilling to admit even
a momentary violation of the hierarchical relationships they strive so

zealously to maintain. Dauphine's somewhat overly enthusiastic mockery in act 4, scene 5, of these two inept antagonists—if Daw and LaFoole can be given even this much credit—is an indication that despite their affectations of detachment and urbanity, the gallants' sense of identity is precarious enough to need constant reinforcement and to be threatened by the actions of individuals who, from our vantage point, do not seem threatening at all.

Whatever their momentary difficulties with Daw, LaFoole, and their other sources of amusement, however, the gallants do not find the fools much of a challenge. The latter are easy marks, scarcely (like the gamester in *Epigrammes* 112) worth competing with and easily defeated. Truewit, Clerimont, and Dauphine have little trouble distinguishing themselves from the other members of the play-world. But just as the relative ease with which Morose is defeated by the other characters leaves those characters free to compete with one another, so two of the gallants, having punished Morose and able easily to manipulate the gulls for their own purposes, turn their attention to each other in order to create distinctions within their own group as well.

Dauphine's plot to gain part of his inheritance from Morose is, in fact, the source of only part of the action depicted in *Epicoene*. A second and, for my purposes, more important cause of the onstage activities is Truewit's attempt (and, less energetically, Clerimont's) to demonstrate his superiority to his friends—both as potential rivals and as audience.[8] If Jonson's young protagonists embody to some extent the detachment and urbanity sought and valued by the aristocratic members of Jonson's audience, they likewise embody that audience's equally pronounced tendencies toward rivalry (see Finkelpearl 1969, 67–73). Wit is something "men doe best with the best Gamsters," Beaumont says in his verse epistle to Jonson, and that is certainly true in *Epicoene*. Rivalry is once again generated by what might be described as the threat of equality, and the more clever the opponents, the more extraordinary the performances elicited by the rivalry.

That the most obviously competitive individual in this play is called

Truewit is simply one more indication that competitiveness is—according to Jonson and Beaumont, anyway—an essential component of wit and so of that character's identity. To be a "true" wit, in other words, is to seek to distinguish oneself from all other wits, to surpass past models and present rivals—to prove, in effect, that one has "written better." Like the epigram on Donne's satires that Jonson addressed to Lucy Bedford, *Epicoene* establishes ever finer distinctions: the opposition between Morose and all the other characters momentarily obscures a more illuminating opposition between the three gallants and the fools they observe and manipulate, and this difference in turn gives way to various attempts to create even subtler distinctions among the fools themselves and, more instructively, the gallants. Much of the comedy might even be described as a chronicle of Truewit's endeavors to demonstrate the accuracy of his own name.

The movement of act 4, scene 1, is a good example of such tendencies. When the scene begins, the gallants are contemplating their triumph over Morose and attempting to make this trick into "a source of continued laughter" (Heffner 1955, 78) or, to put it slightly differently, a memorial to their superiority. They here speak the language of art, for their plot has been an imaginative triumph of considerable extent. To Truewit's question, "Was there euer poore bridegroome so tormented? or man indeed?" Clerimont replies, "I haue not read of the like, in the *chronicles* of the land" (4.1.1–4). Their *"comoedy* of affliction"* (2.6.37) has proved to be excellent indeed; it seems nearly incomparable—a source of wonder and, to echo the Jonson of the "Apologetical Dialogue," despair to all would-be imitators. Truewit apparently has fulfilled his pledge to make the day into a "iest to posterity" (2.6.27).

The parallel between this situation and one in which Volpone and Mosca similarly contemplate the successful completion of their plan to dupe the Venetian judges, not to mention their usual victims, is instructive and worth pursuing briefly. In *Volpone,* Mosca's judgment that he and Volpone have reached a kind of stasis by creating a "master-peece" that they cannot "goe beyond" (5.2.13–14) is quickly set aside in favor of a new plot to vex the gulls. Although, as has often been argued, this decision in general reflects the two characters' unstable identities and need to change constantly from one role to another (see, for example, Greenblatt 1976), these causal factors can be described in somewhat different and more precise terms. As Horace learned to his regret, and as Jonson was beginning to realize, emulation is an endless process. A momentary victory over one's rivals is just that, momentary, and must be followed by new and greater achievements. Volpone and Mosca cannot retain the sense of uniqueness that both value so highly unless each one continues, respectively, to "gaine / No common way" (Volpone at 1.1.32–33) or surpass the ordinary rabble of "Parasites, or Sub-parasites" (Mosca at 3.1.13).

In addition, Mosca's successes have, in Volpone's view of things, complicated the relationship between the two, exalting the servant to a level uncomfortably close to or even above that of his apparent master. Whereas Mosca is apparently willing to speak of their victory at the court in collective terms—it is "our" masterpiece, he says—Volpone stresses, and rather uneasily, Mosca's skill only, replying: "True, / Thou'hast playd thy prise, my precious MOSCA" (5.2.14–15). The opposing attributions of ownership designated by the pronouns Volpone employs—the prize is Mosca's, who should belong to Volpone—implies at least some discomfort on the *magnifico*'s part, discomfort that has its source in his belief that not he but Mosca has been the main author of the plot they have just completed so successfully. Volpone's subsequent decision to vex his suitors becomes, then, an attempt to repay Mosca—he acts, he tells Mosca, "for thy sake, at thy intreaty" (line 55)—but not in a disinterested manner. By concocting a plan of his own, Volpone hopes to regain some of the distinction Mosca has taken for himself and so prove his superiority, in wit as well as in rank. It is an attempt that continues, I might add, until the end of the play. The Volpone who names only himself before the *avocatori* (lines 89–94), who thanks the judges for Mosca's punishment (line 115) while moralizing cleverly on his own (line 125), and who, finally, steps forward to ask our applause in the concluding lines is a character still seeking the kind of distinction—the name—that will mark his superiority to all around him.

A character who is certainly less compromised than Volpone, perhaps even an admirable one, Truewit is nevertheless motivated by a similar uneasiness about sharing glory even with his friends and an equally strong unwillingness to acknowledge any triumph a final one. As a result the collective unity with which act 4 of *Epicoene* begins slowly dissipates as he begins to maneuver—unobtrusively at first, but insistently—to gain the position of authority that should accompany his name. Truewit's chief rival in this instance (and superficially throughout) is Clerimont, and Truewit's efforts to displace his friend initially take a form especially congenial to the members of this society: he simply doesn't give poor Clerimont a chance to talk. During a discussion in which both men comment on women's use of makeup and attempt to advise Dauphine about dealing with potential lovers (4.1.32–128), Truewit speaks some eighty-five to Clerimont's eight. He interrupts his companion when they are in agreement:

CLER.: O, you shall haue some women, then they laugh, you would
     thinke they bray'd, it is so rude, and—
TRUE.: I, and others. . . .
     (lines 47–49)

He corrects him if his analysis falls short of Truewit's notion of the truth. For example, when Clerimont tries to qualify Truewit's statement that women desire to be "ouer-come"—"O, but a man must beware of force," he interjects—Truewit replies that, on the contrary, "it is to them acceptable violence, and has oft-times the place of the greatest courtesie" (lines 83–86). Similarly, after Clerimont mockingly calls Dauphine a "stallion" for being in love with all of the Collegiates at once (line 140), Truewit chooses to ignore Clerimont's obvious intent to be humorous and treats the comment as a serious but misguided judgment that must be rejected: "No," he assures his friend, "I like him well" (line 141).

Once he has satisfactorily distinguished himself from Clerimont and so reestablished his habitual role as the authority to whom the other gallants look for guidance, Truewit can then take on a new and presumably greater challenge than the one just completed (the punishment of Morose). "Thou wouldst thinke it strange," he tells Dauphine, "if I should make 'hem [the Collegiates] all in loue with thee afore night!" (lines 145–47), his words simultaneously indicating the difficulty of this new undertaking and the response (wonder) that its successful completion should receive from an understanding audience (Clerimont and Dauphine). Whereas the gallants, as a group, attempt to establish their superiority to the other characters by adopting the role of a mocking audience that laughs at rather than with the characters it is watching, Truewit would establish his superiority to the two wits who are his friends by becoming an actor/author who elicits from his audience not mockery but admiration.

Truewit, furthermore, is not above appropriating the plots of others in his attempts to command center stage. His wish to make the vexing of Morose "a iest to posterity" (2.6.27) by moving LaFoole's feast to the old man's house is, in part, an endeavor to expand Dauphine's much tidier plot into a form for which Truewit can claim some responsibility. Later, when talking with Haughty, he assures the Collegiate that Epicoene's feigned reticence was a trick "to put her vpon this old fellow, by sir DAVPHINE, his nephew, and one or two more of vs" (3.6.42–44), skillfully hiding his robbery of another's idea under the guise of apparent humility and calling attention to himself in the process.

The corollary of Truewit's eagerness to claim a share in the tricks of others is a determination not to let Clerimont do the same, at least until Dauphine accuses Truewit of vanity late in the play (4.5.251–53). Like his creator, Truewit would possess his stage against all rival claims. "Trust my plot," he tells Dauphine as he proposes to trick Daw and LaFoole (line 19), placing appropriate emphasis, undoubtedly, upon the first-person pronoun. And when Clerimont has the audacity to suggest that he might have something to contribute, Truewit will have nothing of it. "Looke, you'll spoile all," he tells his friend, adding (with unintended irony), "these be euer your tricks," and threatening to withdraw from the game entirely: "I pray forbeare, I'll leaue it off, else" (lines 144–49). Even when poor Clerimont chances to stumble onto something that strikes Truewit's fancy—bringing the ladies to witness Daw's and LaFoole's idiocy—Truewit rather ungenerously appropriates the idea in a way that minimizes Clerimont's authorship and, of course, the stature that might accompany it: "Well, I will haue 'hem fetch'd, now I thinke on't, for a priuate purpose of mine: doe, CLERIMONT, fetch 'hem" (lines 247–49).

Nor does Truewit's willingness to have Dauphine designated the author of this trick, after Dauphine chides him (lines 251–55), alter matters significantly. For one thing, Dauphine is not, in Truewit's mistaken view, so likely a rival as Clerimont. For another, the only audience Truewit seeks to please in this play is composed of his two companions; whatever the other characters may think, these spectators are well aware of his responsibility for what follows. That Truewit's "fit audience, though few" contains at least one potential competitor is not without its problems however. Truewit, like Jonson, must at once overcome the rival claims of his spectators and acquiesce to their judgment. Without distinguishing himself from (that is, defeating) Clerimont and Dauphine, he cannot claim distinction, yet that distinction can come only from the approval of those he would outdo. Clerimont and Dauphine's approbation of his skill paradoxically both confirms his superiority and denies it, since that superiority is granted only by their applause.

The difficulty of this position is demonstrated very early in the comedy. Having vexed Morose to the point of madness, Truewit returns, seeking his friends' applause: "DAVPHINE, fall downe and worship me," he urges. When that applause is not immediately forthcoming, however, his exuberant hopes quickly degenerate into the puzzlement and resentment, all too familiar to Jonson, of an author frustrated by the response of an audience whose approval he requires: "Why doe you not applaud, and adore me, sirs? why stand you mute? Are you stupid? you are not worthy o' the benefit" (2.4.5, 17–19). At no other point in the play is Truewit so vulnerable; he is, one might say, overcome by the wonder he had hoped to elicit from spectators. Momentarily, he sounds defeated, and when he pleads that his "masters . . . not put on this strange face to pay my courtesie" (lines 34–35), his fear that his former authority is eroding with alarming rapidity is difficult to miss—in the tone with which he now addresses his friends, in the abdication of authority implicit in his use of the word "masters."

Truewit does not, of course, remain in this predicament for long. Cutbeard's news that the gallant's harangue has furthered rather than hindered Morose's desire to marry is all that is required for Truewit to regain control of the action—"Beyond your expectation? by this light, I knewe it would bee thus" (lines 67–68)—and to begin repairing whatever damage may have been done to his reputation.[9] Yet even if this episode is soon forgotten by the participants, and perhaps by some members of the comedy's audience as well, it nevertheless remains an important one: the incident at once anticipates Truewit's, and everyone else's, misjudgment of Epicoene and indicates the precariousness and uncertainty of his attempts—indeed, of all attempts—to gain distinction within a game of life whose rules are not fixed and whose outcome depends so heavily upon the sometimes unpredictable responses of others.

This predicament also explains Truewit's addiction to variety, a quality the gallant associates closely with art (1.1.103–11). As Clerimont sarcastically suggests when he states that his friend's opening disquisition on time and decay stems not from belief but from the wit's latest reading (lines 62–64), Truewit passes quickly from subject to subject, depending upon his interests and the potential for display present in a particular topic. The fund of witticisms provided by Clerimont's satiric commentary on makeup apparently exhausted, Truewit suddenly drops the subject: "No faith, I let her alone, as wee'l let this argument, if you please, and passe to another. When saw you DAVPHINE EVGENIE?" (lines 138–40). The scope given for cleverness by Daw's foolishness having narrowed too greatly, Truewit exits without warning—"God b'w'you gentlemen. I haue some businesse too"—leaving Clerimont confused ("This is very abrupt!" he mutters) and providing us with a vivid sense of Truewit's inability to remain in the same place for very long (1.2.67–68, 85).

We are never sure, as Jonas Barish has argued (1960, 157), "when if ever . . . [Truewit] is speaking in *propria persona*," because his statements and actions are not expressions of firmly held beliefs but performances. That these performances often have their origin in disagreement with others (usually Clerimont) is likewise not a sign of genuine opposition. Rather, it is the result of Truewit's probably correct insight that contradiction provides more fruitful soil for display than does agreement. Truewit's "many plots" (4.5.20) simply afford the frequency and variety of performance necessary to hold the attention of his audience and justify his name. Like Volpone and Mosca, he is always in motion. He cannot rest; his stature is constantly threatened; his achievements do not seem to constitute the monumental jests to "posteritie" (2.6.27) he so energetically attempts to create. "Why, if I doe not yet afore night, as neere as 'tis [make all of the collegiates] . . . inuite thee, and be ready to scratch for thee," he playfully tells Dauphine late in the comedy, "take the mortgage of my wit" (4.5.22–24). Success leads to a claim of possession, a claim that evidently must be constantly renewed by further success. Failure means a loss of ownership and, for this character, identity. A "true wit" commands center stage and defeats his or her rivals by an apparently endless adoption of roles and masks that will delight spectators and garner their approval. There is no conclusion to the "subtle sport" this gallant plays so well.

Furthermore, despite his skill, Truewit does not by his own standards emerge victorious at the end of *Epicoene*. Having proved his superiority to Clerimont, the man who seemed his only serious rival in the play, Truewit finds his achievements unexpectedly overshadowed by those of Dauphine, whose final trick is so successful that it immediately gains the kind of audience response that Truewit noisily seeks for himself. Dauphine's calmly triumphant "How now, gentlemen! doe you looke at me?" (5.4.220–21) echoes in an instructive manner Truewit's earlier, and frustrated, attempt (in 2.4) to prompt a similar reaction from his companions. Dauphine has indeed "lurch'd his friends of the better halfe of the garland" (5.4.224–25), gaining in the process the authority Truewit desires for himself.

The latter's long concluding speech is an attempt to salvage this situation—hence the potential condescension in his congratulations to Dauphine, his somewhat uncharacteristic generosity toward Clerimont, his condemnation of the fools, and his appeal to the offstage audience for applause. Like Volpone, who engages in a similar strategy after his defeat, Truewit is partially successful. His voice dominates at the conclusion as it did through much of the action; he speaks for the remainder of the characters, even Morose, at the end of the play.

Yet the true wit of this comedy has been bettered; his wish to display his abilities has been, in part, manipulated and taken advantage of by another. Truewit has been directing a plot that he did not, in fact, completely control. That he has been pushed out of the spotlight by a character who speaks relatively infrequently in comparison with the other main characters in this drama, and who is, furthermore, not particularly competitive (see 1.3.9–10; 2.4.69, 78) is the most telling irony in *Epicoene*. Dauphine's plot, unlike those of his companion, is limited. He has a practical goal that, once gained, makes subtly artful behavior no longer necessary. He does not seek praise and does not, in contrast to Truewit, continually have to surpass his peers in order to establish his identity. Dauphine would possess his uncle's money, not a stage; and his ability to outdo his friend at the friend's own game, if only momentarily, cannot but cast doubt on the wisdom and perhaps the attainability of Truewit's goals. The "iest to posteritie" turns out to be authored by a secretive, practical heir, not an energetic and competitive gallant.

Truewit is not, of course, totally unsuccessful in the comedy; I certainly do not mean to imply that his displacement at the end of the play by Dauphine encourages us to dismiss him entirely or lessens, to any great extent, his attractiveness. But Jonson's portrayal of this clever man is a highly complex one. Just as, from one perspective, Truewit represents an attempt by Jonson to reconcile his own contradictory attitudes toward reality (Barish 1956, 213–24), so, from another, he is Jonson's vehicle for investigating some of the ambivalent aspects of emulation. That is why Truewit's attitudes are anticipated in large part by *Epicoene*'s first Prologue, which both acknowledges the importance of pleasing its audience (lines 1–3) and asserts the worth of the comedy that follows by contrasting that comedy's various and delightful fare with the more meager dishes of other playwrights: "You shall eate / A week at ord'naries, on his [the author's] broken [but extraordinary] meat; / If his *Muse* be true, / Who commends her to you" (lines 26–29; cf. 4.5.22–24).[10]

Jonson is, ultimately, the true wit of this comedy; it is his art, much more than Dauphine's, that finally is triumphant (cf. Duncan 1979, 66–67). As numerous audiences of the play have affirmed, *Epicoene* more than fulfills the promises made in its Prologue; its author does in fact seem to know the "better way" (line 15) to compose a play. But Jonson's handling of the comedy's major character was the result of what was for him a new recognition that such triumphs are often, and perhaps always, fragile and momentary, and that as a result any attempt to stand apart and claim distinction is fraught with difficulties. Although Jonson may well have created a "iest to posteritie" by undoing in this play the character he most resembled, the career of that character nevertheless testifies to Jonson's knowledge, perhaps not fully conscious, that the course he himself had undertaken was an extremely risky one.

When Gaius Sallustius Crispus turned to the writing of Roman history after an unsatisfactory public career, he began his first work, the *Bellum Catilinae,* not with Catiline himself but with a subject that evidently had personal significance for him: the pursuit of fame. "It behooves all men who wish to excel the other animals," he argues in the opening sentence, "to strive with might and main not to pass through life unheralded like the beasts, which Nature has fashioned grovelling and slaves to the belly" (1.1). Sallust relegates to oblivion the names of the unvirtuous (1.8), and he states that his own glory will come from the difficult task of recording the actions of famous men (1.3). This message is, by his own account, a characteristically Roman one; the early Romans' extraordinary desire for fame was, Sallust explains, the primary reason for his country's ascent to greatness: "Nay, their hardest struggle for glory was with one another; each man strove to be the first to strike down the foe, to scale a wall, to be seen of all while doing such a deed" (7.6), because "citizen vied with citizen . . . for the prize of merit" (9.2). The degeneration into mere avarice of this noble desire to excel (11.1; 14) was what, according to Sallust, made the existence of a Catiline possible. His opening chapters chronicle the gradual corruption within Roman society of the impulses that separate humans from animals and lead to great achievements, a corruption that created, finally, the "monstrous, incredible, gigantic" urges and actions that are his subject (5.5). For Sallust, Catiline's story is a story of perversion. Perhaps influenced by Cicero's repeated references to the immortality of his triumph over Catiline (see, for example, *In Catilinam* 3.11; 4.11), the Roman historian placed the conspiracy within a framework involving rivalry, ambition, and their ambivalent effects. It is a framework, need I add, that must have been especially appealing to Ben Jonson.[11]

There is, admittedly, no way of knowing with any certainty why Jonson selected Catiline's conspiracy as the subject for his second tragedy, or whether he was in fact influenced by Sallust's famous introduction to the *Bellum Catilinae*. But whatever his reasons for selecting this particular story and despite *Catiline*'s significant flaws, the tragedy, like *Sejanus* before it, has an important place in Jonson's development. Just as *Sejanus* deepens and extends Jonson's concern with misinterpretation by making that concern a central aspect of its tragic sequence, so *Catiline* translates the examination of rivalry present in *Volpone, Epicoene,* and *The Alchemist* into a tragic setting and provides in the process a powerful conclusion to that examination.

The world of *Catiline* is a recognizably Jonsonian one, especially when approached in terms of the issues I have been emphasizing in this study. Cicero's opening words define the dangers of envy (3.1–6; cf. 4.875–94), and despite the presence in this tragedy of two major factions vying for power, the members of one of these groups sometimes have a great deal of difficulty acting in concert with one another. Their ability to remain a part of a common endeavor is hindered, if not undermined completely, by their insistence on remaining apart.[12] Cethegus, for example, rejects all aid from his allies when he sets out to murder Cicero. The plot "is my prouince," he tells Curius and Vargunteius, "none vsurpe it," adding, a few lines later: "Safe is your way, then; take it. Mine's mine owne" (3.662, 673). These attitudes should by now be familiar enough, and in the next act we once again find Cethegus grumbling about the conspirators' "many counsells" and wishing that he might go off by himself: "Would I / Had somewhat by my selfe, apart, to doe" (4.594–95).

Nor is this inability to join in a common effort or to accept another as a comrade or equal limited within the play to a madman like Cethegus. With the exception of a few words about her lovers and the desirability of variety (recall Truewit's similar preference), Fulvia spends most of her initial appearance discussing with her servant two rivals, Sempronia and Aurelia Orestilla—most likely in order to be assured that she has become a model for all other women slavishly to imitate:

> in troth,
> As I liue, madame, you put 'hem all downe
> With your meere strength of iudgement! and doe draw, too,
> The world of *Rome* to follow you!
> (2.75–78)

Cicero takes advantage of this same desire for precedence when he and Fulvia meet with Curius in act 3, cleverly telling her lover, "Here is a lady, that hath got the start, / In pietie, of vs all," and promising that her fame will bring her rivals to despair: "What enuy, and griefe in matrons, / They are not shee!" (3.341–42, 348–49), he says, sounding as if he had read some of the passages in *Discoveries* or the "Apologetical Dialogue."

Even Fulvia's betrayal of the conspiracy results from ambition rather than patriotism or moral scruple. Stepping to one side with her lover, she asks:

> doe you think, I'ld walke in any plot,
> Where madame SEMPRONIA should take place of me,
> And FVLVIA come i'the *rere,* or o'the *by?*
> That I would be her second, in a businesse,
> Though it might vantage me all the sunne sees?
> (3.375–79)

For a woman accustomed to being a model for others, accepting equality ("o'the *by*"), much less inferiority ("i'the *rere*"), is out of the question. Although Cicero has earlier told Curius, "'Tis no shame, to follow / The better precedent" (lines 358–59), precedents in Fulvia's view exist only to be surpassed, not echoed. The imitative subservience implicit in the word *follow* is simply not for her, however fitting it may be for others, including her lover. Thus, at the same time that she admits to Curius her unwillingness to accept within the conspiracy a role second to Sempronia, she none too subtly asserts her dominance over him, urging (as Cicero did) that he imitate the model *she* provides but making more explicit the loss of stature such a relationship involves: "Follow the fortune I ha' put you into: / You may be something this way, and with safetie" (lines 382–83). And he does exactly that. "Most noble *Consul,* I am yours, and hers; / I mean my countries" (407–8), Curius tells Cicero, his comic slip of the tongue making clear the extent to which he has agreed to be governed by Fulvia's example. He is indeed hers; he has acknowledged her priority.

Fulvia, Curius, and Cethegus are, of course, only minor players in a game that is being played for the control of Rome. The key gamesters are Catiline and Cicero, and there is much to be said for Gabrielle Jackson's argument (1968, 31) that *Catiline* contains Jonson's most extensive portrayal of conflict between a true and false artist. Catiline and Cicero are competitors, in part because they have moral and political differences but also because they have a great deal in common, not least their desire to distinguish themselves from their contemporaries.[13] As such, they have some important things to tell us about the concerns that are the subject of this book.

Catiline is the more obviously instructive of the two. He is, among other things, a character whose sense of self is rooted in his ability to act, primarily in a violent and destructive manner. To be a spectator is, for Catiline, to be "benum'd" (1.404); resignation to losing the consulship threatens to reduce him to "a shaddow" (3.165). In a Jonsonian world this preference inevitably entails an involvement in imitation and, if one seeks fame, a commitment to its more militant and aggressive forms. Catiline's desire for power leads to rivalries not only with his contemporaries, but also with his immediate predecessors, with models sufficiently authoritative that they must be followed or, if Catiline is to gain distinction, surpassed. Sylla's opening speech provides a catalogue of these models; it indicates that we are watching an action that is in some ways a repetition of past actions and, as such, sketches a generic background against which Catiline will endeavor to define his own identity:

> PLVTO be at thy councells; and into
> Thy darker bosome enter SYLLA'S spirit:
> All, that was mine, and bad, thy brest inherit
> . . . .
> All, that the GRACCHI, CINNA, MARIVS would;
> What now, had I a body againe, I could,
> Comming from hell; what Fiends would wish should be;
> And HANNIBAL could not haue wish'd to see:
> Thinke thou, and practice.
> (1. 16–25)

The list is an impressive one; it is a formidable tradition indeed with which Catiline will need to come to terms.

Catiline's own former actions establish an additional point of departure for his conspiracy. That is why a list of the patrician's earlier "incests, murders, rapes" (lines 27–43) follows the catalogue quoted above. Catiline's greatness must be attained, it seems, by his ability at once to reinvigorate and to surpass a destructive past (both his own and Rome's). Sylla's ghost admits that its spirit is too "weake" for Catiline (line 19); the desires of the Gracchi, Cinna, Marius, and unnamed fiends—what they "would" do—will find fulfillment in Catiline's actual deeds, which will also dwarf the most extravagant wishes of a Hannibal. His "Conscience" of his own former crimes—and the irony surrounding this word choice is intentional—will "prouoke" him to the greater accomplishments (line 29) that Catiline will later fantasize while recalling fondly the executions performed under Sylla: "And this shall be againe, and more, and more" (line 254). The patrician's goal is not simply to destroy Rome and gain power; he seeks a triumph so remarkable that it will become an incomparable and unapproachable standard, one that will displace all past examples of destruction and make even the Furies enviously fear and "grieue," and "wish" the "mischiefe theirs" (line 72). The "transcendent" event he would create will overshadow not only all human acts, but also the imagined monstrosities of nature (3.651–55), and, Cicero notes, "all insolent fictions of the tragick *scene!*" (3.259). Catiline would manufacture a reality beyond human thought.

To do so, Catiline must not allow himself to pause for even a moment. Ambition, the Chorus explains at the end of act 3, is a "neere vice / To vertue" and a "rest-lesse ill, that still doth build / Vpon successe" (3.860–61, 864–65). Curius and Cethegus would multiply without apparent end the worlds they might destroy (3.594–96), and their leader is continually seeking new achievements (1.79–82, 117–20) in order that, in Sylla's words, his "thought [not] find any vacant time / To hate an old, but still a fresher crime / Drowne the remembrance" (1.55–57).[14]

Catiline's ambitions seem also to require that he, like Volpone, sever all natural bonds with others. Just as Volpone's "family" is a menagerie of grotesques, so Catiline's past is filled with his bloody violations of familial relationships (1.30–43; cf. 1.232–33). In addition, he finds it necessary to reject the land that nurtured him, the "common mother" that, Cicero says, "doth challenge / The prime part of vs" (3.366–67). In a sense, Catiline must become self-begotten, the parent of a new land (1.283–91) rather than the son of one that already exists. Priority usually confers authority; according to Catiline, the past must be destroyed if the present is to wrest power from it. The grisly ritual with which act 1 concludes is thus more than the product of his ghoulish monstrosity: it at once symbolically reenacts past attempts to destroy the authority of the motherland, and attempts to guarantee success in the present. Rome will become its own altar (3.623–25) as the conspirators rise up to slay their parent and take for themselves the power which that parent now wields, leaving her, Catiline pledges, "as bloud-less, / As euer her feares made her, or the sword" (1.493–94). That such a sacrifice will occur during the Saturnalia is only fitting. In essence, the conspirators intend to make final and actual the momentary and symbolic overthrow of social hierarchy associated with that festival, sweeping aside all currently sanctioned differences in order to create new and more acceptable ones.

Yet even if Catiline had successfully overthrown the country that gave him birth, he likely would have proved as heartless toward his spiritual children and followers as he is to the members of his family and his homeland. Like Truewit in *Epicoene,* and Cethegus and Fulvia in this play, Catiline does not easily engage in a common effort. He scorns the men and women of whom he makes use; his involvement with them, he tells Aurelia, is but a disguise that can be removed as quickly as a visor in the theater, a momentary and necessary hazarding of his honor for a greater good (1.169–71, 180–85). And even this admission does not do justice to Catiline's desire to distinguish himself from all others—including, most likely, Aurelia herself. "The cruelty, I meane to act," he soliloquizes, "I wish

> Should be call'd mine, and tarry in my name;
> Whil'st, after ages doe toile out themselues,
> In thinking for the like, but doe it lesse:
> And, were the power of all the fiends let loose,
> With fate to boot, it should be, still, example.
> (3.746–51)

The initial litany of first-person pronouns, the emphasis upon the continuing dominance of his action over all future actions—these details and others indicate clearly enough what Catiline desires: not simply power but a distinction so pronounced as to be inimitable and eternal, a distinction that is his and his alone. His goal is the one Quintilian establishes for all who emulate: "For this glory also shall be theirs, that men shall say of them that while they surpassed their predecessors, they also taught those who came after" (*Institutio Oratoria* 10.2.28). It is a serious and infinitely more destructive version of Truewit's "iest to posteritie," and, as with the gallant's plots, the success of Catiline's conspiracy will be an assertion of identity, of name. The destruction of Rome, Sylla's ghost whispers to him in act 1, "is thy act, or none" (line 48). That is, the catastrophe will both provide proof that Catiline is truly himself (it is the only act fit for him) and that he is unique (the action is suitable to Catiline and no one else). Or as Cicero laments upon first hearing the details of the conspiracy: "His former drifts partake of former times, / But this last plot was onely CATILINES" (3.243–44). The assessment is one that the consul's opponent undoubtedly would have welcomed.

Catiline's habit of talking about the conspiracy in terms of models and imitative endeavors explains why it is so easy to see him as a kind of artist, if only a flawed one; Alexander Leggatt is surely right to argue that "all the huffing and puffing of the conspirators suggests that it [the conspiracy] is . . . a bad overdone play" (1981, 7). Such talk is the stuff of emulation, and both Catiline and Cethegus describe the conspiracy using dramatic metaphors (1.180–85; 5.272–77), which intimate a potential connection between their desire to control the world-stage and that of a writer like Jonson to dominate an artistic one.

This does not mean, certainly, that Catiline is an artist, much less that he is Jonson. Nor does it mean that Jonson sympathized with this character. Obviously, he did not. But Catiline's search for distinction does have much in common with that of his creator (as well as with the actions of such characters as Truewit and Volpone), and it is surely significant that almost all of the passages from this play that I have considered above are Jonson's invention; they are not in his sources.

Moreover, there is a certain, although somewhat disturbing, decorousness to Jonson's decision to portray within a particularly brutal setting the urge to be "still, example" for others. We may recall that classical and Renaissance writers often employ military metaphors when discussing emulation (see Pigman 1980; Cave 1979, 35–77). We might note as well that even Jonson's apparent admirers sometimes describe his relations with other writers in a similar way. Thomas Carew, for instance, dwells on "the bloud of mayrtird Authors, spilt" into Jonson's ink, continuing, "Nor thinke it theft, if the rich spoyles so torne / From conquerd Authors, be as Trophies worne." And John Dryden notes in a widely known passage that his great predecessor "invades Authours like a Monarch, and what would be theft in other Poets, is onely victory in him" (Herford, Simpson, and Simpson 1925–52, 11:336, 515).[15] The resemblance between these comments and Sylla's admonition to Catiline, "Make all past, present, future ill thine owne; / And Conquer all example, in thy one" (1.53–54), is both remarkable and instructive. By making the monster of Sallust's chronicle a monster who talks a great deal about standing apart, defeating models/rivals, and providing an example for future generations to follow, Jonson made Catiline an embodiment, albeit a ruthless and bloodthirsty one, of some of his own impulses.

Given this partial connection between Catiline and the dramatist who created him, it is especially significant that Catiline does not fail to achieve what he wants simply because he is evil and destructive—because, in other words, he deserves to. He fails also because there is something inherently contradictory and self-defeating about the plan to which he has committed himself. For one thing, Catiline can never completely separate himself from the Rome he would destroy and is, as a result, a potential victim of his own mayhem. When the Chorus at the end of act 1 states that Rome has become "both her own spoiler, and owne prey" (1:586), it points to a paradox that perhaps undermines all of the patrician's efforts. Catiline, the lines imply, may be both victim and victor simultaneously; his actions may in fact be suicidal. By attempting to destroy completely his past and his origins, he threatens to destroy himself, becoming a force of pure negation and nothing more. The patrician cannot exist apart from the Rome he would destroy, yet the name he seeks can be acquired (so he thinks) only through that act of violence.

This predicament is reinforced by another problematic aspect of Catiline's activities, one much closer to Jonson's own situation. Some ten years before Jonson wrote his second tragedy, Thomas Dekker had argued in *Satiromastix* that Jonson's attempt to distinguish himself from other writers caused him to ignore important distinctions among those he sought to leave behind—a danger exemplified by Dekker's Horace, who strikes out indiscriminately at all around him in order to gain a reputation. *Catiline* suggests that Jonson was at last willing to grant the possibility that Dekker had been right; his conspirators embody the same contradiction. According to their own explanations, the conspiracy was made necessary in part by the erosion of hierarchical distinctions within Roman society. Too often, the conspirators complain, they have been "hearded with the vulgar" (1.355). Sempronia's defense of the privileges of the nobility (2.131–38) can best be understood within this context, as can the conspirators' seemingly excessive hostility toward the "new man," Cicero. The gods, Catiline tells the Senate, would prefer to return to a completely undifferentiated world—"the first, rude, indigested heape" out of which all things and all differences arose—"Ere such a wretched name, as CICERO, / Should sound with theirs" (4.486–88).

Yet the conspirators' solution to this confusion is an act of almost totally indiscriminate destruction, a more chilling counterpart to the scattershot calumnies of Dekker's Horace. Their frenzied descriptions of the glories of Sylla's era (glories they hope to surpass) are chronicles of mindless violence. "All hate had licence giuen it: all rage raines," Catiline exults, and Cethegus adds: "No age was spar'd, no sexe" (1.234, 239). "All dyed," since "To strike but onely those, that could doe hurt, / Was dull, and poore" (244–46): that is, insufficient to gain the glory sought by the perpetrators of this massacre. Even the distinction between living and dead was no longer absolute: Charon's boat was filled with "men, yet liuing, / Whose flight, and feare had mix'd them, with the dead" (252–53). For the conspirators, as for Dekker's Horace, there is only one difference that matters: that between the self and all others. Catiline's ruthlessness is based upon his acceptance of this attitude; the one distinction essential to him is to be achieved by ignoring all others.

Like Catiline, Cicero is a man seeking fame, an endeavor whose success requires that the orator distinguish himself from his peers and immediate predecessors. Just as Jonson carefully provides Catiline with a tradition to imitate and surpass, so he provides Cicero with one that the new consul will transcend, and much more successfully than his opponent, through a series of events that is already in progress when the play begins. Cicero's tradition is composed of heroes who have sacrificed themselves for Rome (2.391–96), and he is both a continuation and a new form of that tradition. There have been virtuous consuls prior to his election, but (as Cicero repeatedly emphasizes when he first enters) "new men, before me, none" (3.25). The language of difference fills his opening speech: "I have no vrnes," he states (line 14); and he continues the enumeration of what he is "wanting" (line 16) for several lines, wants that constitute one aspect of his newness and continue a process of definition that will distinguish him ever more clearly from those who have held a similar position.

Cicero's progress through the play delineates his increasing success in this activity, from the auspicious beginning provided by his election to the consulship, to his demonstration that he is not simply a "talker" like his "gentle enemy" Sempronia (line 781; cf. lines 776–80), to his final triumph not only over Catiline but also over the earlier members of the tradition to which he belongs. He brushes aside the destructive visions of Catiline and in effect recreates the country that gave him birth.[16] No longer the child of Rome, with the secondary status such a relationship implies, Cicero becomes its progenitor. "He is," Cato announces, "the onely father of his countrey" (5.313), that *onely* acknowledging Cicero's privileged status and echoing, ironically, Catiline's earlier claims to exclusivity (3.746–51), claims that Cicero himself had acknowledged (3.243–44). Cicero's exclusive fatherhood differentiates him sharply and forcefully from the heroic Scipios and Brutuses of the Roman past; never one to let such differences go unnoticed, he emphasizes precisely this point at the end of the play. Noting the extraordinary honors he has been granted, he asks:

> why should not, then,
> This day, to vs, and all posteritie
> Of ours, be had in equall fame, and honor,
> With that, when ROMVLVS first rear'd these walls,
> When so much more is saued, then he built?
> (5.321–23)

The question is, obviously, a rhetorical one; despite Cicero's apparent acknowledgment that his own achievements and those of Romulus are roughly equivalent (not a humble assertion in itself), he is really seeking a very different relation between his deeds and the earlier hero's initial act of creation. "So much more" having been saved, it is only just that the recognition accorded him should proportionately surpass that given his great predecessor. And so, evidently, it will. Cicero's example will nourish past, present, and future: "the old men of the citie," the "matrons," the "youths, and maids" (5.611–13). When he concludes the play by once more noting *"my* labours, / *My* watchings, and *my* dangers" (lines 694–95, emphasis added), Cicero's words stress in good Jonsonian fashion his awareness of the position he has attained, a position of authority and preeminence dependent upon an achievement related to yet clearly distinct from other achievements, a position that is his alone.

Cicero's career in *Catiline* is not, however, the product merely of Jonsonian wish-fulfillment; his triumph is not as complete as this discussion has so far implied. Nor is he an unambiguously virtuous character. Although *Catiline* may indeed present the triumph of virtue over evil, true art over false, the exemplar of the positive values is flawed and his triumph qualified in important ways. [17] Plutarch had described Cicero as a man who, despite knowing better, was often overcome by a desire for glory. Cicero's potentially beneficial recognition "that the fame towards which he was emulously struggling was a thing that knew no bounds and had no tangible limit" was, Plutarch explains ("Life of Cicero" 6.4–5), undermined by "his excessive delight in the praise of others and his too passionate desire for glory [that] remained with him until the very end, and very often confounded his saner reasonings." Indeed, Cicero too frequently spoke, Plutarch tells us, "as if he were impetuously vying with Isocrates and Anaximenes the sophists, instead of claiming the right to lead and instruct the Roman people" ("Comparison of Demosthenes and Cicero" 2.2).

Although Jonson was certainly more sympathetic to the Roman orator than was Cicero's classical biographer, his Cicero does retain the competitive urge so central to Plutarch's characterization, together with an itch for praise. In *Catiline,* Cicero's unceasing search for approval may to some extent result from his uneasy status as a "new man" (Leggatt 1981, 154), but that status is also, as noted, an advantage. The orator's actions more probably stem from an aware-ness, like Truewit's, that spectators play an important role as judges between competitors for distinction.

It is therefore one of this tragedy's most telling ironies, as well as a major qualification of Cicero's triumph, that the dominant onstage audience is hostile to him. For even though this audience has only two members, Caesar and Crassus, it is an extremely powerful one: our knowledge of the future that awaits both Rome and Cicero after the defeat of Catiline cannot but reinforce the authority often afforded relatively detached observers in Jonson's plays. The admitted purpose of the two men is a recognizably Jonsonian one—they will "watch the watcher," Caesar says (3.108)—and their comments provide a somewhat disturbing analysis of Cicero's ploys and weaknesses, as well as (in the case of Caesar) a reminder that today's victor will be to-morrow's victim. Caesar stands both above and apart from the rival-ries between the play's major antagonists. He is the consummate Ma-chiavellian in the drama, a role befitting his detachment, and it is probably no exaggeration to say, with J. A. Bryant (1954, 270), that the conspiracy "is not really Catiline's after all, but Caesar's." If by the end of the tragedy he has lost one battle in a war for control of Rome, we know all too well, if Cato and Cicero do not, that there will soon be another.

Jonson qualifies the triumph of his hero in one other way. When the English playwright turned to Dio's *Roman History* to gather ma-terials for this tragedy, he would have encountered an especially in-triguing statement. Having reported the details of Catiline's con-spiracy, Dio concludes by stating that the patrician's failure was not as complete as it might have been: "Such was the career of Catiline and such his downfall; but he gained a greater name than his deeds deserved, owing to the reputation of Cicero and the speeches he de-livered against him" (37.42.1). Cicero, in other words, gave Catiline the immortality and fame that the conspirator so energetically, at least in Jonson's play, sought. Catiline's cruelty has, as he hoped, "tarried" in his name (3.746–47); we need only note that Jonson's tragedy is called *Catiline,* rather than *Cicero's Triumph* or the like, to recognize that the drama affirms Dio's judgment. Just as Shakespeare's Antony and Cleopatra wrest a kind of victory from their defeat by Octavius, in a play written only a few years before this one, so Jonson's Catiline gains stature in defeat, looked on at last by the divine audience he is always seeking and becoming almost literally monumental in his "braue bad death" (5.655–57, 688).

However, the reason for Catiline's "triumph" is not, as is Antony's and Cleopatra's, his ability imaginatively to transform the world he inhabits; it is the actions of his opponent. Cicero immortalizes Catiline in his attempt to immortalize himself. The orator's glory is dependent in a very fundamental way on the enormity of the danger he faces; one might go so far as to say that Cicero needs Catiline, a paradox that in Jonson's play Caesar clearly understands. Hearing Catullus mention rumors of a major internal threat to Rome, Caesar turns to Crassus and says:

> Doe you not tast
> An art, that is so common? Popular men,
> They must create strange monsters, and then quell 'hem;
> To make their artes seeme something. Would you haue
> Such an HERCVLEAN actor in the scene,
> And not his HYDRA?
> (3.95–100)

Caesar's comment is certainly self-serving and, in important ways, inaccurate: Catiline does represent a destructive force that must be opposed; he is not a creation of Cicero's imagination. But there is also more than a little truth in what Caesar says. Without a Catiline, Cicero is nothing, one of a long line of relatively undistinguished and sometimes nameless consuls. For Cicero to attain glory, Catiline must be an internal threat equal to—or, ideally, greater than—the external enemies defeated by the great Romans of the past, that list of heroes whom Cicero hopes to join or perhaps to surpass. Cicero's recognition of this dependence may even explain why he is so ready to credit Catiline with the stature the conspirator seeks (3.243–44).

The two opponents are inseparably and ironically linked. Cicero's plan to defeat Catiline has to be successful if Cicero is to take his place as a hero in the chronicles of Rome, but Catiline's own assertion of greatness must also be acknowledged to some extent in the process. Catiline's victory in defeat thus provides a particularly suitable balance to Cicero's defeat in victory—an ambiguous outcome that could not have given Jonson much comfort. That he was able to write a play which held out this fate to two powerful men seeking fame is one more indication of his consciousness of his own predicament and, more generally, the predicament of anyone who seeks distinction. Jonson had learned a great deal since the opening salvos of the War of the Theaters.

5

COMING TO TERMS

Shortly after the fourth act of *Bartholomew Fair* begins, Quarlous and
Winwife enter with drawn swords, having sacrificed both their
friendship and their detachment for the hand of a woman who asks
no such offering. "I am no she," Grace tells them, "that affects to be
quarell'd for, or haue my name or fortune made the question of mens
swords" (4.3.3–5). The presence of yet another quarrel in a play in
which "almost every episode culminates with a scrimmage" (Barish
1960, 231) is hardly surprising. But that Tom Quarlous and Ned
Winwife are the participants is somewhat unexpected, despite the
implications of the former's last name; and the rapidity with which
these two friends become enemies is remarkable.

Their absurd attempt to maim each other over a woman neither
of them really knows originates, in fact, only a few scenes earlier, when
Quarlous's characteristically witty and, in this instance, perhaps even
innocent lament that he has not studied Grace's case at the Inns of
Court (3.5.277–80) is interpreted by Winwife as a sign that his companion wants Grace for himself—"I, Master *Quarlous,* are you prof-
fering. . . . (I'le looke to you i' faith, Gamster)" (lines 281, 283)—
and Quarlous, with more justification, suspects that Winwife's hesitancy to acknowledge his interest in Dame Purecraft reveals that the
target of the gallant's search for a suitably wealthy spouse is now Grace
rather than the widow: "Cry you mercy, is the winde there? must not
the widdow be nam'd?" (lines 305–6).

These suspicions quickly metamorphose into the theatrical expression of hostility that we see before us in act 4, primarily because the participants have so much in common. "How can I iudge of you, so farre as to a choyse, without knowing you more?" Grace protests, "You are both equall, and alike to mee, yet: and so indifferently affected by mee, as each of you might be the man, if the other were away" (4.3.31–35). The two are in her view indistinguishable, and, even granting Quarlous's greater volatility and cynicism, she is for the most part correct. That is one reason why Quarlous ends up with the marriage-partner his friend was initially pursuing.

The competition between Quarlous and Winwife is a less impressive version of the rivalries central to the four plays that precede *Bartholomew Fair*. Like Cicero and Catiline, or Truewit and his companions, Quarlous and Winwife are the most intelligent characters in the drama in which they appear. Like Volpone and Mosca, or Face and Subtle, their quarrel is a "difference" whose purpose is to create difference.

But the resolution of this particular rivalry has nothing to do with the skill or efforts of the two opponents. The victor is determined by the whim of a madman, "a figure of destiny at its most capricious" (Cope 1984, 81), and from its inception this solution is described in a decidedly ambivalent manner. When Grace calls her plan "a motion of mine" (4.3.41), her description anticipates another and equally foolish "motion"—the puppet play John Littlewit pens for Leatherhead—with the person pulling the strings in this case a half-crazed victim of Overdo's faulty justice rather than one of the fair's cleverest thieves. And when Trouble-All marks the tablet in order to satisfy Grace's "longing, (and multiply him)" (line 95), we should be reminded of Win's "longing" for pig and the apparent connection between that longing and her pregnancy (multiplying), a parallel that is hardly flattering. It is no wonder, then, that Quarlous, the drama's closest approximation to a Volpone or Truewit, decides late in the comedy that "there's no playing with a man's fortune!" (5.2.83–84). Although the game of life may in fact be no more unpredictable here than in Jonson's previous plays, the Quarlouses of this world, unlike the Moscas and Catilines of the earlier dramas, acquiesce to that capriciousness without attempting to shape it.

Whether such acquiescence is a sign of wisdom or cynicism or both is one of the most difficult questions raised by this wonderful yet puzzling play—a question that I am not, at this point, ready to answer. But however one finally decides to resolve the dilemma, Jonson's portrayal of rivalry in *Bartholomew Fair* is obviously even more pessimistic than is his depiction in *Catiline* of the conflict between Cicero and the Roman patrician. The intimation in Jonson's second tragedy that there may not always be a clear distinction between victory and defeat becomes in his last great comedy a suggestion that there may be no point in seeking distinction at all, given the disorder of a world beyond human control. That suggestion may explain why rivalry is much less central to this play than it is to the four that precede it. And it recalls the viewpoints of Thomas Dekker and Samuel Daniel, two writers with whom Jonson probably would not have been comfortable acknowledging agreement (see Chapter 1).

Furthermore, this apparent "reconciliation" takes place in a play whose lines, incidents, and structure frequently echo—as none of the plays of the 1616 folio does[1]—the works of another English playwright. That playwright, of course, is Shakespeare, for as several critics have noted, *Bartholomew Fair* contains an extraordinary number of Shakespearean allusions in addition to the Induction's explicit (and seemingly disparaging) references to *Titus Andronicus, The Winter's Tale,* and *The Tempest.*[2] Knockem's comments on the relation between malice and body type (2.3.22–33) recall Caesar's similar comments on Cassius (*Julius Caesar,* 1.2.190–95). Overdo, like Prospero, is very much concerned with selecting the proper moment, his "due time" (3.3.39; 5.4.19–21; cf. *The Tempest* 1.2.22–23, 36–37); each man acknowledges a "thing of darkness" (Trouble-All, Caliban) to be partly his creation. The name Grace repeats a word that is constantly on Hermione's lips when she first appears in *The Winter's Tale* (1.2.80, 99, 105); Cokes's experiences while listening to ballads parallel those of the country bumpkins in the same romance. Purecraft's belief that Trouble-All is "mad in truth" (4.6.169–74) and Cokes's lament that he no longer knows who he is and has "lost" himself (4.2.78–86) sound like the sentiments of an Antipholus of Syracuse, an Orlando, or a Ferdinand, as he wanders through a topsy-turvy world the confusion of which ultimately will be salutary and redemptive. And finally, the puppet play at the end of *Bartholomew Fair* probably has as its model the play-within-the-play at the conclusion of *A Midsummer Night's Dream*.

As several of these parallels suggest, *Bartholomew Fair* works "off and within a quintessentially Shakespearean pastoral/romance pattern of withdrawal and return" (Cartelli 1983, 152).[3] The characters move from their presumably structured and orderly everyday life in London into the confusion and misrule of the fair and then back again, a movement that apparently resolves the problems with which the play begins by revealing, among other things, those characters' common humanity. Their journey thus repeats in a general way the journeys of the lovers in *A Midsummer Night's Dream* and of the noble families of Milan and Naples in *The Tempest,* to cite only two of several possible Shakespearean parallels. This kind of journey, furthermore, is nowhere present in Jonson's earlier plays.

Jonson's adaptation in *Bartholomew Fair* of an essentially Shakespearean structure seems especially fitting, given the pessimistic implications of the rivalry between Quarlous and Winwife. What better way for a dramatist to embody the futility of attempting to stand apart from one's peers than by portraying that futility within a dramatic form closely associated with a potential or former rival? As a play whose "exhilarating finale . . . rebaptizes the repressive spirits in a communal joy" (Barish 1960, 236), *Bartholomew Fair* might thus become, through its acceptance of human frailty and equality, both a kind of agreement between Jonson and, say, Daniel or Dekker about the foolishness of Jonson's former competitiveness, and "a living memorial to the influence of his rival and master [Shakespeare]" (Cartelli 1983, 172). No longer feverishly endeavoring to separate himself from his contemporaries or obsessed with making ever finer distinctions, no longer a man committed to the reformation of both art and society, Jonson may at last have come to terms with his audience, his native tradition, and its greatest artist.

Perhaps so. But as satisfying as such an account of Jonson's "reformation" may be, the play is more complex than a reading of this sort admits. The Shakespearean allusions are there, of course, as is the essentially Shakespearean structure; the mere presence of these materials is, at the very least, a testimonial to Shakespeare's importance and power. The key question that remains to be answered, however, is whether Jonson's use of a popular dramatic tradition associated with Shakespeare is the sign of a somewhat belated recognition of the value of that tradition or an indication of cynicism—a question that dovetails, in turn, with the questions raised by his portrayal of the rivalry between Quarlous and Winwife. Moreover, both issues are related to the significance within the play itself of the characters' confrontation at the fair with what is most basic in human nature. What, finally, are we to make of these movements—Jonson's, his characters'—toward a somewhat un-Jonsonian emphasis upon similarity rather than difference? Are they beneficial, perhaps even redemptive? Or do they reveal, as one reader has argued, "not our common bond of humanity but the commonness, the baseness, and enormity of our humanity" (Ornstein 1969, 46)?

Jonson himself encourages these very questions in *Bartholomew Fair* by employing the verb "reduce" in two apparently contradictory yet not totally dissimilar ways. Both have a bearing on this discussion. The first usage occurs near the beginning of act 5. Fresh from his latest misadventure, Overdo encounters Quarlous, disguised as Trouble-All, and is heartened that the madman seems to be overcoming the effects of Overdo's earlier and now much regretted severity. Although Overdo characteristically is wrong once again, Trouble-All's apparent recovery allows the justice to turn his attention to what is perhaps his favorite project in the play, the reformation of Edgeworth: "Now, for my other worke, reducing the young man (I haue follow'd so long in loue) from the brinke of his bane, to the center of safety" (5.2.132–34). The verb "reduce" in this case has the sense of leading back or recalling from error, of restoring or taking something back to its origins.[4] It implies that Edgeworth's evil represents a deviation from what is usual and natural, and that the better future which Overdo hopes to create for the young man will in fact be a return to an original and uncorrupted past. Returns of this sort are often the stuff of romance (in *As You Like It,* Orlando's father connects the young man with a beneficent past that precedes the usurpation of Duke Frederick), and thus it is particularly appropriate that Overdo should conclude his plans in Prospero-like fashion: "I will waite the good time" (lines 135–36), he says.

A scene later, Jonson employs the same word much more negatively. Explaining Littlewit's reworking of Marlowe's *Hero and Leander*, Leatherhead notes: "I haue entreated Master *Littlewit,* to take a little paines to reduce it [the original poem] to a more familiar straine for our people" (5.3.115–17). "Reduce" has in this speech its more usual modern meaning of bringing down or diminishing. Littlewit's "reduction" of Marlowe's poem is an act of debasement; it makes that distinguished poem common and ordinary, fit for the foolish audience that Leatherhead must entertain. And he does so in part by clothing the poem in native garb, by making it "familiar." It hardly seems the kind of reducing that Overdo had in mind.

Yet the two speeches are more alike than is apparent at first glance. Leatherhead is, after all, endeavoring to translate Marlowe's poem into a more popular form by correcting the poem's unfortunate deviation from what is natural and familiar and so, to paraphrase Justice Overdo, bringing it back from the "brink" of danger (the poem's distinctiveness, what sets it apart) to the "center of safety." He is in the business of destroying difference; his goal is a perfectly egalitarian poem, "grounded," one might say, in the common humanity of his poorest and least educated spectators.

A return to what is basic and fundamental is also the subject of a third passage by Jonson that employs this verb. The passage occurs in *Discoveries* (rather than in *Bartholomew Fair*) as part of a long discussion of laughter, which is defined as "a kind of turpitude, that depraves some part of a mans nature without a disease" (lines 2632–33). The primary examples of this "turpitude" are the comedies of Aristophanes—in particular, the Greek playwright's controversial portrayal of Socrates in *The Clouds.* While the presence in *Discoveries* of comments condemning a dramatist who was in other ways an important model for Jonson is certainly notable in itself, this discussion is especially relevant to *Bartholomew Fair* because the comedy is, as several scholars have argued, a decidedly Aristophanic play. If it does not imitate Aristophanes' interest in and portrayal of rivalry, as do so many of Jonson's earlier dramas (see Chapter 4), it does reproduce as well as any play in English the Greek dramatist's pervasive emphasis upon the most basic aspects of human nature.[5]

The account in *Discoveries* of Aristophanes' mockery of Socrates, "that Example of all good life, and honesty, and vertue" (line 2663), ends as follows:

> This was *Theatricall* wit, right Stage-jesting, and relishing a Play-house, invented for scorne, and laughter; whereas, if it had savour'd of equity, truth, perspicuity, and Candor, to have tasten a wise, or a learned Palate, spit it out presently; this is bitter and profitable, this instructs, and would informe us: what neede wee know any thing, that are nobly borne, more then a Horserace, or a hunting-match, our day to break with Citizens, and such innate mysteries? This is truly leaping from the Stage to the Tumbrell againe, reducing all witt to the originall Dungcart. (lines 2667–77)

Even though this passage is translated in part from Daniel Heinsius and we cannot therefore be sure that it represents Jonson's own views on the subject, he was evidently interested enough in Heinsius's comments to note them down, and in doing so he both expanded and intensified them (the section I have just quoted, for example, is based upon only two short sentences in the original).[6] What is particularly instructive for my purposes is that Aristophanes' debasement of Socrates is described not only as a sop to the masses ("relishing a Playhouse, invented for scorne and laughter") but also as a return to origins, to a more primitive and, presumably, communal form of drama. The "Tumbrell" and "Dungcart" of the final sentence allude both to Thespis, the legendary inventor of Greek drama, and to the medieval beginnings of the English stage (Herford, Simpson, and Simpson 1925–52, 11:290). Aristophanes' mockery of Socrates is thus presented as an instance of the theater reversing the history of its own development as it returns to the undifferentiated matter from which it sprang. This example of "reducing" may, in a sense, be regenerative—it is, after all, a "Dungcart" that is being leapt into—but it is surely defiling as well. And the agent that has brought about this regression is laughter.[7]

Jonson's willingness to entertain criticism of a playwright he seems greatly to have admired in other respects indicates the complexity of his attitude toward Aristophanes, a complexity often present in classical and Renaissance comments on the Greek dramatist.[8] His ambivalence may explain why *Every Man out of His Humour* is only "somewhat like *Vetus Commoedia*" (Induction, lines 231–32), the differences between that play and its presumed model perhaps being a function not only of historical change and Jonson's need to preserve his own voice but also of his desire to disassociate the laughter his play elicits from the "turpitude" described above (cf. Campbell 1938, 5–14). Similarly, when Asper, himself no mild-mannered satirist, promises in the Induction to that play that our eyes will "flow with distilled laughter" (line 217), he may be pointing out, among other things, that the laughter of the English play has been cleansed of the maliciousness and buffoonery attending Old Comedy.

However, the most important point made in the lines based upon Heinsius is not limited to Aristophanes; at a more general level the passage examines the nature and effect of laughter—or, to be more precise, of a certain kind of laughter, in this instance associated with Old Comedy. Moreover, that Ben Jonson, the author of some of the greatest and most humorous comedies in English, was somewhat ambivalent about what many people would consider the most important aspect of his art is not as inconsistent as it may seem.

Robert Weimann's distinction between "laughing at" and "laughing with" (1978, 254–60)—the former detached and critical; the latter communal and accepting, "the laughter of solidarity rather than of satire"—provides an instructive gloss on Jonson's attitudes in this matter. Jonsonian laughter is predominantly a version of what Weimann calls "laughing at." It is not sympathetic; it does not join together. Rather, it is often scornful, judgmental, and alienating. Laughter within Jonson's plays is usually employed to establish difference and hierarchical relationships: those who laugh hold a position both apart from and superior to those who are are the object of their laughter. Thus, even in the apprentice play *The Case Is Altered,* a detached onstage audience laughs at the emotional outbursts of the Count, Jacques, and Christophero not with sympathy (only Phoenixilla does this) but with scorn: "Ladies . . . will you laugh / To see three constant passions?" Francesco asks (5.11.27–28). In *Every Man out of His Humor*, Puntarvolo hopes—as do so many of Jonson's characters—to "laugh with iudgement" (4.8.96) at someone who is his inferior (in this case, Saviolina); and Clerimont's description in *Epicoene* of Truewit's plan to vex Morose—"it will be an excellent *comoedy* of affliction" (2.6.36–37), he says—provides both an epigraph for that play and a fairly accurate description of the qualities of much of Jonsonian laughter as well.

Yet laughter does not always work only in this way, and perhaps it never does completely. If laughter can create distance and order, it can also undermine by its very nature the detached, careful, and individual response Jonson seems to have wanted from theatergoers. Although the spectators are asked in the Induction to *Bartholomew Fair* (lines 97–98) to pledge "that euery man heere, exercise his owne Iudgement, and not censure by *Contagion,* or upon *trust*," laughter, as Jonson knew very well, is inherently social—or, as he would say, contagious. That is why comedy so often recalls its own communal and popular origins. That is why, too, laughter can be and often is subversive, ridiculing what is usually taken seriously or claims importance for itself (Socrates, for instance) in order to sweep away our arrogant claims to superiority and distinction by reminding us of the inescapable humanity and folly we all share.

This "reductive" form of laughter—a laughter that destroys socially created, and thus unnatural, distinctions in order to reveal an original and fundamental equality—is the subject of the passage quoted above. Moreover, it is this laughter that pervades *Bartholomew Fair,* for Jonson's play presents as devastating a critique of various claims to authority as *The Clouds* directs at Socrates (Heffner 1955, 89–90). Jonson's return in his last great comedy to a form of drama often seen on the seventeenth-century English stage, his apparent reconciliation with the greatest of his contemporaries and, more generally, with his audience, is accomplished in a play whose structure and incidents recall the inclusive reconciliations of Shakespearean romance and whose pervasive and egalitarian emphasis upon flesh and blood owes a great deal to Aristophanes. To understand more fully the implications of this extraordinary mixture, we must look more closely at the play itself.

According to Walter Ong (1977, 136–39), movement along a scale of the senses ranging from seeing to hearing, smelling, tasting, and touching is a movement toward concreteness, matter, indistinctness, and subjectivity. Because the desire "to consider intellectual knowing . . . by analogy with vision responds to the need to 'formalize' intellectual knowledge, to give it definition, distinctness, edge, precision, clarity," the "movement from the analogy of touch to the analogy of sight is a movement from the generic to the specific." Thus, as I have already argued, the Jonson so concerned with judgment and separating himself from his peers is a Jonson who fills his works with visual images and spectators who watch and comment upon the world around them (see Chapters 1 and 2). The Jonson of *Bartholomew Fair*, on the other hand, seems as interested in the other senses as he is in sight, for the play depicts a world in which the sounds and smells of peddlers hawking their wares—toys, food, drink, women—rival the visual splendors of the wares themselves. There is, of course, more than enough to see at the fair, but the other senses—smell, taste, touch—make their claims with an insistence that the characters cannot ignore.

If Father Ong's account of the relation between the various senses is correct, then the sensory barrage that is Bartholomew Fair should move the play-world and its characters away from clarity, order, difference—values that had previously been important to Jonson—and toward their opposites: obscurity, disorder, likeness. And so it does. The power and authority that often accompany the role of spectator in Jonson's earlier plays can no longer be present in this one, because such qualities are predicated upon the distance, in all the various senses of that concept, between onlookers and those they watch. Even so obtuse a character as Adam Overdo recognizes the importance of this distance, though not its impossibility within the world of the play. That is why he announces his plan, to spy out "enormities," in language that asserts the absolute uniqueness (and, unintentionally, the absurdity) of his enterprise—"defie *all* the world," he tells himself; "They may haue seene many a foole in the habite of a Iustice; but *neuer* till now, a Iustice in the habit of a foole" (2.1.2, 7–9; emphasis added)—and comically describes his activities in imagery that connects him with the most powerful and distant spectator of all: God (see Cope 1984, 77–78). So, too, Wasp's ability to watch over Cokes is based upon the apparent gap between his abilities and intellect and those of the fool he is supposed to protect—a gap that gradually erodes as the play progresses and Wasp proves himself at least as foolish as his young companion: he becomes, like Cokes, mesmerized by the sights of the fair—in this case, the game of "vapours" (4.3.116–18)—falls victim to the skills of Edgeworth, and ends up in the stocks. In the process he loses all his authority over the "child" entrusted to his care.

Perhaps the most instructive example of how the fair seems to dissolve the detachment upon which the role of spectator is necessarily based is the experience of Winwife and Quarlous during the play. By virtue of their intelligence and wit both men seem very different from most of the other characters in the comedy and therefore have a much greater claim to the distinction and authority pursued by Overdo, Wasp, and Busy. Indeed, their purpose in going to the fair recalls the attitudes of Truewit and his friends. "These flies cannot, this hot season, but engender vs excellent creeping sport" (1.5.140–41), Winwife says to Quarlous, dehumanizing the fools who will entertain them in order to emphasize the distance between the gallants and the potential objects of their mirth, just as in *Epicoene* Truewit denigrates those he would watch and ridicule.

The moment the two young men enter the fair, however, these differences are no longer so easy to see. Much to Winwife's disgust, they are immediately taken to be the very sort of fools they have come to mock. "That these people should be so ignorant to thinke vs chapmen for 'hem" (2.5.13–14), he complains to Quarlous, his emphasis upon the stupidity of Trash and Leatherhead being an attempt, one suspects, to erect yet another distinction between the gallants and those they encounter.[9] The two hucksters, Winwife might have said, are not intelligent enough to see straight. Unfortunately, the gallant's newly created difference proves as tenuous as did its predecessor. Another of the peddlers recognizes the two men as former companions: "Who's yonder!" Knockem shouts, *"Ned Winwife?* and *Tom Quarlous,* I thinke. . . . will you take a pipe of tabacco with vs?" (lines 20–23; cf. 3.2.4–21). Although Winwife's reaction to this undesired familiarity is to keep his distance—he will neither eat nor drink with those he has met (2.5.50–53)—Knockem transforms even this expression of displeasure into a sign of similarity rather than difference by equating it with an activity especially prevalent at the fair: it is a kind of "vapours" (line 55), he says. Moreover, if a few lines later Quarlous and Winwife mock Ursula's obesity in a manner typical of the detached spectators in Jonson's earlier plays (lines 73–82), they do not do so with the same impunity. There is simply not enough space—literally—between the young men and their target: Ursula overhears their comments and hurls back some of her own, and another of the play's many quarrels ensues. One could scarcely find better support for René Girard's argument that we must learn to think of "violence in terms of a loss of distinctions, or a loss of distinctions in terms of violence" (1977, 56).

In fact, the omnipresent if comic violence at the fair is a corollary of what might be called the fair's egalitarian emphasis on flesh and blood. Ursula strikes back at Quarlous because she will not grant any real difference between the gallant and herself, just as Quarlous and Winwife will later quarrel because Grace cannot distinguish between them. The free-for-all with which Leatherhead's puppet play concludes also accompanies, and is generated by, various denials of difference: between the puppetmaster and the tools of his craft (the puppets attack Leatherhead); between the stage and its audience (Cokes interrupts the puppets, and Busy debates one of them); between "calling" as vocation and as a way of getting someone's attention (5.5.52–53); between male and female (the puppets have no sex). The puppets' battles among themselves and with their human opponents are, as Knockem says (5.4.354), merely additional versions of the endless and nonsensical contradictions of the game of vapours, that quintessential pastime for the denizens of the fair and absurdly appropriate symbol of the sound and fury that is generated within a world lacking clear distinctions. As Thomas Hobbes would argue with more seriousness and urgency several decades later (1968, 185), "during the time men live without a common Power to keep them all in awe, they are in that condition which is called Warre; and such a warre, as is of every man, against every man." In the comic world of *Bartholomew Fair* this "condition" is named "vapours."

The puppet play is in many respects the climax of *Bartholomew Fair*, a play-within-the-play that reduces the happenings at the fair not simply by echoing them on a smaller scale and in a shorter period of time but also by presenting a less sophisticated (more natural? more basic?) version of the events we have been watching onstage. It is not an alternative to the fair but its epitome. Cokes can suggest that the characters "bring the *Actors* along" in order to "ha' the rest o' the *Play* at home" (5.6.114–15) because the puppet play has, in a sense, always been home. It is not a portrayal of what might be or should be; rather, it is a replica, albeit an exaggerated one, of the characters' own experiences. Furthermore, this sort of redundancy is exactly what Leatherhead wanted: "Your home-borne proiects proue euer the best," he tells Filcher and Sharkwell, "they are so easie, and familiar" (5.1.14–15).

The "familiarity" between the world of the puppet play and that of its audience is one more example of the overall emphasis within *Bartholomew Fair* upon what is basic and common. The same is true of an analogous and more important similarity between the ostensibly strange world of the fair and the London society in which the characters spend their everyday lives. I do not mean, of course, that the fair is indistinguishable from London, but the differences between fair and city are for the most part differences of appearance rather than substance, the product of a sophistication that is in this play both superficial and fragile. The quarrels at the fair, for instance, are anticipated by Wasp's obscene sputterings in the fourth scene of the play. Littlewit associates women with horses (1.1.24–25) long before Knockem comes on stage; and Whit's offer to help Quarlous to a "vife vorth forty marks" (3.2.6–8) is only a more straightforward version of Winwife's ongoing pursuit of rich widows and Overdo's attempts to sell Grace to the highest bidder (3.5.273–76). Busy is stuffing himself while still in London, and Winwife anticipates the olfactory overload that the London visitors are about to encounter when he announces the end of his interest in Dame Purecraft by saying that he is "quite off that sent" (1.3.104).

As these parallels suggest, Jonson's handling in this play of what might be called primary and secondary worlds (London and the fair) differs, in a way I find particularly instructive, from that of many other writers of the period—the Shakespeare of the comedies and romances most important among them. In *A Midsummer Night's Dream,* for example, the forest contrasts markedly with the characters' normal society in Athens, and both Northrop Frye and C. L. Barber have taught us that the movement of the characters from Athens to the forest and back again exemplifies a pattern typical of Shakespearean comedy and romance: "The action of the comedy begins in a world represented as a normal world, moves into the green world, goes into a metamorphosis there in which the comic resolution is achieved, and returns to the normal world" (Frye 1957, 182; cf. Barber 1959). The comic resolution Frye describes is usually dependent upon the differences between the green or holiday world and normal society; by moving outside the attitudes and rules that structure their everyday lives, the characters are able to recognize and/or experience "something of great constancy," something that is somehow more natural and fundamental than the socially sanctioned attitudes which within the comedy have tended to obscure or deny that truth. Their journey outside normal society might be described as a return to a more basic kind of existence, which society has in its development and sophistication obscured or left behind. As such, it is a necessary and redemptive yet momentary experience of what the anthropologist Victor Turner has called "communitas," an experience that will enable those involved to reenter and endure the relatively rigid structures of their everyday lives with less frustration and with greater wisdom and understanding: "In human history, I see a continuous tension between structure and communitas. . . . Structure, or all that which holds people apart, defines their differences, and constrains their actions, is one pole in a charged field, for which the opposite pole is communitas, or anti-structure, the egalitarian 'sentiment for humanity' . . . representing the desire for a total, unmediated relationship between person and person" (1974, 274).

Bartholomew Fair, following a Shakespearean model, seems at first

to portray just this opposition between structure and "communitas."
It appears to trace a "reduction" akin to Overdo's plans to reform
Edgeworth: that is, a beneficial return to a more natural past characterized by equality and an acceptance of our common humanity.
But a key feature is missing from Jonson's depiction of this pattern,
and that absence complicates and qualifies the pattern's usual implications. The fair is, as I have suggested, not very different from the
London in which the characters live. Furthermore, their journey is
not a momentary yet necessary and beneficial movement from structure to its opposite and back again; their experience of equality does
not serve finally to reinforce, by making more acceptable and flexible,
the rules and distinctions upon which their society (like all societies)
is founded. On the contrary, their experiences at the fair seem irrev-
ocably to undermine the differences that formerly organized their lives.
What proves momentary, in other words, is not the fair and what it
represents but the system of distinctions that both constitutes the
London with which the fair initially seems to contrast and provides
the basis for that contrast. Unlike the secondary worlds we encounter
in *As You Like It* and *The Tempest,* this one cannot be circumscribed
or left behind. *Bartholomew Fair* implies what Shakespearean comedy
and romance do not: that the apparently coherent structure of its
characters' everyday society is a sham, merely a subtle and sophisticated cover-up of the confusion we see in the last four acts of the play.
The similarities between the fair and London may not at first be as
apparent as the differences, but by the end of the comedy they prove
more important.

As a result, the "communitas" or misrule experienced by the characters ultimately is not, as it usually is in Shakespearean comedy and
romance, conservative. Shakespeare's comedies and romances begin
and end, if only figuratively, with what is for the characters everyday
society. The structure of these dramas is circular because, although
both rule and misrule, court and green world, structure and anti-
structure "are indispensable for human social continuity . . . [and]
neither can exist for long without the other" (Turner 1974, 268), it
is the former half of the dichotomy that takes precedence. In *Bartholomew Fair* there is no such precedence—indeed, no such coexist-
ence. We do not get a mutually beneficial alternation between two

different realms, each necessary, each lacking in itself. We get the triumph of one over the other or, perhaps more accurately, a suggestion that there is in fact really only one world: undifferentiated, disordered, and uncontrollable, the world represented by Bartholomew Fair.

The characters' willingness to forgive and accept one another at the end of this play thus has implications very different from those of similar actions by characters in Shakespeare. Their behavior does not result from a beneficial recognition that human society will wither and stultify if within its structure of differences we fail to make room for human frailty and what human beings hold in common; rather, it stems from the recognition that in a world without important distinctions there is never anything to forgive. As Katherine Maus has argued (1984, 133), nonjudgmental endings in Jonson "are always bought at a price, and that price is human dignity." Overdo will no longer concern himself with discovering "enormities" when the characters return to London (5.6.109), not simply because he has been exposed as the fool he really is but also, and more importantly, because the concept "enormity" presupposes a relatively clear opposition between right and wrong, good and bad. One can hardly speak of deviation in a world that lacks such distinctions.

The meaning of the phrase most obviously associated in this play with forgiveness—Trouble-All's often repeated *Quit yee* (4.1.112–13, for example)—tends to lose its positive aspects for the same reason. In *Bartholomew Fair* to "quit" someone is not so much to deliver or redeem that person from responsibility for a serious crime as it is to dismiss or depart from that person or responsiblity altogether.[10] The former meaning depends, as does the concept "enormity," on distinctions between correct and incorrect, acceptable and unacceptable, whereas the latter implies just the opposite: that one forgives merely because nothing is important enough to be worth remembering for very long.

The final casualty in this relentless dismantling of difference is Jonson himself, not only the Jonson who wrote to instruct and teach—goals that would be difficult, if not impossible, to maintain in a play with the characteristics I have described—but also the Jonson who set out to distinguish himself from his fellow playwrights. As I have already argued, a change in Jonson's attitude toward his own goals was perhaps one reason for his choice of an essentially Shakespearean dramatic form for this play, as well as for the way in which he depicts the competition between Quarlous and Winwife. In addition, Jonson appears to mock his former attitudes throughout the comedy. The Stage-Keeper's fear that he might be overheard by "the *Poet* . . . or his man, Master *Broome,* behind the Arras" (Induction, lines 7–8), for example, echoes Dekker's caricature in *Satiromastix* of Jonson's habit of watching and criticizing the staging of his own plays (see Chapter 2); and Overdo's penchant for making orations, his fondness for Horace, and his exaggerated expressions of stoic endurance sound suspiciously like a parody of both the hero of Jonson's preceding tragedy (Barish 1960, 212–13) and the writer who created him and put Overdo onstage as well.

This self-mockery also colors Jonson's portrayal of John Littlewit, who cannot get through his first scene without displaying an unmistakably Jonsonian contempt for his artistic rivals: "A poxe o' these pretenders to wit! your *Three Cranes, Miter,* and *Mermaid* men! Not a corne of true salt, nor a graine of right mustard amongst them all" (1.1.33–36). The "salt" and "mustard" of which Littlewit speaks are presumably present in the proctor's puppet play, although it is rather difficult for this reader, at least, to discover them. Littlewit's travesty of *Hero and Leander,* we might recall, is an attempt to "reduce" the poem to "a more familiar straine for our people" (5.3.115–17), Leatherhead having earlier commented that "your home-borne proiects proue euer the best, they are so easie, and familiar" (5.1.14–15). We are not expected, of course, to applaud Littlewit's naturalization of Marlowe's great poem. It is simply one more example of the destruction within *Bartholomew Fair* of anything that claims distinction. And Ann Barton has even argued that Jonson's play "directs the attention of its audience" toward this and other English works "in order to remind it that . . . there are better ways of feeling and behaving in difficult personal situations than those displayed by Quarlous, Winwife and Grace Wellborn" (1984, 218).

Yet there are significant connections between Littlewit's rewrite of Marlowe and Jonson's of Shakespeare. The former's handling of his model is in some ways only a much less complex and skillful version of Jonson's use of Shakespearean romance, a similarity that can perhaps be best understood by noting the paradoxical relation between the comments about Shakespeare in the Induction to *Bartholomew Fair* and the play that follows those comments. While the author may say that he is "loth to make Nature afraid in his *Playes,* like those that beget *Tales, Tempests,* and such like *Drolleries*" (Induction, lines 128–30), the play he places before us contains incidents and characters that often seem more bizarre than those the passage criticizes. *Bartholomew Fair* in effect supplies the very things its Induction mocks, and within the same structure as that found in the "*Tales*" and "*Tempests*" toward which the Scrivener is so condescending. However, Jonson's comedy does so—and this is a point that deserves special emphasis—in a native garb. The comedy is, to borrow Leatherhead's recipe for success, a "home-borne proiect." Its setting is England, not Bohemia or some unknown island in the Mediterranean; its wonders are guaranteed to reproduce accurately those the author's countrymen might see at the fair that his play promises to depict (Induction, lines 113–17).[11]

In essence, one might say, Jonson has simply taken "a little paines to reduce" Shakespearean romance "to a more familiar straine" for his audience in order to make it "a little easie, and *moderne* for the times" (5.3.115–17, 121). If he imitates Shakespeare by connecting his art with native and popular traditions, he also retains a vestige of his former competitiveness by "reducing" his story to, or "grounding" it in, a more recognizable and contemporary setting than is usually found in the comedies and romances of his greatest contemporary. *Bartholomew Fair*'s ability to reproduce the qualities of the theater in which it first appeared—"the *Author* has obseru'd a speciall *Decorum,* the place {the theater} being as durty as *Smithfield,* and as stinking euery whit" (Induction, lines 158–60)—is only one more indication that it has been written exactly to the Stage-Keeper's "*Meridian,* and the *Scale* of the grounded Iudgements here, his Play-fellowes in wit" (lines 56–57). For this particular Stage-Keeper "kept the *Stage* in

Master *Tarltons* time" (lines 36–37), a distant golden age of popular and native theater, long since superseded by the more complex, sophisticated, and learned dramas of the Jacobean stage, Jonson's not least among them (cf. 5.1.15–16). Having evidently learned the error of his ways and, consequently, both following and—in the extent of his return to what is common and basic—surpassing Shakespeare, Jonson now pledges to reverse that evolution and writes a play that in its own wickedly comic way leaps "from the Stage to the Tumbrell againe, reducing all witt to the originall Dungcart." Tarlton, it seems, may once more have his day.

That this affirmation of everything that Jonson had spent much of his life opposing is suffused with irony is, it seems to me, unquestionable. Jonson's apparent willingness, finally, to give his audience what it wanted, as well as his use of English rather than classical models, was more the result of frustration over the failure of *Catiline* than a sign of a change in attitude. Stung by the unpopularity of a play that he believed to be one of his greatest achievements and that, ironically enough, reflects Jonson's own growing awareness of the difficulties inherent in the career he had envisioned, Jonson responded by creating a drama that is a *reductio ad absurdum* of Shakespearean romance. And if that comedy seems more genial and good-humored than some of his earlier works, its geniality is a function not of acceptance but of disillusionment (cf. Maus 1984, 134; Ornstein 1969, 46; Sweeney 1985, 188).

Bartholomew Fair is, then, as combative a play in its own terms as are the "comicall satyres" in theirs; it is yet one more attempt to demonstrate, this time indirectly, the superiority of Jonson's art to that of his fellow dramatists. But the subtlety with which *Bartholomew Fair* makes this claim is also to some extent that claim's undoing. Jonson's assertion of superiority is complicated and even undermined by the technique he employs. As noted in Chapter 4, after writing *Every Man in His Humour* Jonson turned away from the Terentian and Plautine models followed by many of his contemporaries and sought an alternative classical tradition in order both to distinguish his plays from those of most other English playwrights and to avoid creating ambiguities of the sort that surround *Every Man in*, a play whose reliance on the conventions of New Comedy widely accepted and imitated by other English dramatists seems to undermine the claims to distinction made in its Prologue.

The clarity that Jonson had endeavored so energetically to create in the period following *Every Man in His Humour* is obscured once more in *Bartholomew Fair*, however, because parody cannot avoid providing a measure of authority to whatever it would debunk. By borrowing the form of his play from one of the traditions that he intended to criticize, Jonson could not avoid calling attention to the influence and power of that tradition. Parodying something that is unknown or has no importance makes no sense, after all, and a parody thus acknowledges by its very existence the stature of whatever it ostensibly attacks. *Bartholomew Fair*'s direct involvement with Shakespeare, then, cannot help but constitute a recognition— grudging and hostile, but present nevertheless—of Shakespeare's importance, and perhaps even of the importance of popular dramatic traditions in general. The *reductio ad absurdum* of Shakespearean romance is an implicit admission that those traditions cannot simply be dismissed.

As such, it is also potentially a first step toward using them in a more positive way—and that is just what Jonson did in much of the remainder of his career. With the exception of *The Magnetic Lady*, whose point of reference is Jonson's own works rather than the works of other dramatists, the plays that Jonson completed after *Bartholomew Fair* draw upon native and popular traditions: *The Devil Is an Ass* and *The Staple of News* upon what Alan Dessen (1971) has called the "late moral play"; *The New Inn*, once again and much less ambivalently, upon Shakespearean romance. (This generalization also applies to *A Tale of a Tub* if, in fact, that play was written toward the end of Jonson's career rather than at the beginning.) The assertions of difference between Jonson and other writers remain, certainly, and Jonson does not really become comfortable with what he is doing (if he ever does) until he writes *The New Inn*. But after what might be called the all-embracing and purgative cynicism of *Bartholomew Fair* and until the disastrous reception of *The New Inn*, Jonson's work displays an increasing willingness to come to terms with English dramatic traditions.

Although I do not intend to chart at length Jonson's use of native traditions in these three plays—that has already been done in detail[12]—I do want to examine briefly some indications in both *The Devil Is an Ass* and *The Staple of News* of Jonson's characteristically self-conscious attitude toward this accommodation, as well as discuss in somewhat more depth his splendid approximation in *The New Inn* of Shakespearean romance—an approximation that is, finally, everything that *Bartholomew Fair* is not: a sincere and admiring tribute to the greatest playwright of Jonson's or anyone else's time.

Although it is a much less successful play than *Bartholomew Fair, The Devil Is an Ass* is closely allied to the masterpiece that precedes it in one important way: it both employs and satirizes an important native dramatic form—in this case the morality play, rather than romance.[13] However, Jonson's treatment of dramatic antecedents in this play is less cynical and corrosive than is his handling of romance in *Bartholomew Fair*. As a result, *The Devil Is an Ass* is for the most part only an up-to-date version of the form it criticizes, and Jonson's alterations carry with them none of the ironies that accompany and complicate what might be described as the "modernization" of older works and traditions in *Bartholomew Fair*. *The Devil Is an Ass* is not a *reductio ad absurdum* of other devil plays; it represents from Jonson's viewpoint a genuine and needed improvement in a dramatic tradition that had become passé.

That is one reason why the drama's most important subject is not greed or folly but the inevitability of change both in society and in a theater whose function is, at least in part, to hold a mirror up to that society. Nothing is forever, Merecraft tells Fitzdottrel, sounding the keynote of the play. "Wee see those changes daily," he explains to his uncomprehending victim. "Nature hath these vicissitudes. Shee makes / No man a state of perpetuity, Sir" (2.4.33, 38–39). The same is true, the drama implies, of literary conventions. Merecraft is only one voice of change in a play that is, among other things, a meditation upon the relation among novelty, anachronism, and cliché both in the playhouse and in society at large. *The Devil Is an Ass* at once employs old stage devices as part of its plot and examines the ability of those devices to represent the complex world of Jacobean England. Not surprisingly, they are found wanting. But Jonson's play does not stop with the diagnosis of this problem; it supplies the cure as well, or so Jonson thought.

These concerns are first brought to our attention in the Prologue, which translates a potential conflict over space between actors and onstage spectators into a commentary both on the play's audience and the play's relation to the tradition of which it is a part. At issue, both literally and figuratively, is whether there will be "room" for Jonson's play, since, the actor tells the onstage spectators, *"This tract* [the stage] / *Will ne'er admit our* vice *because of yours* (lines 8–9). Clearly, this problem cannot be solved merely by getting the spectators out of the way so that the play can begin. Affording room is as much a matter of audience expectations and attitudes as it is of physical movement. Given that the comedy these spectators are about to watch is a *"new* Play," not only because they have not seen it before but also because it represents a new version of a old tradition, it is particularly important that the drama's actors not be forced to perform *"in compasse of a cheese-trencher"* (line 8)—that is, not be forced to conform to the preconceptions and superstitions of their audience. The spectators' "vice" is thus more than their habit of sitting onstage; it is in addition the "vice" of the old moralities, a character that this audience has apparently made its own through yet another "vice": its desire to see only what it has seen before and its general hostility toward innovation.

Within *The Devil Is an Ass* itself, Pug and Fitzdottrel exemplify all three of these "vices." The former character belongs in an interlude; the latter is fond of upstaging whatever play he attends, whether or not he actually gets in the way of the actors' movements. He is also addicted to a form of theater long since past. Both lack that quintessential Renaissance discovery—a sense of anachronism—and both are therefore hopelessly lost in the society of seventeenth-century London.

The first time we see Pug, for instance, he is mesmerized by the skill of Iniquity, a character who may be even more old-fashioned than Pug is, and he ironically praises that equally shopworn refugee from an interlude with a word that designates just what Iniquity is not: "Rare, rare!" (1.1.76), Pug exclaims, only to be corrected by his master Satan, who has a much better understanding of the forces of change: "Peace, dotard," Satan snarls at him, "Remember, / What number it is. *Six hundred* and *sixteene*" (lines 76, 80–81). Pug is both morally and artistically indecorous—"not for the manners, nor the times" (line 120), as Satan says—and that is why he disappears from the play before its conclusion, having had no real effect on the play-world or its inhabitants. He is banished, as it were, to an earlier time and an earlier form of drama, carried away on the back of his fellow anachronism, Iniquity, in a scene that at once recalls and reverses an old morality convention in which the vice did the carrying, not the other way around. Jonson admits Pug and the conventions of which Pug is a part only to reject both as unusable and irrelevant—in other words, as lacking in verisimilitude.

Fitzdottrel is the theatergoing equivalent of the outmoded conventions Pug represents, a spectator whose foolish obsession with the past is precisely what has allowed, so Jonson suggests, those conventions to remain on the Jacobean stage long after they have lost their usefulness. The silliest playgoer in all of Jonson, as well as one of the most disruptive (1.6.31–38; see Chapter 2), Fitzdottrel ironically displays what might be called a Jonsonian disregard for the opinions of others, asserting even in defeat his own demented individuality: "I will be what I am, *Fabian Fitz-Dottrel*, / Though all the world say nay to't" (4.7.93–94). His sense of self is dependent upon his living in a world gleaned from old plays, a world in which devils have cloven hooves (1.3.7–9) and masters beat foolish vice figures (as Fitzdottrel does Pug). As Wittipol notes in speaking of his foolish opponent's habit of borrowing or buying old clothes to wear about town, Fitz-dottrel "thinkes / Himselfe still new, in other mens old" (1.4.24–25). Once more, the central issue is the importance and inevitability of change. Like Pug, Fitzdottrel is absurdly indecorous; he neither speaks nor sees in accordance with the times in which he lives. He is, in effect, out of context, and that fact makes him both a victim of those who understand change and an enemy of a drama that reflects it.

However, understanding and accepting change does not mean in this play that one should mindlessly seek novelty at any cost. Despite its satiric depiction of its own dramatic heritage, *The Devil Is an Ass* does not reject that heritage completely; rather, it preserves the older drama in the only way possible, by transforming it in a manner determined by the demands of a different time and context. In doing so, the play both acknowledges and limits change. Although the comedy's relation to English models may not yet replicate the mostly unproblematic relation between Jonson's works in general and their classical antecedents, it is certainly a step in that direction.

So, too, is *The Staple of News,* which lacks for the most part even the satiric handling of outmoded antecedents that we encounter in *The Devil Is an Ass*. The comedy is one of the last in a long list of English prodigal-son plays—plays that Jonson, together with Chapman and Marston, seems to have mocked some two decades earlier in *Eastward Ho!*—and it takes its place within this tradition with relative ease.[14] Jonson's play does not, of course, simply repeat the elements of that tradition without altering them. Any spectators who came, as did Tatle, to see once more the most popular features of sixteenth-century prodigal-son plays (Intermean after act 2, lines 10–13) were unquestionably but deservedly disappointed: *"That was the old way, gossip, when* Iniquity *came in like* Hokos Pokos," Mirth tells her, *"but now they are attir'd like men and women o' the time, the* Vices, *male and female"* (lines 14–17). Mirth's comments echo those in the Prologue to *The Devil Is an Ass,* with one important difference: her explanation of Jonson's alterations of "the old way" lacks the satiric bite so often present in the earlier play's handling of its dramatic antecedents. Her statement contains little, if any, adverse criticism of the "Hokos Pokos" of earlier prodigal-son plays. A new time requires a somewhat altered version of an old story, Mirth suggests, and what mockery there is in her speech is directed not so much at anachronistic dramatic forms as at those who, like Tatle, wish to see those forms and nothing else.

Jonson is simply not very much interested in differentiating *The*

Staple of News from its literary models, and for good reason. If his play is a new version of an old story, both its novelty and the reasons for that novelty must be distinguished carefully from the headlong obsession with news that propels so many of the characters in the play. "*Looke your Newes be new,* Mr. Prologue, *and untainted,*" Tatle threatens before the comedy even begins (Induction, lines 24–25), introducing a concern that is not only the reason for the Staple's existence within the play proper but also the underlying cause of Peniboy Junior's prodigality. For in Peniboy's opinion, virtue is old-fashioned and conventional moral statements clichés. "No more o' your sentences, *Canter,*" he tells his disguised father, "they are stale, / We come for *newes,* remember where you are" (3.2.14–15). [15]

Unlike Jonson's more careful assimilation and reworking of past dramatic traditions, moreover, the news the characters seek often turns out to be not really very new at all. Most of the individuals who come to the Staple seeking news are in fact seeking what they want to hear. "News" for them is anything, no matter how false or outrageous, that fulfills or confirms beliefs and needs already present. That explains why Censure can paradoxically find the Staple's products at once "*stale! and too exotick*" (Intermean after act 3, lines 14–15), a comment suggesting that in this play apparent novelty may often be only a repetition of a past that has been forgotten. Similarly, the news Peniboy seeks early in the play—"Fresh, from the forge (as new as day, as they say)" (1.5.81)—turns out to be disappointingly familiar. He is told of his own coming of age and his father's death, news that is dated (he knows it already), partially untrue (his father is not really dead), and virtually a commonplace of the English Renaissance theater ("*here's nothing but a young* Prodigall, *come of age,*" Expectation complains in the Intermean after act 1, lines 5–6).

Appropriately, one of the first signs of Peniboy's reformation is his twofold realization that such news has little value (5.1.22–35) and that he must accommodate himself to a past which he had formerly dismissed (his father). He does not simply repeat that past, nor is he completely subservient to it (Peniboy, after all, saves his father from being swindled by Picklock), but he does acknowledge its importance. Like many Renaissance versions of the parable of the prodigal son, this one is basically conservative, a story that chronicles a reconciliation between young and old, present and past. The typical prodigal-son narrative emphasizes the value of what is traditional and established. Within its world innovation is usually a function of the necessary and beneficial connection between new and old rather than a radical separation between past and present. The prodigal discovers and understands his identity by returning to his or her origins and establishing a relationship with them.

These characteristics, in turn, explain why Jonson's choice of this particular dramatic form was perfectly suited to his own situation when he wrote *The Staple of News*. Peniboy Junior's story is in its general outlines a mirror of that of his creator; Peniboy's reconciliation with his father repeats in less complex fashion Jonson's reconciliation with his own native dramatic traditions. With the *Staple of News* that most impressive of seventeenth-century artistic prodigals signaled that he had returned home. [16]

In a similar fashion, when the Prologue to *The New Inn* raises the question of that play's originality by welcoming us *"all, to the new* Inne; / *Though the old house"* (lines 1–2), the apparently contradictory description of the play as both new and old emphasizes its relation to a dramatic past composed both of the works of its author—*"we ha' the same Cooke, / Still, and the fat"* (3–4)—and of Shakespearean romance. In Ann Barton's words, the drama is Jonson's "most impressive and memorable lament for the age of Elizabeth and for the dramatist who was best in it. . . . Shakespeare—with some help from Chaucer, Sidney, Spenser, Lyly, Kyd, and Donne—presides over *The New Inn"* (1979, 417–18). [17]

Barton's list is a remarkably inclusive one; the number of English writers who contribute in one way or another to Jonson's play is an unmistakable indication of his desire to establish a strong link between *The New Inn* and English literary traditions. Nor is this inclusiveness limited to his use of English literary antecedents. In a remarkable reversal of the tendencies that dominated both his life and the plays he created, and without the corrosive irony which suffuses that complex *reductio ad absurdum* of romance called *Bartholomew Fair,*

Jonson condemns in *The New Inn* forces that separate and divide, not those that join together. The characters in this play do not attempt to make distinctions; they endeavor to overcome them.

Lovel's initial activities annoy the Host, for example, primarily because they are connected in various ways with difference. Lovel spends too much time, the Host complains, looking at things through a "multiplying glasse," for instance (1.1.29), and making "*Speculations /* That doe become the age" (lines 32–33; emphasis added). He values analysis and accuracy: "measuring," to the Host's dismay, "an Ants egges, with the Silke-wormes, / By a phantastique instrument of thred, / Shall giue you their iust difference, to a haire" (lines 34–36). He is also disturbingly unlike the other visitors at the inn. Lovel's melancholy is out of place; he is a "sullen ghest" (1.2.31) in a world set apart for merriment, a bad spectator at the theater the Host has created (1.3.126–36). Lovel's sadness is heavy, like the earth (1.2.30–32); his seriousness is, one might say, deadly; his gravity reminds us of the grave. Lovel's interest in "recouering o' dead flyes, with crums" (1.1.37) is at once ironic and futile, for in this play life and fertility are functions of the inclusive forces of merriment. "I must ha' iouiall guests to driue my ploughs, / And whistling boyes to bring my haruest home" (1.1.22–23), the Host explains.

As we might expect, the laughter the Host values so highly is the laughter of acceptance, not of judgment, a "laughing with" that acknowledges our common humanity without reducing that humanity to an Aristophanic "dungcart." Significantly, it is the marvelous unity-in-variety of human behavior, the "throng of humors" (1.3.131–36), that the Host finds so attractive and even attempts to protect from mockery. He is, for example, shocked that Lovel would think that his laughter is directed *at* the young man's frustrations (4.4.275–80); and when Latimer reacts to Beaufort's marriage to Frank in a manner that sounds suspiciously like satire—"Raise all the house in shout, and laughter, a boy" (5.4.50)—the Host immediately interrupts him, most obviously to call the others' attention to the Nurse but also to prevent the intrusion of an alien, and alienating, tone into the merriment.

The business of the first act of the play is to move Lovel somewhat haltingly in the direction of the "whistling boyes" the Host mentions in the opening scene. Lovel must put aside his discordant melancholy and, like Shakespeare's Bassanio, "hazard" in the name of love, turning away from the careful measurements and observations of his experiments in order to "throw the dice." "Cheare vp," the Host tells him; and when Lovel answers "I doe" (1.6.171), he marks the beginning of a series of events that will transform the play's opening expression of anger and discomfort—"I am not pleas'd," the Host tells Ferret in the first line of the comedy—into the song with which it concludes.

Lovel's melancholy and his attraction toward experiments involving measurement and analysis are only, of course, the first of several kinds of separation that the play must heal (cf. Cheney 1983, 183). The Host's anger stems in part from his own previous addiction to Lovel-like activities (5.5.93, 100), and the story of the Frampuls is, as he states, an account of "a strange division of a familie," "scattered," Lovel adds, "as i' the great confusion" (1.5.75–76). There are other divisions as well: between Lovel and the woman he loves, a division generalized both by Beaufort's half-remembered account of Aristophanes' speech in the *Symposium* (3.2.79–84) and Lovel's own account of love as union (see 3.2.152–54); between what Lady Frampul says and what she feels; between the feigned and actual identities of the Host, the Nurse, and Frank.

Paradoxically, the characters are able, unlike Lovel's poor insects, to "recover" from these deathlike divisions (cf. 1.1.37 with 5.5.104–5) because they are involved with two others: the separation between the inn and their normal society, and that between the everyday life of the inn itself and the game over which Pru presides. In each case the secondary world (the inn, the game conducted by Pru) is a place where divisions are healed and problems are solved. Both represent, to borrow Victor Turner's terminology once again, a moment of "communitas," an experience of unity that is difficult if not impossible to repeat within the rules and structures of normal society. Furthermore, the characters' journey into these special worlds is, like that of so many of the characters in Shakespearean comedy and romance, circular. Their movement outside the structures and differences of everyday society concludes with a return to that society. More than anything else, it is the limited nature of the characters' involvement with "communitas" that makes their involvement conservative and socially beneficial. Even the Host leaves the inn at the conclusion of the play and takes his place within the social hierarchy, thereby exchanging the divisions among the members of his family and between his feigned and real identity for social ones. *The New Inn* avoids the all-inclusive dismantling of distinctions of *Bartholomew Fair* by allowing room for, but at the same time carefully limiting, the characters' involvement with a world that unites and brings together. At the same time as it demonstrates that division is unavoidably both painful and deadly, the play also intimates that social order is necessarily based upon making and preserving distinctions.

This double recognition explains why the conclusions both of the Court of Love and the characters' visit to the inn are tinged with sadness: the characters must leave the idealized comfort of these games and reenter a reality that is both divisive and painful (cf. Barton 1979, 415–17). Lovel's discourses on love and valor may depict, in the first instance, a perfect unity between two once separate individuals and, in the second, a self-sufficiency so total as to be impervious to fortune, but these ideals—roads to a "quiet heart," like the inn in which they are affirmed—fully exist only in the special realms the characters have created. Beaufort's contemptible attitudes are proof enough that idealistic love is in short supply, and his vow to appeal to the "*Star-chamber*" (5.5.43–45) in order to get what he wants represents an important and unnerving intrusion of social power and authority into the world the Host has constructed with such care. Lovel himself lacks the fortitude he praises so eloquently (cf. Leggatt 1981, 40–43; Beaurline 1978, 271). The Court of Love ended, he turns in despair to experiments even more absurd than those that the Host criticized in the opening scene, sounding like a bitter version of the Prospero who becomes so caught up in his own art that he forgets momentarily the plot that Stephano, Trinculo, and Caliban have hatched against him:

> how like
> A Court remoouing, or an ended Play
> Shewes my abrupt precipitate estate,

By how much more my vaine hopes were encreas'd
By these false houres of conuersation?

. . . .

I will goe catch the wind first in a sieue,
Weigh smoak, and measure shadowes, plough the water,
And sow my hopes there, ere I stay in *Loue*.
(4.4.251–71)

Even the Host is disillusioned after Pru dismisses the Court: "All failes i' the plot" (5.1.27), he laments.

Although these difficulties are soon dispelled by the extraordinary events with which the play ends, they provide—like the comments on old plays in the final scenes of *The Winter's Tale* or the silence of Antonio and Sebastian as *The Tempest* comes to a close—a glimpse of what lies ahead for the characters once they leave behind the special world in which they have sojourned and reenter their normal society. Secondary worlds like the inn or the Court of Love "are useful only if they proclaim their hypothetical status. . . . However much they attract us in and for themselves, their ultimate purpose is to lead us beyond them" (Berger 1965, 78). We must never, in other words, confuse a golden world with a brazen one.

Jonson complicates the apparently harmonious conclusion of *The New Inn* in one other way. To each of Lovel's two long speeches in the Court of Love, Lady Frampul responds with passionate expressions of admiration. After the first speech, she finds that Lovel "breathes the true diuinity of Loue" (3.2.209); after the second, she desires to "clip the wings of time" so that his speech can continue without end (4.4.226). Her reactions reflect, at one level, the power of the special world in which the characters have immersed themselves. Lovel's earlier silence in the presence of the woman he loves has been transformed within the context of the Court of Love into an eloquence so powerful that it destroys the division between them. Yet because Lady Frampul's speeches occur at the boundary of the "game" Pru leads, they are taken as part of the game itself, not as expressions of her true feelings. "How I am changed," Lady Frampul exclaims, when Lovel completes his discourse on love (3.2.171), only to have that change denied by comments that attribute any alteration in her behavior to her acting skills. "Well fain'd, my Lady," Pru says and, turning to Latimer, adds, "now her parts begin" (line 178; cf. 210, 214–15, 236–37). And although Latimer initially expresses doubts that Lady Frampul is really playing a role (lines 214, 254–56), Pru finally convinces him that "All is personated, / And counterfeit comes from her" (lines 259–60).

As might be expected, Lady Frampul is outraged by her companions' inability to distinguish between game and reality: "Dull, stupid, wench! / Stay i' thy state of ignorance still, be damn'd / An idiot Chambermayd" (4.4.311–13). Though the anger is certainly misplaced (the confusion is more her fault than anyone else's) Lady Frampul's insults are the product not merely of her arrogance but also of the frustration often generated by yet another kind of division, a division that might be called misunderstanding. Frampul's anger is directed at an audience that has failed to comprehend the meaning of her words and so has failed to give her the support that comprehension would provide. When she tells Pru, "Go thy wayes" (line 316), her command makes concrete the gap that now exists between Pru and herself, a gap which is in Lady Frampul's opinion the result of the chambermaid's inability to construct a common bond between them by understanding the true significance of her mistress's statements.

The difficulty that the most intelligent character in this play has in comprehending a woman she knows quite well is perhaps Jonson's subtlest way of calling attention to the fragility of the unions with which the play concludes. The division between Pru's (and Latimer's) understanding of Lady Frampul's words and the intended meaning of those words may be bridged relatively easily, as are the other divisions in the comedy, but it quietly yet insistently predicts the frustrations that may be ahead for the characters once they leave the inn. They will unavoidably and often be divided one from another by misunderstandings, large and small.

Ironically and, to this reader, sadly, the prediction implicit in Pru's inability to understand her mistress turned out to apply all too accurately to the situation of the man who created her. *The New Inn,* like *Sejanus* before it, proved uncannily prescient about a future Jonson could not have envisioned when he wrote the play. As is well known, *The New Inn* was rejected by its Caroline audience, and in "The Dedication, To the Reader," with which Jonson prefaced the published version of the play, he describes this rejection in a manner that reemphasizes some of the concerns I have just now been tracing: "If thou canst but spell, and ioyne my sense; there is more hope of thee," he tells his potential readers, "then of a hundred fastidious *impertinents,* who were there present the first day, yet neuer made piece of their prospect the right way" (lines 3–7). Understanding is here, as it is in the comedy that follows, a matter of piecing together or "joining," but the play's spectators, according to Jonson, were not interested in creating such unions. His most important attempt to accommodate his art to that of his contemporaries was rejected, by his account, because his audience failed to make an accommodation of an analogous sort: between their own needs for self-expression and display on the one hand, and the demands of the play they had come to watch on the other. As Jonson knew, such an accommodation is to some extent an acknowledgment of subservience; it requires a willingness to follow and imitate. He had shown this willingness in writing *The New Inn:* the play turns toward, not away from, the work of other English authors. But the spectators in the playhouse had not come to join his sense by submitting themselves to his drama and its (his) meaning; they had come instead, Jonson states, to "possesse the Stage, against the Play" by replacing its theater with their own: "as the *Stage*-furniture, or *Arras*-clothes, they were there, as Spectators, away" (lines 14–16).

If Jonson's view of his audience mellowed somewhat after the failure of *Catiline* (and I am not convinced that it did), both this dedication and, more spectacularly, the "Ode to Himself" that follows the published version of *The New Inn* announce a return of the open hostility toward spectators that is characteristic of his early plays.[18] Jonson had attempted for much of his career to stand apart from his fellow writers in order to establish his difference from and superiority to them, only to learn to his displeasure that he would probably never succeed in making such distinctions. That knowledge seems to have encouraged an attempt to make peace with native dramatic traditions, an attempt that began in earnest with *The Devil Is an Ass* and culminated in the disaster I have recounted above. Both strategies failed, from Jonson's perspective, because of the fickleness, ignorance, and self-absorption of the spectators in the theater. The division between his plays and the attitudes and needs of the typical seventeenth-century playgoer must have seemed, given the fate of *The New Inn,* unbridgeable.

Jonson's frustrations with his audience may have been compounded, moreover, by his recognition that his attempt to ally himself with native traditions had been made at tremendous cost to his art. His finest dramas are characterized by, among other things, an extraordinary amount of tension and ambivalence—qualities resulting largely from the complex mixture of arrogance, competitiveness, and envy that has been a major concern of this study. As Jonson became less driven by these emotions—as he became, in other words, less concerned with distinguishing himself from other English dramatists—his plays began to lose energy and vitality. What may thus have been, from one perspective, a praiseworthy but somewhat belated realization that his former goals were unattainable and perhaps even morally questionable was, from another, a major cause of the deterioration of his dramatic art. Jonson the dramatist could attain greatness only in opposition to others. And while we can never know with certainty whether Jonson felt that the plays he wrote after *Bartholomew Fair* were inferior to those preceding it, I believe his anger at the reception of *The New Inn* stemmed in part from a realization that he had sacrificed too much of what was best about his plays in a largely unsuccessful attempt to come to terms with his contemporaries.

This knowledge, or something like it, may also explain why in the "Ode to Himself" Jonson's scorn for English theatergoers metamorphoses at one point into scorn for Shakespeare. "No doubt some mouldy tale, / Like *Pericles*" will please those whose "palate's with the swine," Jonson sneers early in the poem (lines 20–22). The contemptuous reference to Shakespeare's first romance may at first seem surprising, given the resemblance between that romance and the one

Jonson is in these lines defending; and Owen Felltham was all too happy to point out this contradiction, noting that Jonson's jests in *The New Inn* "do displease / As deep as *Pericles*" (Herford, Simpson, and Simpson 1925–52, 11:339). In addition, the reference to *Pericles* is certainly self-serving, not to mention inaccurate and perhaps even dishonest.

But Jonson, one suspects, felt that he had no choice if he wished to regain some semblance of the qualities that had characterized his finest dramas. However unfair or hypocritical his criticism of *Pericles*, its function is easily identified: to assert that Jonson's art is radically different from that of his greatest contemporary, despite the obvious and important connections between *The New Inn* and Shakespearean romance. By denigrating *Pericles*, Jonson in effect transformed the essentially imitative relation between his play and its Shakespearean model into an emulative one, reintroducing as he did so the envy and hostility so often associated with rivalry. Accommodation was no longer his goal. [19]

As a result, when Jonson returned to the stage once again, nearly four years after the failure of *The New Inn*, he brought a play that not only contains his most penetrating examination since *Every Man out of His Humour* of the potential antagonism between author and audience (see Chapter 2) but also finds its antecedents in Jonson's own dramatic career rather than in Shakespearean romance or some other popular native tradition:

> The *Author*, beginning his studies of this kind, with *every man in his Humour*; and after, *every man out of his Humour*: and since, continuing in all his *Playes*, especially those of the *Comick* thred, whereof the *New-Inne* was the last, some recent humours still, or manners of men, that went along with the times, finding himself now neare the close, or shutting up of his Circle, hath phant'sied to himselfe, in *Idaea*, this *Magnetick Mistris* (Chorus 1.99–106)

Even if it is not in fact his last finished play, Jonson intended that *The Magnetic Lady* signal the official close of his career, just as he wished to have the revised version of *Every Man in His Humour* announce its beginning.[20] The play completes the circle of his life and works by once more emphasizing the self-sufficiency and exclusivity of his achievement. And in doing so, it reaffirms a personal truth that Jonson had set aside when writing the three dramas that preceded this one: making distinctions is not only an important concern in Jonson's most successful plays; it is their prerequisite.

In this need to make distinctions, as in so many things, Jonson differed markedly from his greatest contemporary. Shakespeare seems to have had relatively little interest in continually distinguishing himself from other English dramatists. Although competitive impulses are sometimes present in his works—the somewhat antagonistic relation between his early dramas and those of Lily and Marlowe come to mind, as do the sonnets dealing with a rival poet—in general, Shakespeare seems to have avoided the militant assertions of distinction that form such an important part of Jonson's career; in one instance he seems even to have commented, indirectly but forcefully, on the futility of such assertions. The occasion was the War of the Theaters, the instrument *Troilus and Cressida,* and I would like to conclude by examining briefly what that extraordinary play has to say about some of the major issues I have been discussing.

Admittedly, Shakespeare's actual role, if any, in the Elizabethan War of the Theaters has remained (like so much of the conflict) something of a mystery. A passage in *Hamlet* (2.2.329–62) seems to indicate more than a passing interest; a statement in the Prologue to *Troilus and Cressida*—"hither am I come, / A prologue arm'd, but not in confidence / Of author's pen or actor's voice" (lines 22–24)— very probably mocks the armed Prologue to *Poetaster.* More intriguing still is a comment by the character Will Kemp in the last of the Parnassus Plays: "O that *Ben Ionson* is a pestilent fellow, he brought vp *Horace* giuing the poets a pill, but our fellow *Shakespeare* hath giuen him a purge that made him beray his credit" (lines 1170–72).

I suggest that *Troilus and Cressida* is the "purge" Kemp mentions—not because, as some critics have suggested, the play contains caricatures of Jonson and his adversaries but because it presents a powerful, if indirect, analysis of the causes, characteristics, and ultimate futility of the theatrical quarrel itself.[21] References to emulation are scattered throughout the play, a fact that may not seem particularly important until it is placed within the context of the entire Shakespearean canon. Although Shakespeare employs the words *emulation* and *emulous* only sixteen times in his works, eight of those usages occur in this play (Spevack 1973, 350), and two of them in passages that are likely to be central to any interpretation of its overall meaning: Ulysses' speech on degree in act 1, scene 3; and his discussion of the destructive effects of time in act 3, scene 3. Whatever else *Troilus and Cressida* may portray, it is a play about (to quote Ulysses' words) the "envious fever / Of pale and bloodless emulation" (1.3.133–34), an "emulation [that] hath a thousand sons / That one by one pursue" and hope to "rush by" and "o'errun" those who have already achieved greatness (3.3.156–63).

As with the literary quarrels at the end of the sixteenth century, a major cause of this competitive behavior is the disappearance of difference, or what Ulysses calls the vizarding of degree (1.3.83; cf. Girard 1975, 142). Within the Greek camp, he argues, an inability to recognize and unwillingness to accept socially established distinctions have led to a form of imitative rivalry in which members of each rank emulate those above them, attempting (like Jonson's Crispinus) first to deny the differences between themselves and their apparent superiors and then to overthrow those superiors altogether and create a new set of hierarchical relationships in the process. Achilles' and Patroclus's penchant for mimicking the words and actions of their leaders (1.3.146–51)—an activity imitated in turn by others (lines 185–96)—is one sign of this unfortunate situation. Another is the Greeks' inability, even after Patroclus's death, consistently to "draw together" (5.5.44), as Nestor urges. In fact, only eleven lines after the aged warrior expresses his hope for cooperation, we see Ajax and Diomedes absurdly arguing over the right to fight Troilus (5.6.9–10), neither one capable of admitting the desirability of a common effort. The inability of potential heroes, like that of rival poets, easily to distinguish between themselves seems inevitably to lead to conflict, even among those who should be allies.

The characters' fondness for making comparisons—from Pandarus's assertion that Cressida "look'd yesternight fairer than ever / I saw her look, or any woman else" (1.1.32–33), to Agamemnon's hope that Achilles' victory over Hector will be "bragless," since "Great Hector was as good a man as he" (5.9.5–6)—also results from their desire to surpass one another. Comparisons in *Troilus and Cressida,* as in the War of the Theaters, are expressions of rivalry: the characters tend to measure themselves and those around them against models (Helen, Hector, Achilles) whom they often hope to displace as well as imitate. While Paris may argue that Helen is someone whom "the world's large spaces cannot parallel" (2.2.162), Pandarus's many comparisons between his niece and this most famous (or infamous) of women imply that, on the contrary, Helen can be imitated and surpassed. And in this play, at least, he is right. Just as Ajax becomes even more vainglorious than his chief model and rival, the presumably inimitable Achilles (5.4.12–17), so Cressida manages to earn a reputation which promises to obscure that of her putative competitor; Cressida, according to Troilus, is a new and extraordinary pattern of fickleness and perfidy:

> O Cressid! O false Cressid! false, false, false!
> Let all untruths stand by thy stained name,
> And they'll seem glorious.
> (5.2.178–80)

Cressida has become, one might say, incomparable; she has achieved the status that Quintilian, we might recall, grants to all successful emulators: "For this glory also shall be theirs, that men shall say of them that while they surpassed their predecessors, they also taught those who came after" (*Institutio Oratoria* 10.2.28). Yet the model Cressida provides is hardly praiseworthy. The ironies that suffuse her victory over Helen, together with those that accompany the analogous triumphs of Ajax over Achilles and Achilles over Hector, suggest that the goals sought by rival poets at the end of Elizabeth's reign might not be worth attaining—more specifically, that the career upon which Ben Jonson had embarked was a hazardous one indeed.

Shakespeare's critique of competing poets has one additional aspect. When Ulysses tells Achilles that an individual's worth is dependent upon the responses of others to that individual (3.3.112–23), he is talking about the power of audience, a power that would finally determine both the outcome of the War of the Theaters and the success of the artistic journey Jonson had mapped for himself. Moreover, Ulysses' message is hardly an encouraging one. Shakespeare seems to have known—both more profoundly and much earlier than Jonson did—that this dependence upon the responses and judgments of others is, at best, problematic and, at worst, self-defeating. "The present eye praises the present object" (line 180), Ulysses warns Achilles and, I would add, Jonson; human judgments are nothing if not changeable; good deeds are "forgot as soon / As done" (lines 149–50). And we need look no further than Shakespeare's handling of his sources to find support for Ulysses' statements. By transforming the heroes and heroines of Homeric epic and Chaucerian romance into figures who invite contempt rather than admiration or sympathy, Shakespeare shows, in effect, that no reputation is lasting and that all victors become victims. Even the creations of the two authors who stand, respectively, at the beginnings of the European and English literary traditions are subject, evidently, to the destructive power of "envious and calumniating Time" (line 174), a power here represented by Shakespeare's uncharacteristic but telling subversion of his own artistic heritage.[22]

Jonson, obviously, would have had much to learn from his greatest contemporary if he had been willing to listen. But though both *Catiline* and *Bartholomew Fair* approach from somewhat different directions the message *Troilus and Cressida* conveys, Jonson was never able, or willing, to accept fully the implications of that message. The unfortunate results are all too easy to list: envy and calumny became his constant companions; his defeats were frustratingly numerous; his victories too often proved, in Ulysses' words, "forgot as soon as done."

Yet this is not, finally, the whole story. If Jonson never attained the stature he sought, his efforts nevertheless have earned for him an important and, yes, distinguished place in the history of English literature. If his career was, by his own standards, a failure, it was a magnificent and fascinating one. And if that career attracted, then as now, sizable portions of both blame and praise, the complexity of this mixture is a testimony to the special complexity of the man himself. Jonson, after all, is not Shakespeare—but then, that is exactly what he spent so much of his life trying to prove.

Notes

CHAPTER 1

1. The Hall-Marston controversy has been detailed by Arlice Davenport in Hall 1949, xxviii–xxxiv. For recent accounts of the War of the Theaters, see Hoy 1980, 1:179–98; and Ingram 1978, 43–54.

2. See Helgerson 1978, 893–911; 1979, 193–220; and 1983, 101–84. As is perhaps already apparent, my view of Jonson complements Helgerson's, and the pages that follow provide additional support for his account of Jonson's "laureate" ambitions. Roger B. Rollin and Don Wayne have examined Jonson from a similar perspective: the former analyzes the English writer's poems on Donne and Shakespeare in order to demonstrate that Jonson's relationships with his contemporaries represent an " 'anxiety of identification' arising out of a strong poet's need to come to terms with his strong contemporaries" (Rollin 1982, 151); the latter argues that for Jonson subjectivity is a form of property that "can be acquired only at the expense of others; and once acquired . . . must be protected in what becomes a struggle to a figurative death in all one's relationships" (Wayne 1979, 93; cf. 1984, 146–60). I have also learned a great deal from Stephen Greenblatt's seminal study, *Renaissance Self-Fashioning from More to Shakespeare* (1980).

3. In Smith 1904, 2:312. Unless otherwise noted, all quotations from Elizabethan critics are from this collection and cited in the text by volume and page.

4. All quotations from Jonson's works are taken from Herford, Simpson, and Simpson (1925–52). They are cited in the text by act, scene (when

available), and line numbers (for plays), line numbers only (for poems and prose works with continuous lineation), or volume and page. I have not followed this edition in the use of the long "ſ" and have spelled out all abbreviated words; otherwise, I have retained Jonson's own spelling and emphasis.

5. See Partridge 1973, 190–95; and Elsky 1982, 97–99.

6. See also Barish 1981, 132–54. Leggatt (1981, 58) comments that in Jonson's plays "at times it seems that what Nature has created is not a collection of individual fools or knaves but a vast amorphous mass of undifferentiated material." Jonson's fear of a loss of distinctions and his ambivalence toward imitative activities may also have been influenced by the arguments of Roman stoics for whom "a sense of exclusivity is the foundation of the moral sense" (Maus 1984, 130).

7. On this contrast, see Greene 1970; and Danson (1984, 183), who points out that "even a Crites cannot escape playing the social game of endless imitation if he is to be anything more than that metaphysical impossibility, a naked breathing self."

8. My discussion of classical and Renaissance attitudes toward imitation is indebted to the researches of Cave 1979; Greene 1982; LaBranche 1970; Pigman 1979 and 1980; Scott 1920; Trousdale 1976; White 1935. Quotations from classical works (with the exception of passages taken from the plays of Aristophanes; see Chap. 4, n. 4) are cited conventionally in the text, as are those from Jonson's contemporaries (Bacon, Dekker, Shakespeare), so that they may be referred to in any edition; the editions and translations I have used may be found under the author's name in Works Cited (following the notes).

9. On this combative form of imitation, which I call "emulation" throughout this study, see the discussions of Cave and Pigman cited in n. 8, above (although the former does not distinguish between the transformative and combative versions of the concept).

10. See Pigman 1980, 23–24. The negative form of emulation is stressed in the most influential modern theories of imitation. See Bate 1970; Bloom 1973 and 1975; and Girard 1977 and 1978. Emulation (although it is not called such) is also an important concern in Greenblatt 1980.

11. For other accounts of the role that imitation plays in Jonson's works, see Clark 1978; Greene 1982, 264–93; and Manley 1980, 189–95.

12. For the original, see Herford, Simpson and Simpson 1925–52, 11:220. Greene (1982, 274–77) also discusses Jonson's complex and ambivalent

attitude toward imitation, arguing that "the ultimate destructiveness of imitation, which Jonson never portrays, would presumably be the series of endless transformations catalogued seductively and wickedly by Volpone as the final enticement of Celia, the dream or nightmare of the perfectly protean."

13. Envy, of course, is also an important attribute of the satiric persona. See Campbell 1938, 48–61. But the importance of envy within the satiric tradition, while it may explain Macilente's behavior in *Every Man out of His Humour,* is not a sufficient reason for the central place this emotion has in the Jonson canon as a whole.

14. See COMPETITOR *sb.* 1, 2; and CORRIVAL *sb.* A.1, A.2., *Oxford English Dictionary* (hereafter, *OED*). I am especially indebted to René Girard's studies (1977; 1978) for enabling me to grasp the connections among a loss of distinctions, imitation, and violence. Kenneth Burke (1969a, 414) also stresses this interrelationship: "We could state the matter formally by recalling the dialectic formula quoted by Coleridge: *inter res heterogeneas non datur oppositio,* a notion that he also expresses by observing that *rivales* are opposite sides of the *same* stream." Burke (1969b, 131) notes that "competition itself is but a special case of imitation. For when you discuss competition as it has actually operated in our society, you discover that the so-called ways of competition have been almost fanatically zealous ways of conformity. . . . From the standpoint of 'identification' what we call 'competition' is better described as men's attempt to *out-imitate* one another"—a point that Jonson himself might well have made.

Walter Ong (1977, 224–26) has argued that the traditional association of poetry with rhetoric encouraged rivalry precisely because that tradition was dependent upon a limited number of conventions: "Rhetorically colored poetic was a poetic of virtuosity, setting poet against poet. . . . This topical poetic clearly calls for an agonistic stance for, if the poet deals with the common store of awareness accessible to all, his warrant for saying or singing again what everybody is already familiar with can only be that he can say it better than others." When this poetic is replaced by one dependent upon print and emphasizing creativity, "combative involvement of poet with poet weakens. There is no contest, for the common grounds needed for contest have been eliminated or minimized." Similarly, "involvement with a living audience weakens . . . [and] the 'audience' here turns into spectators. Between the spectators and the performers there is no struggle." I would situate Jonson's work near the close of the rhetorical tradition Ong describes. His rivalries both with contemporary writers and with his audience (see Chap. 2) testify to the continued importance of a rhetorical poetic in Renaissance England; his involvement with print and his overall visual orientation indicate an attempt to leave that poetic behind.

15. Cf. Kay 1978–79, 18–28; and Pigman 1980, 26–27. On the importance of comparative modes of thought in the seventeenth century, see Manley 1980; and Foucault (1970, 55) whose description of what he calls the classical episteme often sounds as if it had been made to explicate Jonson: "The activity of the mind [during the classical age] . . . will therefore no longer consist in *drawing things together* . . . but, on the contrary, in *discriminating,* that is, in establishing their identities, then the inevitability of the connections with all the successive degrees of a series. In this sense, discrimination imposes upon comparison the primary and fundamental investigation of difference." Similarly, Burke's discussion of contextual definition (1969a, 25)—a discussion which, significantly enough, is based upon some of the ideas of the seventeenth-century philosopher Spinoza—is also an instructive gloss on Jonson's practices: "Spinoza explicitly held that all definition is 'negation,' which is another way of saying that, to define a thing in terms of context, we must define it in terms of what it is not. And with scholastic succinctness, he formulated the paradox of contextual definition in four words: 'all determination is negation; *omnis determinatio est negatio.*'" Cf. the initial chapter in Greenblatt 1980. This emphasis upon difference can also be found, of course, in the work of modern linguists (notably Ferdinand de Saussure) and intellectuals (e.g., Jacques Lacan and Jacques Derrida).

16. Beaumont's poem is taken from Herford, Simpson, and Simpson 1925–52, 11:374–76. I have spelled out all abbreviated words.

17. Cf. Wayne 1979, 93. Wayne's essay and his book *Penshurst* (1984) are powerful examples of the social and political contextualizing that in Renaissance studies has come to be associated with the "new historicism." My discussion of Jonson has important affinities with Wayne's work in particular and with the new historicism in general, but I am primarily interested in the way Jonson's career and works were shaped by his relations with and attitudes toward other writers and his audience rather than by his involvement with patrons and the crown. The latter context has been well served by recent criticism; I am attempting to add to our understanding of the former.

18. For examples of the strategies employed by the "sons," see Herford,

Simpson, and Simpson 1925–52, 11:390–91, 400–402, 455–59. For Jonson's attempt to dismiss or dominate Brome, see the "Ode to Himself" appended to *The New Inn,* and *Ungathered Verse* 38.1–10.

19. Obviously, I do not agree with Richard Peterson's conclusion (1981, 158–94) that Jonson's criticisms of Shakespeare are made less problematic because Jonson is echoing Horace's comments on Lucilius, however instructive Peterson's reading of Jonson is in this and other areas. Given the ambivalent nature of Horace's own relations with other writers (see Chap. 3), the Horatian background complicates rather than simplifies our understanding of Jonson's attitudes toward his greatest contemporary. At the very least, one might note that the poem (like the epigram to Beaumont) raises the possibility of envy on Jonson's part (this time in the opening line) and that it is filled with competitive impulses toward John Heminge and Henry Condell, William Basse, and, finally, Shakespeare himself. For readings closer to my emphasis, see Lipking 1981, 138–46; and Rollin 1982. Leonard Digges, one of Jonson's contemporaries, was perhaps the first to question Jonson's intent in the Shakespeare poem; see Freehafer 1970.

20. Joyce Van Dyke (1979) has traced this conflict in detail. Jackson (1969) also emphasizes the competitiveness of the world of Jonson's major comedies, but I disagree with her conclusion that Jonson's endings appeal "to the conviction of mediocrity—the belief that real strength is social strength, that real meaning is the meaning of the group." Cf. also Alvin Kernan's discussions (1973; 1976, 173–80) of Jonson's characters as alchemists attempting to transform themselves and their world in a manner that satirizes Renaissance notions of human grandeur and power. I find Jonson's attitude toward competition and human aspiration more complex than this.

21. See Macpherson (1962, 9–106; 1968) for illuminating discussions of this aspect of Hobbes's thought. Wayne (1979) also discusses points of contact between Jonson and Hobbes.

22. Cf. Foucault 1970, 120: "The fundamental task of Classical 'discourse' is *to ascribe a name to things, and in that name to name their being.*"

23. For negative comments from Weever and Marston, as well as the accounts of Drummond and Howell, see Herford, Simpson, and Simpson 1925–52, 1:151; 11:363, 373–74, 419–21; the positive view of Jonson's activities is a constant refrain in *Ionsonus Virbius* (11:429–81). The most notorious modern description of Jonson's personality is Wilson's "Morose Ben Jonson" (1948). For a more sympathetic and instructive assessment see Pearlman 1979.

CHAPTER 2

1. See, e.g., Greenblatt 1976, 103; Sweeney 1982, 233; and Thayer 1963, 58–68.

2. The seminal study of Jonson's attitude toward his audience is, of course, Jonas Barish's "Jonson and the Loathéd Stage" (1981, 132–54). Other helpful studies include Beaurline 1978, 1–34; Carlson 1977; Duncan 1979; Fish 1984; Kay 1970; Leggatt 1981, 233–74; Parker 1977; Pearlman 1979; and Sweeney 1981, 1982, 1985. Also of interest are Katherine Maus's comments on the stoic belief that "all dependency and incompleteness implies moral weakness" (1984, 15).

3. See UNDERSTAND *v. trans.* I.9 (*OED*).

4. This strategy is especially common in the masques. Jonson published his *Masque of Blackness,* he tells us, "in dutie . . . to that *Maiestie,* who gaue them [the spectacles] their authoritie, and grace" (lines 9–10). In *Hymenaei* he finds the skill of the performers such that they *"left it doubt-full, whether the* Formes *flow'ed more perfectly from the* Authors *braine, or their feete"* (lines 313–15). On the relation of Jonson's court entertainments to royal authority, see Orgel 1975. In general, the relationship of Jonson's masques to their audience was much less problematic than was that of his plays to theirs. A masque concludes, after all, by bringing its audience into the spectacle itself, and so "annihilating the barrier between the ideal and the real, and including the court in its miraculous transformations" (Orgel and Strong 1973, 1:1; see also Orgel 1965). No such possibility was available to Jonson in the public and private theaters, where the audience was much more threatening and Jonson far less willing to give up his authority.

5. See OBSERVER *sb.* 2, 3; and REGARD *v.* I.1, I.4a, I.4b (*OED*). At times, Jonson seems to wish to distinguish between an audience that hears and spectators who see—e.g., in the "Prologue for the Stage" that precedes *The Staple of News,* and in both epilogues to *The New Inn.* See Maus 1984, 158–59. But Jonson's usual tendency was to conflate the two activities, because, as Stephan Orgel (1975, 19) has argued, there was no rigid distinction between verbal and visual theater during the period. That is why, in his quarrel with Inigo Jones, Jonson did not deny the importance of spectacle; he simply attempted to keep the visual elements of the masques from overwhelming the verbal ones (see Orgel and Strong 1973, 1–14). Throughout this study, I have used the terms *audience* and *spectators* interchangeably to designate the individuals who respond to the activities of another (whether that other is Jonson or one of his char-

acters). In Jonson, an audience sees as well as hears, spectators listen as well as watch.

A visual emphasis does, however, dominate many of his descriptions of how individuals respond to others, and for good reason. As Walter Ong (1977, 137) has shown at length, "The drive to consider intellectual knowing . . . by analogy with vision responds to the need to 'formalize' intellectual knowledge, to give it definition, distinctness, edge, precision, clarity." These are quintessentially Jonsonian values; moreover, Jonson would have encountered a strong emphasis upon observation and the attitudes associated with it in the work of several men who had an important influence upon him—William Camden, Francis Bacon, and Peter Ramus among them (I discuss such connections later in the chapter). That Jonson calls our attention to hearing rather than seeing in the prologue and epilogues noted above may in part be the result of his difficulties with Inigo Jones; more important, it is also an indication that when writing *The Staple of News* and *The New Inn*, Jonson had momentarily turned away from his former attempts to separate himself from other writers (see Chap. 5).

6. Sweeney (1981; 1982) argues that audiences are usually victimized in Jonson's world, but his analysis overlooks the power and authority that Jonson's spectators often command. The role of audience, like that of author/actor, is, according to this English dramatist, a fundamentally ambivalent one: each role necessarily involves both domination and subservience.

7. For an extended analysis of the political implications of watching and observing, see Goldberg 1983.

8. In Pearlman's words (1979, 377), "Jonson's life and more especially his writings are replete with instances of assertion and attention-getting behavior."

9. The quotation is taken from Jonson's "Dedication to the Reader" (line 10) which precedes *The New Inn*.

10. See Newton 1982, 33–36: "Written for the study but resistant to interpretation, printed books offer to authors two new things: completeness, an assurance of the self-contained work (neither excerpted nor glozed), and eponimity, a name attached to the work—author and authority." Thus, "we find in Jonson a sense of the printed text as an authorized and established object of criticism—implying, and imposing from within, its own rules for reading," which, among other things, discourage "liberty of interpretation and the imposition of allegory."

11. Alexander Gill's description of the opening performance is reprinted in Herford, Simpson, and Simpson 1925–52, 11:346–48.

12. The image of "the skeene of silke" was evidently an attractive one to Jonson. In *Discoveries* (lines 1997–99) he inserted a similar passage into a translation of a section of Vives's *De Ratione Dicendi:* "Our style should be like a skeine of silk, to be carried, and found by the right thred, not ravel'd, and perplex'd; then all is a knot, a heape."

13. At first glance, this discussion seems to exemplify what Annabel Patterson (1984, 11) has called the "hermenuetics of censorship," a set of practices in which on "the one hand writers complain constantly that their work is subject to unauthorized or unjust interpretation; [and] on the other they gradually developed codes of communication, partly to protect themselves from hostile and hence dangerous readings of their work, partly in order to be able to say what they had to publicly without directly provoking or confronting the authorities." That Jonson at times participated in such a system is undeniable, and his repeated emphasis upon the importance of authorial intention and context might thus be described as simply a strategic attempt to protect himself from prosecution. But this is only a partial explanation of a very complex set of attitudes. Jonson's ideas about interpretation need also to be examined within the context of the literary career he sketched for himself and the widespread change in methods of understanding that I attempt briefly to describe below. Jonson's views were protective in ways, and had origins in concerns, other than those Patterson has detailed.

14. Cf. Jonson's comments on the fate of Fletcher's *Faithful Shepherdess,* a play that was mistreated by the "many-headed *Bench*" and suffered, as a result, a *"Martirdome,"* which Jonson vows to revenge by praising his friend's "murdred *Poeme*" ("To the worthy Author M. *Iohn Fletcher*" lines 1, 13–14).

15. The literature on this subject is extensive. Among the many studies of allegorical interpretation during the classical, medieval, and Renaissance periods, I have found the following particularly helpful: Allen 1970; Auerbach 1959; Hanson 1959; Preus 1969; Robertson 1962; Smalley 1964; Trousdale 1973 and 1982; Tuve 1966; and Wallace 1974.

16. For fine analyses of Erasmus's interpretive methods, see Boyle 1977; and Cave 1979, 78–124.

17. On Petrarch, see Greene 1982, 81–103. Boccaccio's doubts can be found in the preface to his *Genealogia Deorum Gentilium*.

18. On Reformation exegesis, see Bornkamm 1969; Forstmann 1962; Lewalski 1979; and Preus 1969.

19. For accounts of this development in addition to Kelley's, see Ferguson 1979; Franklin 1963; Fussner 1962; Felix Gilbert 1965; Levy 1967; Manley 1980; Pocock 1967; and Quint 1983. As Foucault (1979, 159) implies, these tendencies might also be discussed in relation to the emphasis upon property that is one of the hallmarks of capitalism—a connection suggested as well by a Jonson who talks about audiences "possessing" stages and "picking the lock[s]" of scenes, or a critic who uses the phrase "coming to terms" for the final chapter heading in a study emphasizing Jonson's competitiveness. See also Wayne 1979. The language with which we talk about identity and individuality seems inextricably bound up with the language of capitalism, and I certainly do not intend to deny either that connection or its importance. But I have in general found it more useful to place Jonson's beliefs and activities within contexts somewhat more circumscribed than this economic system: the proliferation of English poets and dramatists toward the end of the sixteenth century; the beginnings of historical understanding in England; the works of Horace and Aristophanes, and so on.

20. Wilson Engel (1980, 98) has suggested that "just how the temperaments of the antiquaries as a whole influenced Jonson and the other serious dramatists is a matter for further study." I have attempted to fill in some of the gaps in this area, as have several others. Richard Peterson (1981, 56–59) for example, has linked Jonson's emphasis on praise to Camden, and Edward Partridge (1973, 194) has pointed out that Jonson perhaps received from his teacher "an historian's sense of the holiness of fact." The best modern analyses of Camden's historical methods can be found in Fussner (1962, 230–52), and in Wallace MacCaffrey's introduction to the Chicago edition of Camden's *History* (1970, xxiv–xxxii).

21. Cf. Foucault's comment (1970, 132) that "observation, from the seventeenth century onward, is a perceptible knowledge furnished with a series of systematically negative conditions"—a statement that has some important connections with Jonson's attempts to educate spectators in the theater. Ramus's influence on Jonson's *English Grammar* may also have been due to the French writer's visual emphasis. According to Walter Ong (1958, 151), Ramus's "interest both in logic and explicitness, in an 'object' (of knowledge) rather than a 'subject' (of discourse)

had drawn him further still toward the visile pole with the typical ideals of 'clarity,' 'precision,' 'distinctness,' and 'explanation' itself—and best conceivable in terms of some analogy with vision and a spatial field." The compatibility of these impulses with some of Jonson's is unquestionable.

22. According to Wesley Trimpi (1962, 146), in the epistle to Selden, Jonson's phrase "newnesse of sense" refers to the historian's careful observation of particulars; similarly, Selden's "antiquity of voice" is his "use of recorded history which gives chronological and ethical coherence to the fragments of individual experience."

23. See, e.g., Digby's worries about whether he had accurately reproduced Spenser's intention, as he attempts to explain a stanza of *The Faerie Queene* to Sir Edward Suckling (Tayler 1967, 203–13).

24. See, in addition to Nelson (1973), John Steadman's comments (1974, 85–89) on the potential conflict between neoclassical ideals and allegory: "Neoclassical theory not only rationalized poetic method, but tended to bypass allegorical problems by emphasizing alternative arguments for the moral authority of poetry, and to undercut the traditional allegorical methods by stressing probability and verisimilitude." As a result, "though there is no inherent contradiction between critical insistence on verisimilitude and probability in imitation and an emphasis on hidden allegorical content . . . they frequently coexist in uneasy tension; and in the late Renaissance and during the eighteenth century this sometimes verges on open conflict." Cf. also Hardison 1972. Jonson provides a striking example of the tendencies Steadman has identified.

25. For some classical examples of these associations, see Cicero, *De Oratore* 1.8.31–32, 2.7.30, 2.44.187; Quintilian, *Institutio Oratoria* 10.1.2, 21, 12.1.35–36, 12.9.3; and Horace, *Satires* 2.1.39–41. Renaissance versions can be found in Puttenham 1906, 166, 207; Smith 1904, 1:164; Spingarn 1908–9, 2:19–21, 25; and Tuve 1947, 180–91, 247.

26. Peter Carlson (1977) provides a fine account of Jonson's ideal spectator.

27. My understanding of this aspect of Bacon's system is indebted to Fish 1972, 78–155. Other accounts of the scientist's influence upon Jonson can be found in Beaurline 1978, 198–200; Newton 1977, 176–84; and Trimpi 1962, 86. Bacon's commitment to careful analysis is, of course, everywhere apparent—e.g., in *The New Organon* 1.51: "To resolve nature into abstractions is less to our purpose than to dissect her into parts,

as did the school of Democritus, which went further into nature than the rest."

It is also worth noting that the verisimilitude Jonson apparently sought paradoxically undermined the detachment he required of his readers and spectators by encouraging them to believe too strongly in the reality of the fictions he created. See, e.g., his attack upon the credulity of his audience in "To the Readers," an address he inserted in the published version of *The Staple of News* between acts 2 and 3. Jonson's need to control this potential problem may explain why, in Arthur Kirsch's words (1972, 17), "One of the most persistent and curious results of seventeenth-century theatrical attempts to become more realistic is that the attempts often call attention to their own artifice."

CHAPTER 3

1. Dekker, "To the World" (prefatory letter to *Satiromastix*), lines 14–16. The Horace to whom these lines ostensibly refer is, of course, a caricature of Jonson.

2. On these and related points, see Beaurline 1978, 21–22; Miner 1971; Peterson 1981; and Pierce 1981.

3. Horace's relation to Lucilius has been instructively discussed by Brink 1963, 156–69; Fiske 1920, 126–32; Knoche 1975, 80–81; and Rudd 1966, 86–131. Peterson (1981, 158–94) analyzes Jonson's use in his poem on Shakespeare of material drawn from Horace's criticisms of his predecessor. Horace's attitude toward Pindar may have been characterized by a similar ambivalence. Note, e.g., the complex tone and function of one passage in which he apparently praises the Greek poet: "Whoever strives, Iulus, to rival [*aemulari*] Pindar, relies on wings fastened with wax by Daedalean craft, and is doomed to give his name to some crystal sea" (*Odes* 4.2.1–4). What Horace seems to give with one hand, he takes away with the other.

4. Crispinus's relations with both Horace and Hermogenes parallel in almost every respect the relations between established and upwardly mobile courtiers in the courts of Elizabeth and James. As Whigham (1984, 33, 42, 60) explains: "Those who would maintain their privileged position now had to constitute their own fundamental difference from their ambitious inferiors. . . . On the other side, those who would rise aimed to make themselves indistinguishable from their future peers, if possible by persuading those peers themselves." The presence of imitative

rivalry at court also created a complex and often antagonistic relation between performers (those who wished to ascend the social hierarchy) and spectators (those who presumably had already established a position of authority), because those spectators, like their counterparts in the theater, often were performing as well: "When all audience members are also performers, judgments become performances and are subjected to reinterpretive pressures. . . . what the courtier wants [from his audience] is a sense not only of the rhetorical requirements that confront him but also of his rhetorical success. And it is precisely this latter sense that the situation ultimately denies him." Crispinus (and Jonson) would have had no difficulty understanding this predicament.

5. See RIVALIS II.A and II.B in Lewis and Short 1879; and COMPETITOR *sb.* 1, 2 and PARALLEL *sb.* B.5 in *OED*. Jonson's knowledge of the etymological origin of the English word *rival* is indicated by a passage in *Cynthia's Revels*. Instructing Asotus on the intricacies of giving an opponent the *"dor,"* Amorphus advises: "Your *Rivalis,* with a dutifull, and serious care, lying in his bed, meditating how to obserue his mistres, dispatcheth his lacquay to the chamber, early, to know what her colours are for the day, with purpose to apply his weare that day, accordingly: You lay wait before, preoccupie the chamber-maide, corrupt her, to returne false colors; He followes the fallacie . . . and you giue him the *dor"* (5.2.48–56). See also Chap. 1, n. 14.

6. See Barish's description (1960, 123–30) of Tucca's "bizarre lingo."

7. Jonson's treatment of Ovid has attracted a great deal of critical attention. See, e.g., Campbell 1938, 125–28; Carr 1978; Jackson 1968, 23–30; Thayer 1963, 39–49; and Waith 1951.

8. In several of his poems Horace has a great deal to say about audience, much of it negative. *Epistles* 1.19 is one example; *Epistles* 2.1, addressed to Augustus, is another, a sort of Horatian version of the quarrel between the ancients and moderns. It is worth noting that the latter begins by contrasting the Roman people's ability to praise and respect Caesar, while he is alive, with their tendency to resent and envy all other contemporary greatness: "Yet this people of yours, so wise and just in one respect, in ranking you above our own, above Greek leaders, judges all other things by a wholly different rule and method, and scorns and detests all save what it sees has passed from earth and lived its days" (lines 18–22). Horace then provides a history of poetry, in essence a history of improvement and progress (lines 118–67), until that history

proceeds to the plays of Plautus and the spectators who enjoy them—both equally foolish. Not surprisingly, these spectators have a great deal in common with those Jonson complains about so often: Democritus, Horace tells us, "would gaze more intensely on the people [in the audience] than on the play itself as giving him more by far worth looking at. But for the authors—he would suppose that they were telling their tale to a deaf ass. For what voices have ever prevailed to drown the din with which our theaters resound?" (lines 197–201). Jonson probably felt that nothing had changed in the centuries since these lines were written.

9. On the pessimism of both the conclusion and the "Apologetical Dialogue," see Jones 1967; and Leggatt 1981, 100.

10. See Barish 1965; Boughner 1961; Bryant 1952; Dutton 1978a; Evans 1971; Hamilton 1971; Patterson 1984, 49–58; and Wikander 1979. The most stimulating account is Goldberg's (1983, 176–85), which argues that the play depicts a "sphere in which the body of the ruler, opaque and transparent, extends to the body politic."

11. Jonson's use of his sources in *Sejanus* has been detailed by Barish 1965; Boughner 1958; Bryant 1952; Duffy 1947; and Dutton 1978a.

12. The two aspects of the play are complementary and should be taken into account in order to understand fully what it has to say about interpretation. Sweeney (1981, 68) reads the tragedy as a study of the victimization of audience but says little about the way in which Sejanus maliciously misreads his enemies' words and actions in order to further his own ends. Patterson (1984, 52–53), on the other hand, argues that the trial of Cordus is a dramatization of "the hermenuetics of censorship," a dramatization that "allows Cordus to protest a political climate of overdetermination" in such a way as actually to encourage curiosity about the play's relation to contemporary events and figures, but seems to overlook Tiberius's manipulation of the Roman populace.

13. Goldberg (1983, 176–85) discusses the political implications of Tiberius's inscrutability, a quality affected by James I as well. For other assessments of Tiberius's role as artist, see Duncan 1979, 142; Marotti 1970; and Sweeney 1981, 79–81. The probable source for Jonson's emphasis upon Tiberius's subtlety was Dio's portrait of the emperor in Book 57 of his *Roman History*.

CHAPTER 4

1. Russ McDonald (1981, 302, 298) also stresses the importance of rivalry and competition in *Sejanus, Volpone, Epicoene,* and *The Alchemist,* arguing that "all of Jonson's intriguers are prima donnas, and the competition that determines the endings is a form of the artistic rivalry common to performers." However, I disagree with his contention that in these plays Jonson is satirizing the "impulse to set oneself apart." See also Jackson 1969.

2. For other discussions of Jonson's indebtedness to Aristophanes, see Barton 1984; Dick 1974; Gum 1969; and Thayer 1963. My understanding of the relationship between the two dramatists has benefited greatly from Judith Engle's (1983) excellent study of imitative rivalry in *The Knights.*

3. On Randolph and Aristophanes, see Davis 1967, 105–18. Boas (1914, 322–46) links topical plays performed at Cambridge University to Old Comedy, but the presence of topical allusions in a comedy is not sufficient evidence to place that drama within this tradition. Aristophanes' place in sixteenth-century grammar school curricula has been discussed by Baldwin (1944, 80, 103, 192, 335–36, 457, 539); Boas (1914, 16–18) describes university productions of the Greek playwright's comedies.

4. Quotations from Aristophanes' plays are taken from the translations by Alan Sommerstein and David Barrett (Aristophanes 1964; 1973; 1977). Page references following each quotation refer to the appropriate edition.

5. For example, Demetrius (*On Style* 3.50) praises Aristophanes' skill at burlesque; and Maggi (Weinberg 1961, 377), Minturno (1970, 357), and Scaliger (Padelford 1905, 44, 67–68) comment upon his penchant for defending himself and attacking the works of other writers.

6. Cf. Dick 1974, 50; and Gum 1969, 108–10. Jonson's inductions and choric passages are also indebted to the prologues of Roman comedies (esp. those of Terence), but his practice is much closer to that of Aristophanes, most notably in its combativeness. For a general account of dramatic inductions during the English Renaissance, see Greenfield 1969.

7. On the gallants as exemplars of aristocratic ideals, see Kay 1975–76; and Shapiro 1973.

8. The gallants' competitive tendencies have been instructively discussed from other viewpoints by, among others, Heffner 1955, 87–88; Leggatt 1976, 227–228; and McDonald 1981, 291–92.

9. Anderson (1970, 357) points out that after his initial blunder with Morose, "Truewit's subsequent actions and speeches are motivated by his desire to reinstate himself in the society and good graces of Clerimont and Dauphine."

10. As a result, I would qualify somewhat Leggatt's argument (1981, 108) that *Epicoene* itself is "a festive occasion that brings a cross-section of society together for a common purpose." Cf. Barish 1972, 22–23. Like the Aristophanes of *Peace,* Jonson envisions a celebration that is exclusive as well as inclusive, one that will prove his difference from other playwrights.

11. An extensive listing of Jonson's sources for *Catiline* can be found in Bolton and Gardner 1973, 176–93.

12. See Burke's comments (1969a, 106–7) on the tendency of the phrase *a part of* to become its opposite, *apart.*

13. The most extensive comparison is in Jackson (1968, 152–57), although I do not completely agree with her assessment of the relationship and of the play as a whole.

14. This is one reason for the many condemnations of sleep in the tragedy— by Sylla (1.1–2, 9–10), Cethegus (1.210–13), Catiline (1.81–81, 409–10; 5.379–82), and, for different purposes, Cicero (3.238–42, 438–42), to mention some of the more important instances.

15. It may also be worth noting that Catiline's defiance in the face of what he feels to be mistreatment by his presumed inferiors sometimes has a Jonsonian ring; see, e.g., 3.116–43; 4.497–99.

16. Cf. Lawry's comments (1982, 400–403) on Rome as parent of Catiline and Cicero.

17. For discussions of Cicero's flaws see, among others, Dutton, 1978b; Echuero 1966; Goldberg 1983, 196–202; and Warren 1973.

CHAPTER 5

1. Jonson did, certainly, draw upon English dramatic conventions in his earlier plays. Baskervill (1911), Barton (1979; 1981; 1984), and Dessen (1971), among others, have discussed at length Jonson's use of native traditions. But in the dramas that preceded *Bartholomew Fair,* that indebtedness is unannounced and not a major interpretive issue in the plays themselves. *Bartholomew Fair* differs markedly from the plays of the 1616 folio in both the extent and the openness of its borrowings.

2. On the comedy's relation to Shakespearean drama, see Baskervill 1911, 13; Cartelli 1983; Colley 1977; Cope 1984, 76–77; Donaldson 1970,

51; Hawkins 1966; Leggatt 1981, 69; Rhodes 1980, 151; and Sweeney 1985, 164–73.

3. Cartelli's is the best analysis of the relation between Jonson's play and Shakespearean romance, and I have found his discussion very instructive. However, I disagree with Cartelli's assessment (1983, 171) that in *Bartholomew Fair* "Jonson transforms what starts out as a parodic impulse into wholesale acceptance of the same kind of theatrical extravagance which inspired his earlier diatribe against Shakespeare." Jonson's use of and attitude toward Shakespeare are more ambivalent than this account admits.

4. See REDUCE *v. trans*. I.1, I.2, I.4, I.5, II.8, II.10, III.19, IV.25, IV.26 (*OED*).

5. On the relation between *Bartholomew Fair* and Aristophanic comedy, see Gum 1969, 169–87; Heffner 1955, 97; Potter 1968; Rhodes 1980, 143; and Thayer 1963, 130–39.

6. The two sentences in Heinsius's *Ad Horatij de Plauto & Terentio juidicium, Dissertatio* are as follows: "Risus enim cum atroci alicujus calamitate conjunctus, fit immanis ac barbarus. . . . Quod profecto est a pulpito ad plaustrum redire" (Truly, laughter joined to some horrid injury becomes monstrous and savage. . . . Because it has begun to turn back from the stage to the cart; Herford, Simpson, and Simpson 1925–52, 11:289). Jonson's version is both longer and more scornful.

7. An earlier passage in *Discoveries* (lines 285–93), this one dealing with jeering and lying, also joins an appeal to popular tastes with laughter and the destruction of distinctions: "Hee [a writer] shall not have a Reader now, unlesse hee jeere and lye. . . . the gentle Reader rests happy, to heare the worthiest workes misinterpreted; the clearest actions obscured; the innocent'st life traduc'd; And in such a licence of lying, a field so fruitfull of slanders, how can there be matter wanting to his laughter? Hence comes the *Epidemicall* Infection."

8. A brief account of Aristophanes' critical fortunes during classical antiquity can be found in Alan Sommerstein's "Aristophanes in Antiquity," (Aristophanes 1977, 9–20). See also Campbell 1938, 1–14; and Grant 1924. The most extensive classical attack upon the Greek dramatist is Plutarch's fragmentary "Comparison of Aristophanes and Menander" in the *Moralia*. He likens Aristophanes' poetry to "a harlot who has passed her prime and then takes up the role of a wife, whose presumption the many cannot endure and whose licentiousness and malice the dignified abominate. . . . For the fellow seems to have written his poetry not for

any decent person, but the indecent and wanton lines for the licentious, the slanderous and bitter passages for the envious and malicious" (3–4). Several Renaissance critics—Castelvetro, Robertello, Trissino, and Sidney, among them—were similarly uneasy about the nature of Aristophanic laughter. Heinsius and Jonson belong in this group as well.

9. We see Quarlous attempting to do the same thing later in the play when he hypocritically attempts to detach himself from Edgeworth (4.6), apparently no longer able to realize, as he seems to in this scene, that his involvement with the fair and its inhabitants has undermined whatever authority or superiority he might formerly have claimed.

10. See QUIT *v. trans.* I.i.a, I.2.a, I.5.a, I.7.a, I.9, I.10, I.12 (*OED*).

11. Cf. Cope's comments (1984, 76) on the relation between Overdo and Prospero: "Jonson alludes to [*The Winter's Tale* and *The Tempest*] . . . to orient our attention to the symbolic mode of his own drama of God and man and Providence, but the pattern is of a very different design in a world wherein the staff of quasi-omnipotence is carried by Overdo rather than by Prospero."

12. See, in particular, Barton's studies (1979; 1981; 1984) of Jonson's late plays.

13. On the relation between *The Devil Is an Ass* and the morality play tradition, see Champion 1967, 33–44; Dessen 1971, 223–27; and Herford's introduction to the play (Herford, Simpson, and Simpson 1925–52, 2:151–60).

14. Barton (1984, 241–42), Jones (1973), Kifer (1972), and Savage (1973, 178–84) have discussed this play's use of conventions taken from earlier prodigal-son plays. Ervin Beck (1973) has written the best general account of this tradition. See also Helgerson 1976; and Rowe 1979, 56–61.

15. A mindless pursuit of novelty is an important concern also in three masques that Jonson composed during the decade between *The Devil Is an Ass* and *The Staple of News: News from the New World Discovered in the Moon* (1620), *Time Vindicated to Himself and to His Honors* (1623), and *Neptune's Triumph* (1624).

16. As a result, *The Staple of News* is an important exception to Helgerson's otherwise correct argument in *Self-Crowned Laureates* (1983) that Jonson's literary ambitions led him to reject the prodigal-son role so popular among his amateur predecessors.

17. Several critics have commented upon the indebtedness of *The New Inn* to Shakespearean romance. In addition to Barton 1979, see Cheney 1983,

193–94; Hawkins 1966, 224; Leech 1973, 16; and Thayer 1963, 224–
25. On the other hand, both Champion (1967, 81–102); and Duncan
(1970) argue that the play burlesques its Shakespearean model.

18. McKenzie (1973, 111) argues that this open hostility returns even earlier: "*The Staple of News* is the hardening point of Jonson's isolation [from
his public], and the wholly derisive view he presents of a stupid audience, gullible populace, and false educators . . . is logically climaxed
by a symbolic act of suppression—which is only the mirror image of
wishful thinking—in the destruction of the news office."

19. Barton (1979, 418), on the other hand, finds that "Jonson was defending something more than his own particular artistic reputation when
he reacted so passionately to the denigration and misunderstanding" of
The New Inn.

20. That *A Tale of a Tub* draws heavily upon native traditions and may have
been written after *The Magnetic Lady* (though I, for one, do not think
it was) is not, finally, relevant to the point I am making. The same is
true of the date and characteristics of Jonson's unfinished pastoral, *The
Sad Shepherd*. It is the manner in which Jonson attempted to define the
limits of his career, not its precise chronology, that is important, together with the attitudes upon which that attempt was based. Whatever Jonson may have written after he completed *The Magnetic Lady*, he
obviously wished us to view this play as the final product of a career
that was closed in upon itself; the primary point of reference for ap-
proaching and understanding one of Jonson's dramas, this comedy tells
us, is his other dramas, not the works of other English playwrights or
English dramatic traditions in general. The circle of which the Boy speaks
is an exclusive one.

21. For summaries of the various theories that have been proposed concern-
ing the relation between *Troilus and Cressida* and the War of the Theaters, see Hillebrand and Baldwin 1953, 375–77; and Kimbrough 1964,
20–22.

22. See the stimulating discussion of the drama's radical skepticism in Colie
1954, 348–49.

Works Cited

Allen, Don Cameron. 1970. *Mysteriously Meant: The Rediscovery of Pagan Symbolism and Allegorical Interpretation in the Renaissance*. Baltimore: Johns Hopkins Univ. Press.

Anderson, Mark A. 1970. "The Successful Unity of *Epicoene:* A Defense of Ben Jonson." *SEL* 10:349–66.

Aristophanes. 1964. *The Wasps, The Poet and the Women, The Frogs*. Trans. David Barrett. New York: Penguin.

———. 1973. *Lysistrata, The Acharnians, The Clouds*. Trans. Alan H. Sommerstein. New York: Penguin.

———. 1977. *The Knights, Peace, The Birds, The Assemblywomen, Wealth*. Trans. David Barrett and Alan H. Sommerstein. New York: Penguin.

Auerbach, Erich. 1959. *Scenes from the Drama of European Literature: Six Essays*. New York: Meridian Books.

Bacon, Francis. 1863. *The Works of Francis Bacon*. Ed. James Spedding, R. L. Ellis, and D. D. Heath. 15 vols. Cambridge, Mass.: Riverside.

Baldwin, T. W. 1944. *William Shakspere's Small Latine & Lesse Greeke*. 2 vols. Urbana: Univ. of Illinois Press.

———. 1947. *Shakspere's Five-Act Structure: Shakspere's Early Plays on the Background of Renaissance Theories of Five-Act Structure from 1470*. Urbana: Univ. of Illinois Press.

Barber, C. L. 1959. *Shakespeare's Festive Comedy: A Study of Dramatic Form and Its Relation to Social Custom*. Princeton, N.J.: Princeton Univ. Press.

Barish, Jonas A. 1956. "Ovid, Juvenal, and *The Silent Woman*." *PMLA* 71: 213–24.

———. 1960. *Ben Jonson and the Language of Prose Comedy*. Cambridge, Mass.: Harvard Univ. Press.

———. 1965. Introduction to *Sejanus*, 1–24. The Yale Ben Jonson. New Haven, Conn.: Yale Univ. Press.

———. 1972. "Feasting and Judging in Jonsonian Comedy." *Renaissance Drama*, n.s., 5: 3–35.

———. 1981. *The Antitheatrical Prejudice*. Berkeley: Univ. of California Press.

Barton, Ann. 1979. "*The New Inn* and the Problem of Jonson's Late Style." *English Literary Renaissance* 9:395–418.

———. 1981. "Harking Back to Elizabeth: Ben Jonson and Caroline Nostalgia." *ELH* 48:706–31.

———. 1984. *Ben Jonson, Dramatist*. Cambridge: Cambridge Univ. Press.

Baskervill, Charles Read. 1911. *English Elements in Jonson's Early Comedy*. University of Texas Studies in English. Austin: Univ. of Texas Press.

Bate, Walter Jackson. 1970. *The Burden of the Past and the English Poet*. Cambridge, Mass.: Belknap Press.

Beaurline, L. A. 1978. *Jonson and Elizabethan Comedy: Essays in Dramatic Rhetoric*. San Marino, Calif.: Huntington Library Press.

Beck, Ervin. 1973. "Terence Improved: The Paradigm of the Prodigal Son in English Renaissance Comedy." *Renaissance Drama* n.s., 6:107–22.

Berger, Harry. 1965. "Renaissance Imagination: Second World and Green World." *Centennial Review* 9:36–78.

Bloom, Harold. 1973. *The Anxiety of Influence: A Theory of Poetry*. New York: Oxford Univ. Press.

———. 1975. *A Map of Misreading*. New York: Oxford Univ. Press.

Boas, Frederick S. 1914. *University Drama in the Tudor Age*. Oxford: Clarendon Press.

Boaseand, C. W., and Andrew Clark, eds. 1885–89. *Register of the University of Oxford*. 2 vols. Oxford: Historical Society.

Bolton, W. F., and Jane F. Gardner, eds. 1973. *Catiline*. By Ben Jonson. Regents Renaissance Drama Series. Lincoln: Univ. of Nebraska Press.

Bornkamm, Heinrich. 1969. *Luther and the Old Testament*. Ed. Victor I. Gruhns, trans. Eric W. Gritsch and Ruth C. Gritsch. Philadelphia: Fortress Press.

Boughner, Daniel C. 1958. "Jonson's Use of Lipsius in *Sejanus*." *MLN* 73:247–55.

———. 1961. "*Sejanus* and Machiavelli." *SEL* 1:81–100.

Boyle, Marjorie O'Rourke. 1977. *Erasmus on Language and Method*. Toronto: Univ. of Toronto Press.

Brink, C. O. 1963. *Horace on Poetry: Prolegomena to the Literary Epistles*. Cambridge: Cambridge Univ. Press.

Bruno, Giordano. 1966. *The Heroic Frenzies*. Trans. Paul Eugene Memmo, Jr. Chapel Hill: Univ. of North Carolina Press.

Bryant, J. A., Jr. 1952. "The Significance of Ben Jonson's First Requirement for Tragedy: 'Truth of Argument.'" *SP* 49:195–213.

———. 1954. "*Catiline* and the Nature of Jonson's Tragic Fable." *PMLA* 69:265–77.

Burke, Kenneth. 1969a. *A Grammar of Motives*. 1945; Berkeley: Univ. of California Press.

———. 1969b. *A Rhetoric of Motives*. 1950; Berkeley: Univ. of California Press.

Burton, Robert. 1932.*The Anatomy of Melancholy*. 3 vols. London: J. M. Dent.

Camden, William. 1806. *Britannia: Or, a Chorographical Description of the Flourishing Kingdoms of England, Scotland, and Ireland, and the Islands Adjacent; From the Earliest Antiquity*. 2d ed. Trans. Richard Gough. 4 vols. London: John Stockdale.

———. 1970. *The History of the Most Renowned and Victorious Princess Elizabeth Late Queen of England: Selected Chapters*. Ed. Wallace T. MacCaffrey. Classics of British Historical Literature. Chicago: Univ. of Chicago Press.

Campbell, Oscar James. 1938. *Comicall Satyre and Shakespeare's Troilus and Cressida*. San Marino: Huntington Library Press.

Carlson, Peter. 1977. "Judging Spectators." *ELH* 44:443–57.

Carr, Joan. 1978. "Ben Jonson and the Classics: The Ovid-Plot in *Poetaster*." *English Literary Renaissance* 8:296–311.

Cartelli, Thomas. 1983. "*Bartholomew Fair* as Urban Arcadia: Jonson Responds to Shakespeare." *Renaissance Drama*, n.s., 14:151–72.

Cave, Terence. 1979. *The Cornucopian Text: Problems of Writing in the French Renaissance*. Oxford: Clarendon Press.

Champion, Larry S. 1967. *Ben Jonson's "Dotages": A Reconsideration of the Late Plays*. Lexington: Univ. Press of Kentucky.

Cheney, Patrick. 1983. "Jonson's *The New Inn* and Plato's Myth of the Hermaphrodite." *Renaissance Drama*, n.s., 14:173–94.

Cicero. 1966. *Tusculan Disputations*. Trans. J. E. King. Loeb Classical Library. Cambridge, Mass.: Harvard Univ. Press.

———. *De Oratore*. 1976–77. Trans. E. W. Sutton and H. Rackham. 2 vols. Loeb Classical Library. Cambridge, Mass.: Harvard Univ. Press.

———. 1977. *In Catilinam I–IV; Pro Murena; Pro Sulla; Pro Flacco*. Trans.

C. MacDonald. Loeb Classical Library. Cambridge, Mass.: Harvard Univ. Press.

Clark, Ira. 1978. "Ben Jonson's Imitation." *Criticism* 21:107–27.

Clayton, Margaret. 1979. "Ben Jonson, 'In Travaile with Expression of Another': His Use of John of Salisbury's *Policraticus* in *Timber*." *RES* 30: 397–408.

Colie, Rosalie. 1974. *Shakespeare's Living Art*. Princeton: Princeton Univ. Press.

Colley, John Scott. 1977. "*Bartholomew Fair:* Ben Jonson's 'A Midsummer Night's Dream.'" *Comparative Drama* 11:63–72.

Cope, Jackson I. 1973. *The Theater and the Dream: From Metaphor to Form in Renaissance Drama*. Baltimore, Md.: Johns Hopkins Univ. Press.

———. 1984. *Dramaturgy of the Daemonic: Studies in Antigeneric Theater from Ruzante to Grimaldi*. Baltimore, Md.: Johns Hopkins Univ. Press.

Danson, Lawrence. 1984. "Jonsonian Comedy and the Discovery of the Social Self." *PMLA* 99:179–93.

Davenport, Arlice, ed. 1967. *The Whipper Pamphlets*. 2 vols. Liverpool Reprints 5–6. Liverpool: Liverpool Univ. Press.

Davis, Joe Lee. 1967. *The Sons of Ben: Jonsonian Comedy in Caroline England*. Detroit: Wayne State Univ. Press.

Dekker, Thomas. 1953. *The Dramatic Works of Thomas Dekker*. Ed. Fredson Bowers. 4 vols. Cambridge: Cambridge Univ. Press.

Derrida, Jacques. 1974. *Of Grammatology*. Trans. Gayatri Chakrovorty Spivack. Baltimore, Md.: Johns Hopkins Univ. Press.

Dessen, Alan C. 1971. *Jonson's Moral Comedy*. Evanston, Ill.: Northwestern Univ. Press.

Dick, Aliki Lafkidou. 1974. *Paedeia through Laughter: Jonson's Aristophanic Appeal to Human Intelligence*. The Hague: Mouton.

Dio. *Dio's Roman History*. 1914–27. Trans. Earnest Cary. 9 vols. Loeb Classical Library. Cambridge, Mass.: Harvard Univ. Press.

Donaldson, Ian. 1970. *The World Upside-Down: Comedy from Jonson to Fielding*. Oxford: Clarendon Press.

Donne, John. 1967. *Selected Prose*. Ed. Helen Gardner and Timothy Healy. Oxford: Clarendon Press.

Duffy, Ellen M. T. 1947. "Ben Jonson's Debt to Renaissance Scholarship in 'Sejanus' and 'Catiline.'" *MLR* 42:24–30.

Duncan, Douglas. 1970. "A Guide to *The New Inn*." *Essays in Criticism* 20:311–26.

———. 1979. *Ben Jonson and the Lucianic Tradition*. Cambridge: Cambridge Univ. Press.

Dutton, A. Richard. 1978a. "The Sources, Text, and Readers of *Sejanus:* Jonson's 'integrity in the Story.'" *SP* 75:181–98.

———. 1978b. "'What Ministers Men Must, for Practice, Use': Ben Jonson's Cicero." *English Studies* 59:324–35.

Echuero, Michael J. C. 1966. "The Conscience of Politics and Jonson's Catiline." *SEL* 6:341–56.

Ehrenberg, Victor. 1943. *The People of Aristophanes: A Sociology of Old Attic Comedy.* Oxford: Basil Blackwell.

Elsky, Martin. 1982. "Words, Things, and Names: Jonson's Poetry and Philosophical Grammar." In *Classic and Cavalier: Essays on Jonson and the Sons of Ben,* ed. Claude J. Summers and Ted-Larry Pebworth, 91–104. Pittsburgh: University of Pittsburgh Press.

Enck, John J. 1957. *Jonson and the Comic Truth.* Madison: Univ. of Wisconsin Press.

Engel, Wilson F., III. 1980. "The Iron World of *Sejanus:* History in the Crucible of Art." *Renaissance Drama,* n.s., 11:95–114.

Engle, Judith Margaret. 1983. "Playing about the Stage: Poetics, Ritual, and Demagoguery in *The Knights* of Aristophanes." Ph.D. diss., Princeton University.

Erasmus, Desiderius. 1963. *Enchiridion.* Trans. Raymond Himelick. Bloomington: Indiana Univ. Press.

———. 1978. *The Antibarbarians.* Trans. Margaret Mann Philips. In *The Literary and Educational Writings,* ed. Craig R. Thompson, vol. 23 of *The Collected Works of Erasmus.* Toronto: Univ. of Toronto Press.

Evans, K. W. 1971. "*Sejanus* and the Ideal Prince Tradition." *SEL* 11:249–64.

Ferguson, Arthur B. 1979. *Clio Unbound: Perception of the Social and Cultural Past in Renaissance England.* Durham, N.C.: Duke Univ. Press.

Finkelpearl, Philip J. 1969. *John Marston of the Middle Temple: An Elizabethan Dramatist in His Social Setting.* Cambridge, Mass.: Harvard Univ. Press.

Fish, Stanley E. 1972. *Self-Consuming Artifacts: The Experience of Seventeenth-Century Literature.* Berkeley: Univ. of California Press.

———. 1984. "Authors-Readers: Jonson's Community of the Same." *Representations* 7:26–58.

Fiske, George C. 1920. *Lucilius and Horace: A Study in the Classical Theory of Imitation.* University of Wisconsin Studies in Language and Literature 7. Madison: Univ. of Wisconsin Press.

Forstmann, H. Jackson. 1962. *Word and Spirit: Calvin's Doctrine of Biblical Authority.* Stanford, Calif.: Stanford Univ. Press.

Foucault, Michel. 1970. *The Order of Things: An Archaeology of the Human*

Sciences. Trans. anon. New York: Random House.

———. "What is an Author?" 1979. In *Textual Strategies: Perspectives in Post-Structuralist Criticism,* ed. Josue Harari, 141–60. Ithaca, N.Y.: Cornell Univ. Press.

Fraenkel, Eduard. 1957. *Horace.* Oxford: Clarendon Press.

Franklin, Julian H. 1963. *Jean Bodin and the Sixteenth-Century Revolution in the Methodology of Law and History.* New York: Columbia Univ. Press.

Freehafer, John. 1970. "Leonard Digges, Ben Jonson, and the Beginning of Shakespeare Idolatry." *Shakespeare Quarterly* 21:63–75.

Freud, Sigmund. 1960. *Jokes and Their Relation to the Unconscious.* Trans. James Strachey. New York: Norton.

Frye, Northrup. 1957. *Anatomy of Criticism: Four Essays.* Princeton, N.J.: Princeton Univ. Press.

Fussner, F. Smith. 1962. *The Historical Revolution: English Historical Writing and Thought, 1580–1640.* New York: Columbia Univ. Press.

Gilbert, Alan, ed. and trans. 1940. *Literary Criticism: Plato to Dryden.* Detroit, Mich.: Wayne State Univ. Press, 1962.

Gilbert, Felix. 1965. *Machiavelli and Guicciardini: Politics and History in Sixteenth-Century Florence.* Princeton, N.J.: Princeton Univ. Press.

Girard, René. 1977. *Violence and the Sacred.* Trans. Patrick Gregory. Baltimore, Md.: Johns Hopkins Univ. Press.

———. 1978. *"To Double Business Bound": Essays on Literature, Mimesis, and Anthropology.* Baltimore, Md.: Johns Hopkins Univ. Press.

Goldberg, Jonathan. 1983. *James I and the Politics of Literature: Jonson, Shakespeare, Donne, and Their Contemporaries.* Baltimore, Md.: Johns Hopkins Univ. Press.

Grant, Mary A. 1924. *The Ancient Rhetorical Theories of the Laughable.* University of Wisconsin Studies in Language and Literature 21. Madison: Univ. of Wisconsin Press.

Greenblatt, Stephen J. 1976. "The False Ending in *Volpone.*" *JEGP* 75:90–104.

———. 1980. *Renaissance Self-Fashioning from More to Shakespeare.* Chicago: Univ. of Chicago Press.

Greene, Thomas M. 1970. "Ben Jonson and the Centered Self." *SEL* 10:325–48.

———. 1982. *The Light in Troy: Imitation and Discovery in Renaissance Poetry.* New Haven, Conn.: Yale Univ. Press.

Greenfield, Thelma N. 1969. *The Induction in Elizabethan Drama.* Eugene: Univ. of Oregon Press.

Guilpin, Everard. 1974. *Skialetheia or a Shadow of Truth in Certaine Epigrams and Satyres*. Ed. D. Allen Carroll. Chapel Hill: Univ. of North Carolina Press.

Gum, Coburn. 1969. *The Aristophanic Comedies of Ben Jonson: A Comparative Study of Jonson and Aristophanes*. The Hague: Mouton.

Hall, Joseph. 1949. *The Collected Poems of Joseph Hall*. Ed. Arlice Davenport. Liverpool: Liverpool Univ. Press.

Hallahan, Huston D. 1977. "Silence, Eloquence, and Chatter in Jonson's *Epicoene*." *Huntington Library Quarterly* 40:117–27.

Hamilton, Gary D. 1971. "Irony and Fortune in *Sejanus*." *SEL* 11:265–81.

Hanson, R. P. C. 1959. *Allegory and Event: A Study of the Sources and Significance of Origen's Interpretation of Scripture*. London: SCM Press.

Hardison, O. B. 1972. "The Two Voices of Sidney's *Apology for Poetry*." *English Literary Renaissance* 2: 83–89.

Hawkins, Harriett. 1966. "The Idea of Theater in Jonson's *The New Inn*." *Renaissance Drama* 9:205–26.

Heffner, Ray L. 1955. "Unifying Symbols in the Comedy of Ben Jonson." In *English Stage Comedy,* ed. W. K. Wimsatt, 74–97. English Institute Essays 1954. New York: Columbia Univ. Press.

Helgerson, Richard. 1976. *The Elizabethan Prodigals*. Berkeley: Univ. of California Press.

———. 1978. "The New Poet Presents Himself: Spenser and the Idea of a Literary Career." *PMLA* 93:893–911.

———. 1979. "The Elizabethan Laureate: Self-Presentation and the Literary System." *ELH* 46:193–220.

———. 1983. *Self-Crowned Laureates: Spenser, Jonson, Milton, and the Literary System*. Berkeley: Univ. of California Press.

Herford, C. H., Percy Simpson, and Evelyn Simpson, eds. 1925–52. *Ben Jonson*. 11 vols. Oxford: Clarendon Press.

Herrick, Marvin. 1964. *Comic Theory in the Sixteenth Century*. Urbana: Univ. of Illinois Press.

Hesiod. 1876. *The Works of Hesiod, Callimachus, and Theognis*. Trans. J. Banks. London: George Bell.

Hillebrand, Harold N., and T. W. Baldwin, eds. 1953. *A New Variorum Edition of Troilus and Cressida*. Philadelphia: Lippincott.

Hobbes, Thomas. 1968. *Leviathan*. Ed. C. B. Macpherson. New York: Penguin.

Horace. 1966. *Satires, Epistles, and Ars Poetica*. Trans. H. R. Fairclough. Loeb Classical Library. Cambridge, Mass.: Harvard Univ. Press.

————. 1978. *The Odes and Epodes*. Trans. C. E. Bennett. Loeb Classical Library. Cambridge, Mass.: Harvard Univ. Press.

Hoy, Cyrus. 1980. Introductions, notes, and commentaries to texts in *The Dramatic Works of Thomas Dekker*, ed. Fredson Bowers. 4 vols. Cambridge: Cambridge Univ. Press.

Ingram, R. W. 1978. *John Marston*. Ed. Sylvia E. Bowman. Twayne's English Authors 216. Boston: G. K. Hall.

Jackson, Gabrielle Bernhard. 1968. *Vision and Judgment in Ben Jonson's Drama*. New Haven, Conn.: Yale Univ. Press.

————. 1969. Introduction to *Every Man in His Humor*, by Ben Jonson. 1–34. The Yale Ben Jonson. New Haven, Conn.: Yale Univ. Press.

Jones, Robert C. 1967. "The Satirist's Retirement in Jonson's 'Apologetical Dialogue.'" *ELH* 34:447–67.

————. 1973 "Jonson's *Staple of News* Gossips and Fulwell's *Like Will to Like:* 'The Old Way' in a 'New' Morality Play." *Yearbook of English Studies* 3:74–77.

Jonson, Ben. *See* Herford, Simpson, and Simpson.

Kay, W. David. 1970. "The Shaping of Ben Jonson's Career: A Reexamination of Facts and Problems." *MP* 67:224–37.

————. 1975–76. "Jonson's Urbane Gallants: Humanistic Contexts for *Epicoene*." *Huntington Library Quarterly* 39:251–66.

————. 1978–79. "Ben Jonson and Elizabethan Dramatic Convention." *MP* 76:18–28.

Kelley, Donald. 1970. *The Foundations of Modern Historical Scholarship: Language, Law, and History in the French Renaissance*. New York: Columbia Univ. Press.

Kernan, Alvin B. 1973. "Alchemy and Acting: The Major Plays of Ben Jonson." *Studies in the Literary Imagination* 6:1–22.

————. 1976. *The Cankered Muse: Satire of the English Renaissance*. 1959; Hamden, Conn.: Archon Books.

Kifer, Devra Rowland. 1972. "*The Staple of News:* Jonson's Festive Comedy." *SEL* 12:329–44.

Kimbrough, Robert. 1964. *Shakespeare's "Troilus and Cressida" and Its Setting*. Cambridge, Mass.: Harvard Univ. Press.

Kirsch, Arthur C. 1972. *Jacobean Dramatic Perspectives*. Charlottesville: Univ. Press of Virginia.

Knoche, Ulrich. 1975. *Roman Satire*. Trans. Edwin Ramage. Bloomington: Indiana Univ. Press.

LaBranche, Anthony. 1970. "Imitation: Getting in Touch." *MLQ* 31:308–29.

Lawry, J. S. 1982. "*Catiline* and the 'Sight of Rome in Us.'" In *Rome in the Renaissance: The City and the Myth,* ed. P. A. Ramsey, 395–407. Medieval & Renaissance Texts and Studies 18. Binghamton, N.Y.: Center for Medieval & Renaissance Studies.

Leech, Clifford. 1973. "The Incredibility of Jonsonian Comedy." In *A Celebration of Ben Jonson,* ed. William Blissett, Julian Patrick, and R. W. Van Fossen, 3–25. Toronto: Univ. of Toronto Press.

Leggatt, Alexander. 1976. "Morose and His Tormentors." *University of Toronto Quarterly* 45:221–35.

———. 1981. *Ben Jonson: His Vision and His Art.* London: Methuen.

Leishman, J. B., ed. 1949. *The Three Parnassus Plays.* London: Ivor Nicholson & Watson.

Levy, F. J. 1967. *Tudor Historical Thought.* San Marino Calif.: Huntington Library.

Lewalski, Barbara. 1979. *Protestant Poetics and the Seventeenth-Century Religious Lyric.* Princeton, N.J.: Princeton Univ. Press.

Lewis, Charlton T., and Charles Short, eds. 1879. *A Latin Dictionary, Founded on Andrews' Edition of Freund's Latin Dictionary.* Oxford: Clarendon Press.

Lipking, Laurence. 1981. *The Life of the Poet: Beginning and Ending Poetic Careers.* Chicago. Univ. of Chicago Press.

Lodge, Thomas. 1963. *The Complete Works of Thomas Lodge.* 4 vols. 1883; New York: Russell & Russell.

Luther, Martin. 1955–76. *Works,* ed. Jaroslav Pelikan and Helmut T. Lehman. 55 vols. Philadelphia: Muhlenberg Press.

McDonald, Russ. 1981. "Jonsonian Comedy and the Value of *Sejanus.*" *SEL* 21:287–305.

McKenzie, D. F. 1973. "*The Staple of News* and the Late Plays." In *A Celebration of Ben Jonson,* ed. William Blissett, Julian Patrick, and R. W. Van Fossen, 83–128. Toronto: Univ. of Toronto Press.

Macpherson, C. B. 1962. *The Political Theory of Possessive Individualism, Hobbes to Locke.* Oxford: Oxford Univ. Press.

———. 1968. Introduction to *Leviathan,* by Thomas Hobbes, 9–63. New York: Penguin.

Manley, Lawrence. 1980. *Convention: 1500–1750.* Cambridge, Mass.: Harvard Univ. Press.

Marotti, Arthur. F. 1970. "The Self-Reflexive Art of Ben Jonson's *Sejanus.*" *Texas Studies in Language and Literature* 12:197–220.

Martial. 1968. *Epigrams.* Trans. Walter C. A. Ker. 2 vols. Loeb Classical Library. Cambridge, Mass.: Harvard Univ. Press.

Maus, Katherine E. 1984. *Ben Jonson and the Roman Frame of Mind*. Princeton, N.J.: Princeton Univ. Press.

Miner, Earl. 1971. *The Cavalier Mode from Jonson to Cotton*. Princeton, N.J.: Princeton Univ. Press.

Minturno, Antonio Sebastiano. 1970. *De Poeta*. Poetiken des Cinquecento 5. Munchen: Wilhelm Fink.

Nelson, William. 1973. *Fact or Fiction: The Dilemma of the Renaissance Storyteller*. Cambridge, Mass.: Harvard Univ. Press.

Newton, Richard C. 1977. "'Ben./Jonson': The Poet in the Poems." In *Two Renaissance Mythmakers: Christopher Marlowe and Ben Jonson*, ed. Alvin Kernan. 165–95. Selected Papers from the English Institute 1975–76. Baltimore, Md.: Johns Hopkins Univ. Press.

———. 1982. "Jonson and the (Re-)Invention of the Book." In *Classic and Cavalier: Essays on Jonson and the Sons of Ben*, ed. Claude J. Summers and Ted-Larry Pebworth. 31–55. Pittsburgh: Univ. of Pittsburgh Press.

Norbrook, David. 1984. *Poetry and Politics in the English Renaissance*. London: Routledge & Kegan Paul.

Ong, Walter J. 1958. *Ramus, Method, and the Decay of Dialogue: From the Art of Discourse to the Art of Reason*. Cambridge, Mass.: Harvard Univ. Press.

———. 1977. *Interfaces of the Word: Studies in the Evolution of Consciousness and Culture*. Ithaca: Cornell Univ. Press.

Orgel, Stephen. 1965. *The Jonsonian Masque*. Cambridge, Mass.: Harvard Univ. Press.

———. 1975. *The Illusion of Power: Political Theater in the English Renaissance*. Berkeley: Univ. of California Press.

Orgel, Stephen, and Roy Strong. 1973. *Inigo Jones: The Theatre of the Stuart Court*. 2 vols. Berkeley: Univ. of California Press.

Ornstein, Robert. 1969. "Shakespearean and Jonsonian Comedy." *Shakespeare Survey* 22:43–46.

Padelford, Frederick M., trans. 1905. *Select Translations from Scaliger's Poetics*. Yale Studies in English 26. New York: Henry Holt.

Parfitt, George. 1976. *Ben Jonson: Public Poet and Private Man*. New York: Barnes & Noble.

Parker, R. B. 1977. "The Problem of Tone in Jonson's 'Comicall Satyres.'" *Humanities Association Bulletin* 28:43–64.

Partridge, Edward. 1958. *The Broken Compass: A Study of the Major Comedies of Ben Jonson*. New York: Columbia Univ. Press.

———. 1973. "Jonson's *Epigrammes:* The Named and the Nameless." *Studies in the Literary Imagination* 6:153–98.

Patterson, Annabel. 1984. *Censorship and Interpretation: The Conditions of Writing and Reading in Early Modern England*. Madison: Univ. of Wisconsin Press.

Pearlman, E. 1979. "Ben Jonson: An Anatomy." *English Literary Renaissance* 9:364–94.

Peterson, Richard S. 1981. *Imitation and Praise in the Poems of Ben Jonson*. New Haven, Conn.: Yale Univ. Press.

Pierce, Robert B. 1981. "Ben Jonson's Horace and Horace's Ben Jonson." *SP* 78:20–31.

Pigman, G. W., III. 1979. "Imitation and the Renaissance Sense of the Past: The Reception of Erasmus's *Ciceronianus*." *Journal of Modern and Renaissance Studies* 9:155–77.

———. 1980. "Versions of Imitation in the Renaissance." *Renaissance Quarterly* 33:1–32.

Plutarch. 1914–26. *Plutarch's Lives*. Trans. Bernadotte Perrin. 11 vols. The Loeb Classical Library. Cambridge, Mass.: Harvard Univ. Press.

———. 1956–69. *Moralia*. Trans. Frank C. Babbitt et al. 16 vols. Loeb Classical Library. Cambridge, Mass.: Harvard Univ. Press.

Pocock, J. G. A. 1967. *The Ancient Constitution and the Feudal Law: A Study of English Historical Thought in the Seventeenth Century*. 2d ed. New York: Norton.

Potter, John M. 1968. "Old Comedy in *Bartholomew Fair*." *Criticism* 10:290–99.

Preus, James Samuel. 1969. *From Shadow to Promise: Old Testament Interpretation from Augustine to the Young Luther*. Cambridge, Mass.: Harvard Univ. Press.

Puttenham, George. 1970. *The Arte of English Poesie*. Kent English Reprints. 1906; Kent, Ohio: Kent State Univ. Press.

Quint, David. 1983. *Origin and Originality in Renaissance Literature: Versions of the Source*. New Haven, Conn.: Yale Univ. Press.

Quintilian. 1976–80. *Institutio Oratoria*. Trans. H. E. Butler. 4 vols. Loeb Classical Library. Cambridge, Mass.: Harvard Univ. Press.

Rhodes, Neil. 1980. *Elizabethan Grotesque*. London: Routledge & Kegan Paul.

Robertson, D. W., Jr. 1962. *A Preface to Chaucer: Studies in Medieval Perspectives*. Princeton, N.J.: Princeton Univ. Press.

Rollin, Roger B. 1982. "The Anxiety of Identification: Jonson and the Rival Poets." In *Classic and Cavalier: Essays on Jonson and the Sons of Ben,* ed. Claude J. Summers and Ted-Larry Pebworth, 139–54. Pittsburgh, Pa.: Univ. of Pittsburgh Press.

Rowe, George E. 1979. *Thomas Middleton and the New Comedy Tradition.* Lincoln: Univ. of Nebraska Press.

Rudd, Niall. 1966. *The Satires of Horace: A Study.* Cambridge: Cambridge Univ. Press.

Sallust. *Sallust.* 1955. Trans. J. C. Rolfe. Loeb Classical Library. Cambridge, Mass.: Harvard Univ. Press.

Sandys, George. 1970. *Ovid's Metamorphosis Englished, Mythologized, and Represented in Figures,* ed. Karl K. Hulley and Stanley T. Vandersall. Lincoln: Univ. of Nebraska Press.

Savage, James E. 1973. *Ben Jonson's Basic Comic Characters and Other Essays.* Hattiesburg: Univ. of Mississippi Press.

Scott, Izora. 1910. *Controversies over the Imitation of Cicero as a Model for Style and Some Phases of Their Influence on the Schools of the Renaissance.* Columbia Univ. Contributions to Education 35. New York: Columbia Univ. Teachers College.

Selden, John. 1726. *Opera Omnia,* ed. David Wilkins. 3 vols. London: n.p.

Seneca. 1917–25. *Ad Lucilium Epistulae Morales.* Trans. Richard M. Gummere. 3 vols. Loeb Classical Library. Cambridge, Mass.: Harvard Univ. Press.

Shakespeare, William. 1974. *The Riverside Shakespeare,* ed. G. Blakemore Evans. Boston: Houghton Mifflin.

Shapiro, Michael. 1973. "Audience v. Dramatist in Jonson's *Epicoene* and Other Plays of the Children's Troupes." *English Literary Renaissance* 3:400–17.

———. 1977. *Children of the Revels: The Boy Companies of Shakespeare's Time and Their Plays.* New York: Columbia Univ. Press.

Smalley, Beryl. 1964. *The Study of the Bible in the Middle Ages.* 2d ed. Notre Dame, Ind.: Univ. of Notre Dame Press.

Smith, G. Gregory, ed. 1904. *Elizabethan Critical Essays.* 2 vols. Oxford: Clarendon Press.

Spevack, Marvin. 1973. *The Harvard Concordance to Shakespeare.* Cambridge, Mass.: Harvard Univ. Press.

Spingarn, J. E. 1908–9. *Critical Essays of the Seventeenth Century.* 3 vols. Oxford: Clarendon Press.

Steadman, John M. 1974. *The Lamb and the Elephant: Ideal Imitation and the Context of Renaissance Allegory.* San Marino, Calif.: Huntington Library.

Stern, Virginia F. 1979. *Gabriel Harvey: His Life, Marginalia, and Library.* Oxford: Clarendon Press.

Stone, Lawrence. 1965. *The Crisis of the Aristocracy, 1558–1641.* Oxford: Clarendon Press.

Sweeney, John G., III. 1981. "*Sejanus* and the People's Beastly Rage." *ELH* 48:61–82.

———. 1982. "*Volpone* and the Theater of Self-Interest." *English Literary Renaissance* 12:220–41.

———. 1985. *Jonson and the Psychology of Public Theater: "To Coin the Spirit, Spend the Soul."* Princeton, N.J.: Princeton Univ. Press.

Tacitus. 1925–37. *The Histories and The Annals.* Trans. Clifford H. Moore and John Jackson. 4 vols. Loeb Classical Library. Cambridge, Mass.: Harvard Univ. Press.

Tayler, Edward W., ed. 1967. *Literary Criticism of Seventeenth-Century England.* New York: Knopf.

Thayer, C. G. 1963. *Ben Jonson: Studies in the Plays.* Norman: Univ. of Oklahoma Press.

Trimpi, Wesley. 1962. *Ben Jonson's Poems: A Study of the Plain Style.* Palo Alto, Calif.: Stanford Univ. Press.

Trousdale, Marion. 1973. "A Possible Renaissance View of Form." *ELH* 40:179–204.

———. 1976. "Recurrence and Renaissance: Rhetorical Imitation in Ascham and Sturm." *English Literary Renaissance* 6:156–79.

———. 1982. *Shakespeare and the Rhetoricians.* Chapel Hill: Univ. of North Carolina Press.

Turner, Victor. 1974. *Dramas, Fields, and Metaphors: Symbolic Action in Human Society.* Ithaca, N.Y.: Cornell Univ. Press.

Tuve, Rosemond. 1947. *Elizabethan and Metaphysical Imagery: Renaissance Poetic and Twentieth-Century Critics.* Chicago: Univ. of Chicago Press.

———. 1966. *Allegorical Imagery: Some Medieval Books and Their Posterity.* Chicago: Univ. of Chicago Press.

Van Dyke, Joyce. 1979. "The Game of Wits in *The Alchemist.*" *SEL* 19:253–69.

Vawter, Marvin T. 1973. "The Seeds of Virtue: Political Imperatives in Jonson's *Sejanus.*" *Studies in the Literary Imagination* 6:41–60.

Velleius Paterculus. 1924. *Compendium of Roman History.* Trans. Frederick W. Shipley. Loeb Classical Library. London: William Heinemann.

Waith, Eugene M. 1951. "The Poet's Morals in Jonson's *Poetaster.*" *MLQ* 12:13–19.

Wallace, John M. 1974. "'Examples are Best Precepts': Readers and Meanings in Seventeenth-Century Poetry." *Critical Inquiry* 1:273–90.

Warren, Michael J. 1973. "Ben Jonson's *Catiline:* The Problem of Cicero." *Yearbook of English Studies* 3:55–73.

Wayne, Don E. 1979. "Poetry and Power in Ben Jonson's *Epigrammes:* The

Naming of 'Facts' or the Figuring of Social Relations?" *Renaissance and Modern Studies* 23:79–103.

——. 1984. *Penshurst: The Semiotics of Place and the Poetics of History*. Madison: Univ. of Wisconsin Press.

Weimann, Robert. 1978. *Shakespeare and the Popular Tradition of the Theater: Studies in the Social Dimension of Dramatic Form and Function,* ed. Robert Schwartz. Baltimore, Md.: Johns Hopkins Univ. Press.

Weinberg, Bernard. 1961. *A History of Literary Criticism in the Italian Renaissance*. 2 vols. Chicago: Univ. of Chicago Press.

Whigham, Frank. 1984. *Ambition and Privilege: The Social Tropes of Elizabethan Courtesy Theory*. Berkeley: Univ. of California Press.

White, H. O. 1935. *Plagiarism and Imitation during the English Renaissance: A Study in Critical Distinctions*. Cambridge, Mass.: Harvard Univ. Press.

Whitman, Cedric. 1964. *Aristophanes and the Comic Hero*. Martin Classical Lectures 19. Cambridge, Mass.: Harvard Univ. Press.

Wikander, Matthew H. 1979. "'Queasy to Be Touched': The World of Ben Jonson's *Sejanus*." *JEGP* 78:345–57.

Williams, Gordon. 1978. *Change and Decline: Roman Literature in the Early Empire*. Sather Classical Lectures 45. Berkeley: Univ. of California Press.

Wilson, Edmund. 1948. "Morose Ben Jonson." In *The Triple Thinkers: Twelve Essays on Literary Subjects,* 213–32. New York: Oxford Univ. Press.

Witke, Charles. 1970. *Latin Satire: The Structure of Persuasion*. Leiden: E. J. Brill.

Index